LAMBSHEAD
BEFORE
INTERWOVEN

LAMBSHEAD
BEFORE
INTERWOVEN
A Texas Range Chronicle
1848 – 1878

BY

FRANCES MAYHUGH HOLDEN

DRAWINGS BY
JOHN GUERIN

TEXAS A&M UNIVERSITY PRESS: COLLEGE STATION

Library of Congress Cataloging in Publication Data

Holden, Frances Mayhugh, 1913–
    Lambshead before Interwoven.
    Bibliography: p.
    Includes index.
    1. Lambshead Ranch (Tex.)—History. 2. Matthews
family. 3. Reynolds family. 4. Ranch life—
Texas—Throckmorton County—History—19th century.
I. Title.
F394.L176H64   976.4'735   81-48374
ISBN 0-89096-122-0 (cloth)   AACR2

Manufactured in the United States of America
FOURTH PRINTING 1997

To Curry, my husband and lifetime partner

PUBLISHER'S NOTE

Both the design of *Lambshead before Interwoven* and of its companion volume, *Interwoven: A Pioneer Chronicle*, follow faithfully the design originally created by Carl Hertzog, the master printer and designer of El Paso, for the limited edition of *Interwoven* which he produced in 1958 for his friend Watkins Reynolds Matthews of Lambshead Ranch. The few modifications of this design which appear in the present volumes have been approved by Carl Hertzog.

The covers and jackets for the regular edition of these companion books differ from the limited Hertzog edition, but the boxed limited edition of *Lambshead before Interwoven* and *Interwoven: A Pioneer Chronicle* have Hertzog's cover design of the 1958 edition.

We are grateful to Watt Matthews and Carl Hertzog for making the publication of these books possible, and we are proud that the final page of each bears the CH printer's mark which has appeared on so many important books of the Southwest.

TEXAS A&M UNIVERSITY PRESS

PREFACE

IN THE MIDDLE of Texas, between Albany and Throckmorton, lies Lambshead Ranch, fifty thousand acres under the experienced, strong, and hospitable hand of Watt Reynolds Matthews. It reflects the proud and private character of the family of Sallie and John A. Matthews, who put it all together nearly a hundred years ago. Kept as it was, or restored to its virgin state, the land, the life, and the buildings are mostly as they were from the beginning, with cattle and horses roaming the pastures along with the native wildlife. Buffalo and Longhorns forage on the strong grasses that have always grown there. Except for massive intrusion of prickly pear and mesquite, the landscape is little changed since the Matthews family first came to these valleys of the Clear Fork of the Brazos River. The good permanent water, the protected valleys, and the wealth of prairie grasses make it a cowman's dream.

The land is a natural stage upon which a wide variety of characters have acted out their parts. Names attached to the pastures, the creeks, the canyons, the flats, the gaps, the river crossings, the trails, the parklike bottoms, and the draws serve as clues to the legends, the drama, and the tragedies enacted by those who came before Lambshead was a ranch.

In 1936, Sallie Reynolds Matthews published a personal narrative for her children entitled *Interwoven*. It chronicles the coming of the Matthews and Reynolds families to the frontier in 1858 and 1859 and the putting together of Lambshead Ranch, and concludes with the marriage of her oldest daughter, May, and the birth of her youngest son, Watt, in 1899.

My interest in the history of Lambshead Ranch began when I first read Sallie Reynolds Matthews' delightful book. Later I met members of both the Matthews and Reynolds families and found them superior people and historically minded. Like many others, I was curious as to how the name, Lambshead, had come about, naturally assuming that it had something to do with sheep. Members of the family knew only that it was the name of a man who was in the area in the 1850's. Attempting to track down this elusive man, I found myself exploring the exciting, sometimes tragic, times on the Lambshead range before the arrival of the Matthews-Reynolds families. Some facts about Thomas Lambshead emerged, but it is a larger story that will be told here. The events of that era reveal in microcosm the early pioneer experience: here were explorers and soldiers; settlers, both cowmen and grangers; the Indian ordeal; renegades and rustlers; vigilante justice; and the eventual coming of gentler, more civilized ways to the raw frontier along the Clear Fork.

Participants in this story include many whose names are already well known: Captain Randolph B. Marcy, trailblazer and keen observer; Tecumseh, Comanche chieftain and host-chief on the Clear Fork Reservation; Major Robert S. Neighbors, explorer and federal Indian agent; Lieutenant Colonel Robert E. Lee, guardian of the Comanche reserve and later leader of the South in the Civil War; Charles Goodnight, cowman and plainsman; and Thomas Lambshead, English farmer from Devon. They were followed by the Matthews and Reynolds families and the "two-hat" men, John Selman and John Larn. Others, some of good repute, some of none, also came to the Lambshead range and helped shape its history.

x

I shall endeavor to describe here the events that transpired between 1848 and 1878. Naturally, there will be some overlap with *Interwoven*.

ACKNOWLEDGMENTS

T HE SINGLE MOST IMPORTANT guide and inspiration for this book has been Sallie Reynolds Matthews' warm-hearted pioneer chronicle, *Interwoven*, the story of the families whose lives and spirits shaped, and were shaped by, the Clear Fork country, especially Lambshead Ranch. The children of Sallie and John A. Matthews whom I have known—Joe B., Ethel Matthews Casey, Lucile Matthews Brittingham, Sallie Matthews Judd, and Watt R. Matthews—provided a wealth of primary materials, including interviews and papers that document the history of their interwoven family and the Clear Fork country. Their spouses, children, other relatives, and family friends have also been generous with interviews and documents, especially some of the J. A. Matthews' grandchildren whose parents are no longer living. To each member and friend of the family, I am grateful.

Original sources from the Robert Edward Nail, Jr., Foundation Collection, Albany, Texas, were made available by Joan Farmer, and she and Bob Green have contributed their invaluable objective interpretations of these and other source materials.

Four gifted and generous men have guided this writing of the Lambshead story. Curry Holden, my husband, prolific writer and ranching historian, inspired and encouraged me, skillfully edited the manuscript, and shared throughout his wit and wisdom. Watt R. Matthews, innate gentleman and guiding force of Lambshead Ranch, steadily encouraged and assisted the search for facts to tell the history of the land he loves. He has graciously shown us over Lambshead, where we saw firsthand the sites

xiii

mentioned here. J. Evetts Haley, eminent cowboy historian, furnished original documentation and pointed the way through his honest writings on the West. Carl Hertzog, a genius at designing and publishing books, rode herd on putting this book together. To each I give my respectful esteem and grateful thanks.

Two secondary sources proved invaluable in developing the characters of Major Robert S. Neighbors, John Larn, and John Selman, principals in the early Lambshead story. I am indebted to Dr. Kenneth Franklin Neighbours for much information and the use of passages from his excellent and exhaustive work, *Robert Simpson Neighbors and the Texas Frontier* (Waco: The Texian Press, 1975). Robert E. Davis of the Texian Press, which holds the copyright for the book, kindly granted permission to quote from it. I have leaned heavily on this source for the part played by Major Neighbors in the history of Clear Fork country. I am likewise indebted to Leon Claire Metz, who generously allowed me to use extracts from his book, *John Selman, Gunfighter* (Norman: University of Oklahoma Press, 1980). Mr. Metz graciously assisted in interpretation of facts concerning John Larn and John Selman.

Dr. Rupert N. Richardson's authoritative writings on the Comanche Indians and the history of Clear Fork country were invaluable, as were the rare sources on these subjects that he made available. In addition, his analysis of the characters of John Larn and John Selman guided my interpretation of these two men, and I am grateful for his help.

The two papers in the Addenda dealing with the natural history of Lambshead add considerably to an understanding and appreciation of the region, and I am indebted to the authors for sharing their professional knowledge. Glen L. Evans, international geologist and Southwestern archaeologist, has done considerable field work in the Lambshead area and he graciously prepared the paper on the geology of Lambshead. A. S. Jackson, a longtime friend of the Matthews family, was sent in 1944 to Lambshead by the Texas Parks and Wildlife Department to head a six-year research and management project for the wild turkey. His description in the Addenda of plant and animal life on Lambshead displays an intimate knowledge of nature's ways in the area.

I appreciate the professional assistance of the staffs of the Southwest Collection, Texas Tech University, Lubbock, of the Rupert N. Richardson Library, Hardin-Simmons University, Abilene, and of the Texas State Library and Archives and the Texas Memorial Museum, Austin.

My brother, Roger Pat Mayhugh, made an important and vital contribution to the completion of this work, lending his expertise in grammatical usage and his typing skill to produce the master copy of the manuscript.

I am also grateful to Frank H. Wardlaw, founding director of both the University of Texas Press and Texas A&M University Press, for his interest and encouragement throughout the development of this book.

Finally, to all present and former residents of Clear Fork country, and to those other special persons who have contributed toward the writing of the Lambshead story, I give my warm and sincere thanks.

CONTENTS

ILLUSTRATIONS

LAMBSHEAD
BEFORE
INTERWOVEN

1   *The Land*

L AMBSHEAD, the evocative and, in cattle country, mis-
leading surname of an English immigrant, became
attached to a creek, then to a valley, and eventually to a ranch, a good ranch in western Texas where the footprints
of history cover every square foot of its fifty thousand acres. To
a range with strong grass and a clearwater stream that never
runs dry. The Clear Fork of the Brazos River enters Lambshead
in the southwest corner, makes a vast, undulating half-circle to
the north, and leaves at the southeast corner of the ranch nearly
thirty miles downstream. Creeks flow into the Clear Fork from
either side. Their bottom lands, along with those of the main
stream, have long attracted animals and man.

Evidence of habitation by prehistoric hunters, discovered in
the bend of the Clear Fork on Lambshead, indicates that men
have been here for thousands of years. They camped in the
sheltered valleys along the river beneath towering hardwoods
and other trees. These hunters came and went, following the
seasons and the herds. No doubt they found life good along the
banks of the clear waters and in the luxuriant valleys where
game animals, their main food supply, grazed.

Some four centuries ago, the Spaniards named the Brazos
River, with its three tributaries, *Los Brazos de Dios*, the Arms

3

of God, for good reason. At their sources, the streams were welcome oases to the resolute explorers. But the Double Mountain and the Salt forks, which cut through the Permian formation, pick up gypsum and other salts that make their waters brackish—unfit for man's use and barely tolerable for animals. The Clear Fork, however, as its name indicates, runs fresh and clean, a uniquely desirable stream. Indians knew this for centuries before the arrival of the Europeans. When the Spaniards came, treasure-seeking explorers of the 1700's, and later, in 1848, gold-seekers from over the world searching for an overland route to the California treasure lodes, white men learned what the Indians had known all along. The Clear Fork was the stream to follow to the Southwest.

Captain Randolph B. Marcy of the U.S. Army found it in 1849, returning from escort of a forty-niners' wagon train destined for Santa Fe. Leaving the gold-seekers, he headed southwest to explore, followed down the Pecos River to Horsehead Crossing, thence down the middle Concho to the convergence of the north and south Conchos, and turned northeast to the Clear Fork. His route later became the road for westbound immigrant wagons. Obviously, Marcy was not the first white man to observe the Lambshead portion of the Clear Fork, but he was one of the first to leave a written record of how it appeared in mid-nineteenth century. Marcy's California Road through Lambshead crossed Paint Creek near where it enters the Clear Fork, then skirted the bend of the Clear Fork on the north.

In August, 1854, Marcy, with an escort of cavalrymen, was again in the Lambshead area, this time accompanied by Major Robert S. Neighbors, U.S. agent for the Texas Indians. In accordance with Sam Houston's early policy of settling friendly Texas Indians under government protection, they were seeking desirable locations for Indian reservations for the southern Co-

Lambshead Valley, winter resort of the South-ern Comanches.

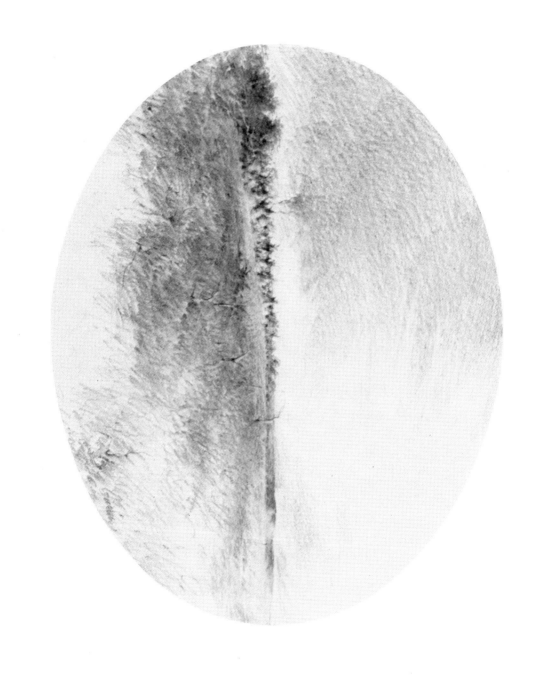

manches and small tribes of other Indians. The party left Fort Belknap and followed the army road to a crossing on the Clear Fork a short distance above the mouth of Lambshead Creek. Pausing atop the high eastern cliff above the river, Captain Marcy was fascinated by the magnificent view.

The valley of the Clear Fork of the Brazos River at this point was one-quarter to two miles wide. Lushly carpeted in thick grasses and verdant plants, in contrast to the rude, barren Salt Fork to the east, it reminded Marcy of "all that is most picturesque and charming in a highly cultivated country." Its clear, pure stream was twenty-five yards wide and flowed rapidly over dazzling white limestone and gravel. The precipitous banks were lined with giant trees, pecan, hackberry, black walnut, and others, which were reflected in the clear waters.

Layers of limestone cropped out in the surrounding hills, shaped by natural causes into convenient shapes and smooth surfaces "already dressed for the hands of the mason." There was plenty of timber for building or fuel. The best varieties of grama and mesquite grasses were everywhere, providing ample winter forage; in fact, animals did better here in the winter than in the summer. There were fewer flies than in timbered districts to the east. Marcy concluded there was "no place in the universe better suited to stock raising."

In the level, rich valley just across the river, Marcy saw a field of oats and corn with a bountiful crop just maturing and, at a short distance, a log house and outbuildings. He was amazed. All this had happened since he was in the vicinity five years previously. He and his party crossed the river. At this place, there was an outcropping of rock and gravel, making a firm bottom, an easy crossing the Indians had used for centuries. Marcy was pleased to find such evidence of civilization in this far western Indian country. The cultivation of the farm and rancho of Colonel Jesse Stem, former Indian trader and agent to the southern Comanches, had been accomplished by simply turning the sod with a prairie plow. No other labor had been required. In 1852 and 1853 Stem had planted oats and corn and, with a ready market and good prices for his produce at Fort Belknap, had profited handsomely. Although Stem had been killed by Indians in February, 1854, someone clearly was tending his land.

Marcy needed no further evidence of the fertility of the soil; this locality could provide for the wants of the Indian. He found numerous remains of old Comanche camps throughout the valley. A map from the Texas General Land Office showed a vacant tract of land large enough for one reservation next to the river above the Clear Fork Crossing, and Marcy and Neighbors determined to examine it.

The party camped for the night at a large spring about half a mile below the Stem ranch house at a place on what is now called Lambshead Creek, which enters the Clear Fork at this point.

The next morning, Marcy, in company with Major Neighbors, went upriver about eight miles to the confluence of another tributary, which the Comanches called Qua-qua-ho-no and the whites, Paint Creek, where Marcy had bivouacked for the night when laying out the California Road five years earlier. Here, in 1849, he had first met Sanaco's band, one of the southern Comanche affiliates friendly to the whites. He pitched his tent under the same tree as before.

Early the next day, Marcy and Neighbors turned toward their camp at Clear Fork Crossing and passed down the north side of the river, carefully inspecting the tract of vacant country. Along the borders of the stream, they found rich valley land well suited to agriculture. The grassy slopes covered with mesquite trees on the rolling hills adjoining would make good pastures.

Returning to their camp, they met two Indians from Sanaco's

band who had come to arrange a council with them. The Indians rode in bareheaded with skin umbrellas hoisted, which caused some merriment. Although Sanaco was acknowledged leader of all the southern Comanches, his band, a small band led by Buffalo Hump, and another led by Tecumseh (spelled "Ke-tum-e-see" by Marcy), were otherwise separate and indepen-dent. Tecumseh was, according to Marcy, "an ambitious and astute leader pursuing a discreet and complaisant policy in the government of his followers," one "calculated to enhance his popularity." This had led to ill will and jealousy between the chiefs. Tecumseh's band usually camped on what later became known as Tecumseh Creek, a few miles north of the Clear Fork Crossing. (As Indian agent, Neighbors had first seen this favored valley resort of the Comanches in October, 1848, when Tecum-seh had joined him on a trip there to counsel with Chiefs Santa Anna, Buffalo Hump, and Can-See-Nothing. He had long ac-quaintance with the Comanches, and his mastery of their lan-guage made him more than welcome to their lodges.)

Sanaco, with several subchiefs, arrived after Tecumseh to hold council with Marcy on the night of August 20, 1854. Marcy and Neighbors assembled all the Comanches, after having an ox killed for them to feast upon. Sanaco was authorized to speak for the southern Comanches gathered at Marcy's camp. The chief was prepossessing in appearance, about five feet eight inches tall, dark-skinned and muscular, "with a countenance mild but decided."

Captain Marcy explained the plan for setting aside a reserva-tion for the southern Comanches and the other Texas Indian bands. Sanaco and Tecumseh were intelligent and had observed enough to understand this message. They realized that change was inevitable, that hunting would have to give way to farming, the chase to the plow. Sanaco, as speaker for the Indian assembly, took a long time to convince his colleagues that this was the only alternative for survival of their people. At last Sanaco announced, with formal dignity, that his people and the other bands represented were willing to try the experiment of farming. They preferred this to moving north and settling among the wild northern Comanches, who were dedicated to hunting and raiding the white and Mexican settlements. Tecumseh, not allowed to speak, left in a black mood.

After finishing the business of the council, Major Neighbors distributed gifts among the Indians, which, with some rations Marcy issued, pleased them greatly. Their camp, pitched in their traditional wintering resort, was a scene of feasting the remainder of their stay. All this took place near Stem's farm and rancho on what was to become Lambshead Ranch.

Having reached agreement with the Comanche bands, Captain Marcy and Major Neighbors surveyed the four leagues of unallotted land for the reservation and reported to the governor and the commissioner of Indian affairs in Washington in September, 1854. The two men, fond of each other and of the Indians they were trying to serve, then separated. The success of the council meeting and the promise of the land they had just surveyed, so evident from the fine stand of corn and oats on the Stem farm, must have given them immense satisfaction.

Curiously, though Marcy and his secretary, W. B. Parker, both comment at some length in their accounts of this episode on the success of Stem's farming venture, neither mentions who was then responsible for the farm, six months after Stem's death. Colonel Stem's widow patented 640 acres to enlarge the rancho on November 19, 1855, but she also left no clue as to the man she put in charge. Had Marcy or Parker said whom they met there, one of the mysteries about the beginning of Lambshead would have been cleared up.

2 *Jesse Stem*

COLONEL JESSE STEM, frontier entrepreneur and agent to the Texas Indians, was the first person of record to obtain, improve, and cultivate land on Lambshead. In 1854, 960 acres in three 320-acre plots, secured from the original grantees, Joseph H. Dalton and Thomas Mounts, were patented in his name. Mrs. Stem added by patent 640 acres in 1855, secured from the original grantee, John Carr. Others filed on small parcels of land, but there is no record that they lived out their claims, though some may have done so.

Little is known of the early life of Jesse Stem other than that he came from a substantial family in Ohio, that he was trained as a lawyer, that he had a respiratory health problem, and that he followed the standard treatment for such illness in the 1800's, to seek a drier climate. He found it in Texas, where in 1850 he was commissioned as federal agent to the Texas Indians. He had two brothers, successful businessmen in Tiffin, Ohio.

Jesse was married, had four daughters, and seemed to be moderately well off. He brought his family to live in Seguin, Texas, in the fall of 1851. There he may have met Major Robert S. Neighbors, as the handsome thirty-six-year-old bachelor had married an eighteen-year-old Seguin beauty on July 15, 1851. Neighbors quickly became a favorite of his wife's family and popular in the community, visiting Seguin often. Perhaps Elizabeth Ann Neighbors and Matilda Stem met in this small German town and brought their husbands together. There is little likelihood the two men ever met on the Clear Fork, though Stem wrote to Neighbors at least once from his agency there. Stem resigned his office and left for Ohio before Neighbors assumed active duty in August, 1853, as supervising agent for the Federal Indian Service in Texas.

Stem's commission as a federal Indian agent in Texas authorized him to supervise and treat with the Indians and to maintain a commissary for trading with them. The government reckoned that a policy of licensed trading was better for settlers and Indians than the stealing the Indians had formerly pursued. Stem's own purpose was to establish an "estate" on the western frontier of Texas, to regain his health, to bring his wife and daughters to Texas, and, ultimately, to lure other Ohioans to form a settlement in the Clear Fork country. He was captivated by the rich valley where he had found the Comanche winter camp site on his first visit to the Clear Fork in June, 1851.

Stem returned to Ohio in late July, 1851 and brought his wife and children back with him. Leaving his family in Seguin, where his daughters could attend school, Stem left in November to make his second reconnaissance. On November 25, he wrote to his wife, Matilda, from Fort Graham (fifty miles south of Fort Worth): "It has been cold . . . I find the Indians have all scattered. . . . I shall have to wait here several weeks . . . and perhaps shall not meet a great number this winter. I shall go out from 6 to 25 miles from here—put up a log house to store my corn & Govt. goods in & a corner for myself . . . make myself comfortable as possible & wait till they [the Indians] come in. . . . I shall . . . contract for beef . . . feed those who come in . . . shall then make what talk seems called for & return to you and the little ones where I should like to be today. . . . You may make yourself easy about me, . . . as I have determined not to go high up in the country. . . ."

Stem must have contracted a serious case of "speculation fever" to think of settling along the Indian trails on the Clear Fork. He wrote to his close friend Rutherford B. Hayes, future president of the United States, on May 2, 1852: ". . . have good horses to ride—and the most delightful country in the world to ride over. . . . I shall probably go up the country in a few days to look after some Indians who have stolen horses, and to look out for some good land in the Clear Fork of the Brazos to locate for speculation and also for a corn farm . . . the two Posts above will make a demand for from 30 to 60,000 bus. corn at 2$ to 3$ pr bus—and I shall give some good fellow 800 or $1000 to pay expenses of raising 150 or 200 acres. He to furnish his quota also. I shall throw it into the wheel and I think it will come out an ace of trumps." This was no idle brag. Stem must have bestirred himself; with luck and a favorable season, he realized his dream by early fall. On October 8, 1852, he wrote Major Neighbors, then a representative in the Texas legislature, that his agency, headquarters, and farm were established on the Clear Fork of the Brazos. He arranged with the Texas General Land Office to purchase nearly one thousand acres at sixteen cents an acre, including two surveys, numbered MD 3-1038, of 320 acres each, and Survey MD 3-1036, another 320 acres. He located his headquarters and agency on the last, about thirty miles from Fort Belknap to the northeast and Fort Phantom Hill to the southwest.

Stem envisioned a bounteous future here, profitable trade and easy counseling with the Indians who wintered in the vicinity. The farm could provide grain and corn; livestock, which could be raised for miles on both sides of the river, could furnish meat for the army posts at Forts Belknap, Phantom Hill, and Chadbourne. He lost no time. Assembling men, equipment, and work stock, with no trees to clear from the rich valley land, he had 120 acres ready to plant by early summer of 1852. Cattle pens were completed and three houses erected, including his log headquarters, the one-room agency to the north, and near the stock pens a smaller bunkhouse for the foreman and the eight men he oversaw.

Lonesome for his wife, Matilda, and their daughters, Stem had brought them to Fort Graham from Seguin in February, 1852. At this outpost, about 150 miles from Stem's farm and rancho on the Clear Fork, Major Henry Hopkins Sibley was in command, and his pleasant wife afforded Mrs. Stem much company. There is no indication that Mrs. Stem or the girls ever lived at Stem's headquarters. A devoted husband and father, Stem likely kept them at Fort Graham, safely removed from his Indian agency and accompanying dangers, yet within visiting distance. He may have brought them to the Clear Fork establishment to visit, but not to live.

Stem's plans reached beyond an Indian agency, however, as we have seen. He wrote further to Hayes: "The land investment is past all doubt—there is none better—& Texas will offer many inducements for a few years to one who will look into titles a little. Just now the chance is in the new field opened on the Clear Fork. . . . one who will look may find doubtless numerous tracts of land which may be located at say 16 cts per acre which are worth from $1 to $10. . . . I must engage in some thing . . . as I expect to get rid of my Office [as Indian Agent] pretty soon."

Stem also wrote to his brother Arthur, extolling the opportunities of the Texas frontier and lauding the climate and its beneficial effects on his health. Arthur replied with some pointed and realistic queries: "How do you succeed with your merchandise? Can you do anything with mine?" Another brother, Leander, wrote in regard to the legal business of the trust company for which Jesse had formerly been the legal counselor.

The northern Comanches continued to be dangerously active, raiding and increasing their horse herds. However, Stem had established friendly relations with the southern Comanches, was their counselor, and accommodated their limited needs at his trading post.

In Colonel Stem's official reports of February and March, 1852, he describes his meeting with the southern Comanches and other tribes. He reports the council convened with most of the Texas Indians present—by the hundreds. He stated that the northern Comanches were again stealing horses from Forts Belknap and Phantom Hill, continuing to raid into Mexico, and invariably murdering and stealing on these long forays as far south as Durango. He also notes that unlicensed traders were selling intoxicating liquors to the Indians.

To the west and south of Fort Belknap, between Stem's agency and Fort Phantom Hill, were remnants of a number of small, little-known Indian tribes, the Wichitas, Caddos, Anadarkos, Keechis, Ionies, Tonkawas, and Kickapoos, relocated there in 1852 by Chief José María. These, like the southern Comanches, were inclined to be more or less friendly with the whites. Stem kept a careful eye on their creditable showing in agriculture— fields of corn, pumpkin, beans, potatoes, and other farm produce. Groups of these Indians under Chief José María came to the agency to "talk" and to eat. So did Koweaka, chief of the Wichitas, for whom Colonel Stem had great respect.

But bitter antipathy was already developing among the whites on the Texas frontier toward Indians in general. Because of the proclivity of the northern Comanches in particular to raid the settlements, steal horses, and take the scalps of the owners, this attitude of the whites is understandable. Sadly, the whites did not, perhaps could not, differentiate between "good" Indians and "bad" Indians. To most white frontiersmen, all Indians were "bad." Certain intelligent white men like Captain Marcy, Colonel Stem, and Major Neighbors, who worked closely with the Indians, understood the friendly smaller Texas bands as well as the free-ranging, unfettered, marauding tribes north of the Red River in Indian Territory.

Jesse Stem took a courageous approach to his duties as agent, with a humane attitude toward the problems of the Texas Indians. He recommended good reservations for the southern Indians and a strengthened line of military posts manned with cavalry, not foot soldiers, to discourage raids from the north. Such a plan would encourage immigration of white settlers to develop agriculture and stock raising.

At his agency, Stem bravely looked after his wards and often achieved the incredible. Once he enlisted a band of southern Comanches to ride with his white employees to capture a party of Waco Indians making away with stolen horses.

Though this Ohio gentleman-lawyer tried to be fair in dispensing beef, presents, "talk," and justice, events sometimes have a momentum of their own, and good men can do wrong.

In February, 1853, Stem had summoned Koweaka, the Wichita chief, to come to the Clear Fork for a talk on horse thieving. Koweaka then volunteered to "take the talk" to his people and do what he could to stop their stealing horses. On the same day, a month later, Stem was amazed to see Koweaka returning with eight men, women, and children, driving a herd of stolen horses down the steep east bank of the Clear Fork Crossing and on up to Stem's corrals. The Wichita leader, using his own novel interpretation of Stem's idea of returning stolen horses, had stopped by a Caddo village and picked up four ponies in order to round out the number to fourteen. Only two of the horses were of value. They were mounts stolen some weeks previously from the dragoons at Fort Croghan.

Earlier that day, Major Henry Sibley, Stem's friend and former commandant at Fort Graham, appeared at the Clear Fork agency, hot in pursuit of the Wichitas, who, he had been told, had stolen nine of his dragoons' finest horses from Fort Croghan a few nights before. When he saw Koweaka innocently trailing in two dragoon mounts, Sibley exploded. Koweaka's timing could not have been more disastrous.

"I was not to be trifled with in this matter," Sibley wrote afterward. He said that Stem had also lost patience.

Fresh from the Mexican War and fighting the Florida Seminoles, Major Sibley now faced a different enemy on the Texas prairies, and one he little understood. Stem later realized this, but at the time he allowed Sibley to sway him. Confronted with reports charging the Wichitas with stealing, looting, and occasional murder, Sibley and Stem were inclined to deal harshly. However, their orders seemed not only severe, but even puzzling: to hold Koweaka and his band in custody at Fort Belknap until two of the men, released to bring in the nine missing dragoons' horses, returned with the animals.

The officers badly misread the situation and misjudged the Wichita leader. Had Koweaka not been acting in good faith, he would simply have ignored Stem's request and fled with the horses into the wilderness of the Wichita Mountains. Instead, he came to deliver the horses to Stem. He was "the only Wichita chief who had shown any disposition to comply with the orders of the white men."

Sibley and Stem told the Indians what they were to do. No violence erupted, but a solemn mood prevailed. Chief Koweaka requested a private talk with Major Sibley. He calmly explained how hard it was to control his young men, whose way of life revolved around stealing horses. He asked to be sent alone as emissary to his tribe to settle the matter of the dragoons' horses.

Sibley refused. Arrogant and unyielding, he miscalculated the hazards of holding any Plains warrior as prisoner, especially a respected chieftain. Koweaka appeared to accept the decision stoically. Disarmed by Sibley's men, the Indians retired quietly to their lodges on the banks of the Clear Fork. Sentries were posted to see that no Indian escaped.

Koweaka walked with dignity into his lodge, where his wife and young son awaited him. Ceremonially, he placed his moccasins at the head of their bed of skins. This was the traditional sign of a warrior not to depart a place, but to fight to the death. At midnight, an Indian noiselessly rushed a sentry, who fired with deadly aim, rousing the camp. As though prearranged, Koweaka strode over his dead comrade and threw himself at the sentry, stabbing him to death before a bullet entered his own heart. In the ensuing melee, most of the other Wichitas escaped.

Those who later parted the flaps of the tent found Koweaka's wife with their small son lying in her arms, a robe pulled up to their breasts, both stabbed to the heart. An old Wichita woman, wailing the death chant, told how Koweaka's wife had calmly assented to her fate. Major Sibley, repentant, described the finale in a letter to his wife: "Nothing in romance or history that I have ever read approximated this act of devotion and self sacrifice. . . . The bright moonlight upon the beautiful countenance of the young mother . . . with her innocent boy by her side . . . the husband, father, and warrior still stretched upon the sod . . . the sentinel not five feet away from him, his cold blue eyes looking to heaven." Their liberty lost, Koweaka and his wife had chosen to walk their ancestral path.

During the following months, Stem continued to plan and press the authorities in Washington for reservations for his Indians. He reported that the Indians showed a willingness to settle down, provided a reservation could be set aside for them. His proposals laid the groundwork for the reservations Captain R. B. Marcy and Major Robert S. Neighbors later established.

However, Jesse Stem never lost sight of the estate and settlement he planned to develop along the Clear Fork. In letters to Ohio, he had mentioned that he hoped to find a reliable man to take charge of his farm and ranch on a cash- or quota-sharing proposition. He must have found one, for crops and herds continued to prosper through 1854, as we have seen. Could it have been Thomas Lambshead he found to be a "reliable man"?

Prospects in Clear Fork country looked bright for the Stem family in the late summer of 1853, when they returned to Ohio to consolidate business interests with Stem's brothers and other associates and to visit family and friends. Stem had sent in his resignation as Indian agent before his departure from the Clear Fork agency.

Finishing his business in Ohio, Stem left his family there and in November, 1853, started back to Texas to expand his holdings on the Clear Fork. Instead of traveling as usual down the Mississippi to New Orleans, thence to Galveston by boat and overland to western Texas, Stem, with a friend, William Leppelman, left the boat at the mouth of the Arkansas River and took another boat up to Shreveport, Louisiana. There they stayed over a few days on business.

They then secured a two-horse wagon with a driver to take a load of supplies to the Texas frontier, 350 miles to the west. For themselves, they purchased a carriage and a team of mules. After their departure from Fort Worth, the wagon broke down fourteen miles east of Fort Belknap. Leaving the driver behind with the wagon, the two men continued on toward Fort Belknap in hope of arriving by early evening on Sunday, February 12, 1854. They never made it.

The next day, a rider arrived at the fort and reported having seen two dead bodies beside the road four miles east of the post. Major H. W. Merrill, garrison commander, sent out a wagon for the bodies. The men had met horrible deaths. Stem's skull and jawbone were broken, and Leppelman's skull was caved in and shattered and an arm also fractured. A rifle, broken and bent, and moccasins and a bow covering identified as Wichita or Waco lay nearby. Only the men's coats and hats had been removed; their watches and money were left on the bodies. The Indians had made off with two mules and a horse. Stem and Leppelman were buried in the Fort Belknap cemetery on February 14.

The deed was traced to the Kickapoos, who were then in Indian Territory. A young kinsman who was with the murderers had told the Kickapoo headmen, who then reported to the army officers when summoned. Why the Kickapoos left evidence pointing to the Wacos and Wichitas is unclear. Perhaps they were trying to express their outrage at the harsh treatment of Wichita chief Koweaka and his people, or perhaps simply laying a false trail.

Major Merrill informed Texas Indian Superintendent Robert S. Neighbors, who was shocked at the cold-blooded clubbing to death of Colonel Stem. Neighbors and Major Merrill, reassured to learn that Brevet Major A. D. Tree was in pursuit of the murderers, offered a reward of five hundred dollars for delivery of the culprits for trial.

However, Indian justice did not wait on the military or a jury. When Major Tree found the Kickapoos in Indian Territory, the tribe had already held council, at which the execution of the Kickapoo criminals had been decreed. One was killed by his nephew, the other by his brother, and all the stolen property was returned. The names of the murderers seem appropriate: Polecat and Thunder.

Rutherford B. Hayes said of the death of his friend: "So good a man, so much beloved, so many to mourn his loss. It is awful, awful; I can't get it out of my thoughts."

The remains of Colonel Jesse Stem were removed from old Fort Belknap Cemetery in 1910, taken to Washington, D.C., and reinterred with honors, according to Joseph Carroll McConnell, who interviewed frontier settlers of the area in the 1920's.

A gap exists in the story of Stem's farm and rancho after 1854, though it was known in Ohio that he had left it in the care of others. Mrs. Stem expanded the holdings in 1855, as we have noted. In *Interwoven*, Sallie Reynolds Matthews picks up the thread in 1885 with an account of the lease and eventual purchase of the Jesse Stem lands by the J. A. Matthews family.

Many questions remain unanswered for the thirty-two years from 1853 to 1885. Who was the "reliable man" who farmed for Stem? Who lived at Stem's headquarters after his murder? Who looked after his livestock? Who plowed his fields and grew the crops that so impressed Marcy and Neighbors and their expedition when they came to the Clear Fork Crossing and described Stem's farm and rancho in August, 1854? The puzzles are intriguing.

Place names are often enigmas, but it is sad that this educated, courageous, enterprising colonizer should be linked by name only with the place of his death, Stem's Gap, and not with the fertile valley and clear stream where he made his mark on the farthest Texas frontier, now known as Lambshead.

3   *Thomas Lambshead*

ORN IN 1805, Thomas Lambshead was a farmer from Devon, England. Just how his name became associated with what is now called Lambshead Ranch is to this day a mystery. Like Jesse Stem, Lambshead was lured to the Texas frontier by visions of fame and fortune.

In the 1840's, glowing descriptions were poured into the Englishman's ears by Sherman Converse, a London promoter for the ill-starred Peters Colony in western Texas. Colonizers in Louisville, Kentucky, organized the colony and negotiated with President Sam Houston in January, 1841, to settle immigrants in the Republic of Texas in the largest empresario colony the Republic ever granted. By July, 1843, the Kentuckians had taken in London partners. The Peters Colony then encompassed what would become twenty-six Texas counties, including nearly all of future Throckmorton and Shackelford counties.

Young Lambshead sailed for Texas with his wife and child, arriving in the Peters Colony, according to company records, before July 1, 1848. Thomas Lambshead and family are listed on the 1850 census of Navarro County (now Johnson and Hood counties) as a forty-five-year-old farmer, born in England; his wife, Eliza, twenty-five; and a "babe, female." Lambshead's moving to the colony from Devon, England, was mentioned in a letter from W. S. Peters to the colony agent, H. O. Hedgcoxe. In 1850, Lambshead was issued a certificate for 640 acres by the Texas land commissioner. No other mention is made of him in the scant records of the Peters Colony, which seems to have been plagued with disaster from its beginning in 1841 until its gradual dissolution in the 1880's.

Lambshead said he came to the Clear Fork region about 1847 and recounts in a letter some of his experiences on a farm there. He must have searched out the country thoroughly before locating and patenting in 1859 one of the most ideal spots for a ranch headquarters. The section he possibly lived on before patenting later, a usual procedure of the times, was bounded on the south by heavily wooded Paint Creek. Round Mountain Creek flowed diagonally across the section from north to south into Paint Creek, which then emptied into the Clear Fork. If Lambshead lived out his patent here, he surely located on the high bluff overlooking Paint Creek with about ten acres of good, level land lying ripe for cultivation between the creek and the small cone of Round Mountain. Being a farmer, Lambshead would have seen the advantages for farming and livestock raising provided by the protected canyons, grassy mesas and bottoms, good water, and rich alluvium. The records show that on May 27, 1859, Lambshead patented this 640 acres in Throckmorton County as original grantee and patentee.

It was in this vicinity that Captain Marcy had camped in 1849 and held council with Sanaco's band of Comanches. The location was crossed by Marcy's California Road and was only eight miles northwest of Stem's farm and rancho near Clear Fork Crossing. It is improbable that Marcy saw any evidence of farming or ranching here in 1854, or he would have remarked upon it, as he did about Stem's farm and rancho. Later, in the 1880's, the Reynolds brothers liked Lambshead's location so well that they established headquarters there on the high bluff, but named it Round Mountain Ranch. Judge J. A. Matthews often remarked that it was Round Mountain Creek that should have borne Lambshead's name.

From "Clear Fork Farm," on May 1, 1856, Lambshead wrote, in his quaint idiom, to the commissioner of Indian affairs, George W. Manypenny, Washington, D.C., on behalf of Superintendent Major Robert S. Neighbors and the Comanche Indians. Now an experienced frontiersman, he spoke with rare, level-headed understanding:

I have taken the liberty for to drop your Honour a fue lines respecting the Indians—settled down on this frontier.

I have been a citizen here nearly ten years & sustained a deal of loss of cattle, & horses & mules by the Comanche Indians & other Bands of Indians & nothing has ever been done for us until this last year.

I came here on this farm in Decr Eighteen Hundred & Fifty-four, in Jany, fifty-five, those savages began for to butcher up my cattle, & steal my Horses & mules. Three or four times a week, I had something killed or my men would find arrows stuck in some of my stock cattle or oxen. At this time I thought it advisable for to move my wife & family at or near the Fort at Belknap, for protection—I did so, seeing their life in danger. I had nine men employed at my farm at this time. I ordered them all for to take their guns to the field at this time we were planting corn. myself with the balance carried our arms until the month of May fifty-five. about this time John Conner arrived here with a fue Comanches from the lower reserve by order of Dr. Hill our late resident agent. Had not Superintendent Major Neighbors arrived here about or shortly after this time an proceeded for to settle down those Indians, nothing but a bloody war must have commenced immediately, which would have caused maney of our familys for to be murdered up by scatered Indians during that time. And also & immense expence to our Government & no credit to a civilized nation for to have butchered up those poor savages which were at this time as Ignorant as the Brutes, and as ravenous as the wolves.

We must acknowledge & do as Citizens of this frontier, that we are highly indebted to Mr. Superintendent for his unweared exertions towards us. The Caddo Indians & some of the other small bands of Indians have begun for to plow with the hoe already, no doubt but all the young ones will in a fue years be able for to support themselves. I do not think that the Old Ones that have been living so many years entirely wild in the woods wil ever work, but I think by this mode of setling them down, we shall derive this benefit that is I think our property will be safe, & our familys also.

Buffalo Hump a Comanche Captain and his band came in a short [time] ago and maney others of the wild Indians it is said will come in shortly at the Comanche reserve. Our resident Agents Capt Baylor & Capt Ross are using every means for to keep those Indians from stealing & commiting depredations and I hope that they will succeed in it which is the only means which will keep peace & harmony between the citizens and the Indians.

Lambshead's remark, "I came here on this farm in Decr Eighteen Hundred & Fifty-four," would indicate it was a different place from where he had been living. The only information to be found on the location of Lambshead's "Clear Fork Ranch" is given by Joseph Carroll McConnell in *The West Texas Frontier*: "Before the [Civil] War Thomas Lambshead bought a ranch four miles north and west of Fort Griffin." Presumably, McConnell meant where Fort Griffin was later located in 1867. If so, he places Lambshead's "Clear Fork Ranch" at the mouth of Lambshead Creek. However, the land records do not reveal that Lambshead ever owned property in this vicinity. It is more likely that he leased the Jesse Stem farm and rancho at this location from the Stem estate.

If Lambshead did indeed farm the Stem lands and made a success of it, people may have begun referring to it as Lambshead's, and the name stuck. On the other hand, as John A. Matthews said, the name could have come from any little thing, like a man's wagon breaking down in the valley near the creek. One bit of contrary evidence does exist. Eliza Johnston, who accompanied her husband, Albert Sidney Johnston, to the Clear

Fork on a freezing night in early January, 1856, noted in her diary that they camped "near a house where the man Skidmore was killed by Indians last year. His wife and children & his brother still live there." The army camp (which would become Camp Cooper, the reservation army post) was several cold miles upstream, and her information was doubtless hearsay, but whether she got the name right or not, a family was living in Stem's house and according to all accounts it was not Mrs. Stem.

Though Thomas Lambshead lived as neighbor to Captain Newton C. Givens and his Stone Ranch, built on Walnut Creek in 1856, he clearly did not share Givens' hostility toward the Indians and Superintendent Robert S. Neighbors' efforts to settle them on reserves along the Clear Fork. At the time when the campaign headed by Givens and others to oust Neighbors from his position and to drive the Indians from the reserves was reaching its peak, Thomas Lambshead again championed Neighbors' cause in a letter signed with J. N. Gibbins. Writing to Commissioner Manypenny "from Clear Fork Ranch" on March 30, 1858, he said: "We the undersigned are in favour of the Comanche Indians and the Caddos and the other small tribes of Indians for still to remain on the present reservation in Texas[.] We the undersigned are in favour of our present Agent Major Neighbors for still to remain in office."

A citizen of the frontier, Thomas Lambshead played a central role in the establishment of Throckmorton County. Created January 13, 1858, the county was named for Dr. William E. Throckmorton, one of the first settlers of North Texas. Thomas Lambshead, William L. Browning, and Robert King were appointed commissioners to organize the county. Their charge was to call an election of county officers and to select not less than three suitable places within five miles of the center of the county to be considered for the county seat. Also, all courts were to be held at Tarrant and Gibbons Ranch on Elm Creek until a suitable building for a courthouse could be erected. However, the removal of the Indian reservation in 1859 and the outbreak of the Civil War in 1861, together with Indian outrages, delayed the county's organization until 1879.

The whereabouts of Thomas Lambshead after 1858 is tantalizing and confusing. In September, 1858, the Butterfield Overland Mail began operating a biweekly stage service from Saint Louis to San Francisco. The route entered what is now Lambshead Ranch at the Clear Fork Crossing, went up Lambshead Creek, passing very near the present headquarters, and left the ranch through the Butterfield Gap to the southwest. The Butterfield line had stage stations from twelve to twenty-five miles apart where teams could be changed and food obtained by the passengers. Local legend has it that Thomas Lambshead kept the station at the Clear Fork Crossing or the Butterfield relay station on the west side of the Clear Fork across Lambshead Creek a short distance from the crossing, whose stone foundations can still be seen. However, the Butterfield Overland Mail records show the station at the crossing was kept by John Irwin and T. E. Jackson, according to R. P. Conkling's *The Butterfield Overland Mail*. When the Butterfield Mail made its first run from east to west in October, 1858, the *New York Herald* sent along an adventurous twenty-three-year-old reporter, Waterman L. Ormsby, to observe and send back stories of the trip. Arriving at the Clear Fork station on September 22, Ormsby wrote that a Dr. Birch was mail agent there and that a log hut was being erected for the station keeper and help on the banks of the river. He did not report a relay station on the west bank. J. C. Irwin, who came with his family in September, 1859, to live in a house they built at a big spring downstream from Camp Cooper, where his father had a contract to supply beef, recalls that Henry McClus-

key herded the stage horses kept at the Clear Fork station, but
he makes no mention of a relay station.

However, Watt R. Matthews heard from his family and others
that the stone ruins on the west side of the river mark the site of
the relay station and that Thomas Lambshead kept the Butterfield stage stand on the Clear Fork. He explained how logical it
was for the remount or relay station to be located there. The
Clear Fork can be filled bank to bank with raging waters, carrying dangerous debris from torrential rains and floods during
spring and summer. It made sense to put a stage stand on the
east bank and a relay station on the west bank of the river. When
the stream was up, travelers and mail on the Butterfield Stage
could cross by boat or raft to continue their journey by stage
from either side of the river.

Only a few yards from the ruins are three graves whose weath-
ered stones, similar to those chiseled with 1850 dates in the old
Fort Belknap cemetery, give no clue as to who lies there. If
Thomas Lambshead did indeed keep the relay station or operate
Stem's farm or rancho, it is possible that he knew or held a clue.

The Conkling account does state that Butterfield records reveal that a Mr. Lambshead, in September, 1858, kept the station
at Mountain Pass some seventy miles to the southwest, eleven
miles south of present-day Merkel. Ormsby also speaks of stopping at Abercrombie Peak (Conkling's Mountain Pass) for breakfast, which was prepared by a Negro woman and consisted of
tough beef, butterless shortcake, and coffee. A year later the
woman was killed by Indians. Ormsby goes on to say that the
keeper of this station, as well as the next one, Valley Creek, fifteen miles farther along, was named Lambshead. The appella-
tion was suitable, he thought, because Lambshead was running
300 head of sheep on the public domain without expense to himself while he was attending to his other duties at the two stage

stations. This is the last available reference to Thomas Lambshead.

With the outbreak of the Civil War in early 1861, the stage line was abandoned, and so were Camp Cooper and the line of frontier forts from Belknap to the Rio Grande. The entire Texas frontier had little or no organized protection for about a year. Settlers on the extreme, exposed frontier began a general movement fifty to a hundred miles eastward, to more protected, densely settled regions. Much confusion prevailed, and families lost sight of one another. A few of the more courageous moved together on the frontier and "forted up." One such group was at Fort Davis, several miles down the Clear Fork from present Fort Griffin, and another, called Picketville, was near the present town of Breckenridge.

During this chaotic period, the Thomas Lambshead family is not mentioned. No marriage, death, or other records were left in Throckmorton County connected with Thomas Lambshead until ten years after he was listed as Butterfield Stage keeper. Then, on June 11, 1868, Eliza E. Lambshead signed a deed recorded as abstract 223 in the Throckmorton County Courthouse. She was listed as a resident of Bryan, Brazos County, Texas. Was she Thomas' wife, who would have been forty-eight years old, or his daughter? Eliza acknowledged the sale of the land patented by Thomas Lambshead on Paint Creek to Walton and Hill. From them, the property went to Mart Hoover; in 1880, to Matthews and Reynolds; in 1883, to Reynolds Brothers; then to Reynolds Cattle Company; and, in 1940, to Ross Sloan, present owner of Round Mountain Ranch, with headquarters still located on Lambshead's original patent. No other clues concerning Eliza, his daughter, or those three unmarked, stone-bordered graves near the old remount station on Lambshead Creek have come to light.

In 1897, John A. Matthews located and built his camp on the banks of Lambshead Creek near its source. During 1906, he made headquarters out of the camp and began calling it Lambshead Ranch. He was able to purchase Lambshead Valley from the Jesse Stem estate in 1909; he had been leasing the property from them since 1886. The Matthews family moved out to live all year around at Lambshead headquarters in 1915. As was the custom, they called all the land they owned Lambshead Ranch because of its headquarters location. By whatever quirk of fate the valley and creek became identified with Thomas Lambshead, this is how Lambshead Ranch was named.

4   *Robert S. Neighbors*

ROBERT S. NEIGHBORS was born November 3, 1815, in Charlotte County, Virginia. His father, a tobacco planter, minister, and college professor, died when Robert was quite young. The son inherited many of the father's characteristics. He was six feet two inches tall, with broad shoulders, square chin, blue eyes, and red hair. An adroit good humor redeemed a quick, stern temper. His stock of amusing stories and affable manner gained him innumerable friends, and his honesty, integrity, and firmness of character earned him respect.

He came to Texas by way of Louisiana, where, in 1836, he joined the Free and Accepted Masons, Saint Alban's Lodge No. 28, an event that enhanced his endeavors the remainder of his life. Masonry, like religion, was a vital bond in relationships on the frontier during the mid-nineteenth century. In Texas, the young Virginian soon became a close friend of President Sam Houston, also a Mason. Neighbors was named quartermaster of the Army of the Republic of Texas with the rank of major, serving from 1839 to 1840. In 1842, he enlisted in Captain John C. Hay's Company of Mounted Gunmen. In a border incident, he was captured by the Mexican Army along with other Texans and marched to San Carlos Perote prison near Veracruz. There he languished with the fifty-two other Texans until they were released in 1844. He received a hero's welcome when they returned to Galveston.

It is to be remembered that Houston served as president of the Republic of Texas from 1836 to 1838, Mirabeau B. Lamar from 1838 to 1841, and Houston again from 1841 to 1844. The attitudes of the two men toward the Texas Indians were diametrically opposed. Houston, who had lived for a while with the Cherokees and had had an Indian wife, understood the Indians, was sympathetic to them, and had, therefore, little Indian trouble during his first administration. Lamar, however, reversed all that Houston had done. His objective was to get the Indians out of Texas, dead or alive. It was during his term, in 1840, that a great blunder in the history of Texas Indian relations occurred in San Antonio: the Council House Massacre, in which twelve Comanche chiefs, sixty to seventy warriors, and several women were wantonly shot down. When Houston returned to office, he set about repairing the damage, and he involved his friend Major Robert S. Neighbors in the Indian cause. Their teamwork continued after Texas joined the United States and Houston went to Washington as one of the first two Texas senators. The two men worked as partners on behalf of the Texas Indians for fourteen years, Houston backing their cause in Washington and Neighbors in Texas.

The Indian policy Neighbors would pursue as agent for these years had been launched by Houston at his second inauguration as president of Texas on December 13, 1841. Immediately, President Houston sent out his agents to assist the Indians and to persuade them "to walk the white path of peace." The agrarian tribes gathered on the Trinity River near Fort Worth September 28, 1843, to sign a treaty. Exactly one year later, at Torrey Brothers Trading House near Waco, Houston himself concluded a peace treaty between these Indians and the southern Comanches and the Republic of Texas. Central to Houston's peace policy was the setting up of frontier trading houses, licensed by the government. It was hoped that with Indians able to trade for fair prices, plundering would decline. The lesser tribes also promised to remain north of the trading posts. Still smarting from the Council House Massacre, the Comanches refused to accept any boundary.

After Texas entered the Union on February 16, 1846, Neighbors, retained as agent, immediately participated in making the first United States treaty with the other Texas Indians. The Comanches, still wary, refused to talk with the new U.S. commissioners. As a show of good faith, Sam Houston, now senator, had Neighbors bring the Comanches the "ring and the casket," symbols Houston had previously told them would identify the bearer as the lawfully authorized agent of the government. On May 15, 1846, the U.S. commissioners and chiefs of the southern Comanches, Ionies, Anadarkos, Caddos, Lipans, Tonkawas, Keechis, Tawacanos, Wichitas, and Wacos signed a treaty, which was witnessed by Robert S. Neighbors and other agents. The terms of the treaty, which encompassed Houston's earlier Indian policy, guided Neighbors throughout his career.

Fortunately, Neighbors, who had learned to speak Comanche by the mid-1840's, was chosen to escort a group of Indian leaders, among whom were Santa Anna and Old Owl of the Comanches, and José María of the Anadarkos, on a visit to Washington. His duty was to show the Indians the power and wealth of the United States and how the national government worked. Neighbors proved to be a proficient guide and considerate chaperon. The party rode to Washington horseback. Houston, undoubtedly dressed in his own Indian regalia, received the colorful delegation in the halls of the Senate. The chiefs spent a month in the nation's capital. When they returned, Neighbors gave them the horses they had ridden on their state journey, and the chiefs hurried to rejoin their bands.

By appointment of the federal government, Neighbors became special agent to the Texas Indians on March 20, 1847. At that time the status of Indians in Texas was unique; they could own no land and were regarded as "tenants at will" as established by the Republic of Texas. When Texas became a state, no intercourse laws were passed and none were extended to the Texas Indians by the United States. Texas Governor J. Pickney Henderson did attempt to set up intercourse laws by drawing a temporary line about thirty miles above the last settlement, beyond which "no white person should be allowed to go unless for legal purpose." This arrangement brought down the anger of both Indians and whites, with Neighbors often caught in the middle. Old Owl was especially agitated by the unilateral line and invited Neighbors to come "talk" with a gathering of the friendly and hostile bands he had managed to bring together at the main Comanche camp near present-day Seymour.

Neighbors was met on the prairie by Old Owl, who escorted him to camp and introduced him both to old acquaintances among the southern Comanche, Tonkawa, and Wichita tribes and to the hostile chiefs. Old Owl entertained Neighbors and all the chiefs that night in his tepee. Neighbors wrote of this council of February 14, 1848: "I found them to be a jovial set, and the evening was spent in eating and smoking, and the discussion of the usual themes among the prairie bands, viz: 'war and women,' finding myself, in the end, upon good understanding with them."

In 1849, Neighbors was sent by General W. J. Worth in charge of a party, which included John S. ("Rip") Ford as assistant, to lay out a wagon road from San Antonio to El Paso. This he did, going out in twenty-two days. The route was roughly the same

Indians approaching Stem's trading post at Clear Fork Crossing.

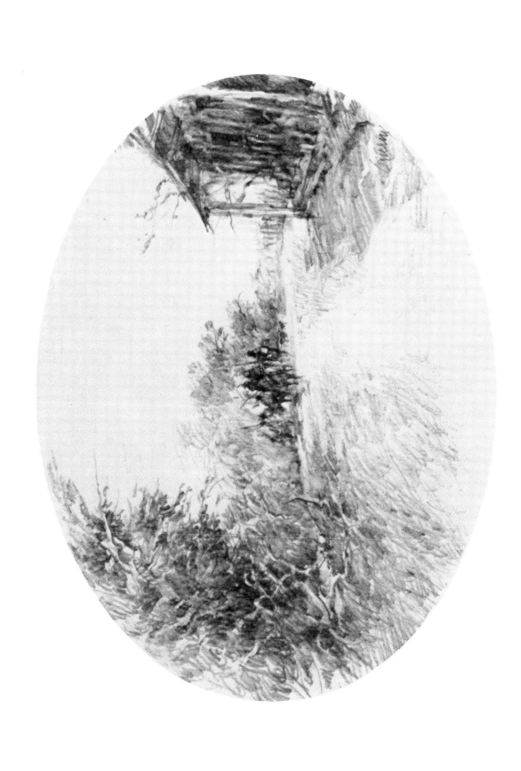

as present-day U.S. Highway 90. Returning, he came by the Upper Route, later used by the Butterfield Overland Mail, to the Middle Concho River and thence to Austin. He calculated the distance from El Paso to Austin as 598 miles, practically the same as on today's road maps. He estimated the mileage by the distance traveled by a mule at four miles an hour.

When he returned from El Paso, Neighbors was ordered to Washington to help draw up a satisfactory policy for dealing with Texas Indians. He was ready for this long-anticipated opportunity with five proposals: "(1) for the government to extinguish the Indian title to as much land as the state needed for immediate use; (2) to acquire from Texas sufficient land for permanent settlement of the Texas Indians; (3) to extend the intercourse laws of the United States to the Indians of Texas; (4) to establish a general agency with at least three sub-agents and interpreters to reside among the Indians; and (5) to establish the necessary military posts in the Indian country to assist the agents in carrying out all laws and treaties." He further suggested that the government extend "such services as carpentry, blacksmithing, agricultural instruction for adults, academic education for the children, and the supplying of cattle, tools, seeds, and utensils until the Indians became self-sustaining." His proposals, which essentially extended Houston's policy, were well received and later implemented.

Returning from Washington, Neighbors visited Sam Houston at his plantation, Raven Hill, near Huntsville, Texas. Lusty stories, plans, and possibilities for Texas and its Indians must have flavored the meeting—as well as a sprinkling of politics.

With the inauguration of the Whig administration in March, 1849, Neighbors was replaced as federal Indian agent for Texas. However, Governor P. H. Bell had a job for him. The western boundary of Texas had been in limbo since Texas entered the

Union, though the state claimed everything north and east of the Rio Grande to the river's source in Colorado. She also had the fifteen-million-dollar debt incurred by the Texas Revolution and its aftermath. Bell sent Neighbors in the fall of 1849 to organize El Paso County and Santa Fe, if possible. He was successful with El Paso County. The political climate in Santa Fe, however, thwarted his efforts there. The boundary question was later settled in the Compromise of 1850, when Texas gave up her claim to the part of New Mexico east of the Rio Grande and a strip in Colorado in exchange for the federal government's assuming the Texas debt.

In 1851, Major Neighbors was elected to the Texas legislature, and he took his lovely young wife with him to Austin. With the welfare of the Texas Indians in mind, he successfully sponsored a resolution opening the way to establish the Texas Indian reservations, though two bills he introduced failed to pass.

Along with his other attainments, Major Neighbors was a surveyor. The Texas Emigration and Land Company, which was locating and surveying the lands of the massive Peters Colony where Thomas Lambshead was a settler, employed Neighbors in February, 1853, to survey a connecting line from a point near Goldthwaite in Mills County to Fort Belknap. With equipment and a party of Delaware and Shawnee Indians, he ran the line up Pecan Bayou to the fort, a distance of seventy-eight miles. Many subsequent surveys were later hung to this survey. In April, 1853, the *Texas State Gazette* commented: "We think the Company very fortunate in securing the service of so competent and worthy a gentleman as Major Neighbors for this difficult duty, and we hope he will do much towards adjusting in a satisfactory manner the land matters of this colony." Neighbors, however, said he was "embarrassed in his work" because earlier surveys were so irregular he could not connect with them. But he thought the land the finest he had seen in the state and regretted that it had been tied up for such a long time.

Upon election of President Franklin Pierce, Major Neighbors was again appointed federal Indian agent on May 9, 1853. He then established his wife comfortably in San Antonio and left for a reunion on the western frontier with Indian friends, traders to the Indians, and military leaders.

5   *Stone Ranch*

WHEN FOUNDED IN 1855, the Stone Ranch was the last ranching outpost between the frontier line of Texas forts—Belknap, Phantom Hill, and Chadbourne—and the small rock or adobe houses on the plains or the fort-like haciendas of the Rio Grande Valley in New Mexico. It became a notable landmark, and for a quarter of a century it served a series of diverse purposes.

Its builder was Lieutenant, later Captain Newton C. Givens, who was to become Neighbors' adversary in the matter of the Texas Indians. Givens was adventurous, imaginative, and shrewd, with a flair for architectural design and building. Handsome and outgoing, he was well known and highly regarded. Stationed in a frontier garrison, where life was boring for other officers, he found it exciting and stimulating. Amply provided with funds, he engaged in various rewarding endeavors.

We first learn of Lieutenant Givens from Marcy's secretary, W. B. Parker, who mentions him when Marcy was at Fort Belknap in August, 1854. Givens' presence, personality, and appearance must have impressed Parker, for he wrote of the lieutenant at length. He described him as an ardent sportsman and was amazed by the pack of thirty-five hounds he had bred, "the finest on the continent." Givens had crossed several breeds to produce a strain best suited to the vast open spaces of West Texas, combining the sense of smell of the foxhound with the speed of the greyhound and the courage of the bull-terrier. In addition, he always ran his pack in company with a bull-terrier, whose example taught them bravery. He was particular to keep pure strains for the crossing. The most convenient game for the dogs to chase were wolves and jackrabbits.

Mr. Parker accompanied Givens on a rabbit chase. Soon the hounds, by their sounds and actions, indicated they were after something more exciting than rabbits. They bayed at a post oak tree and, when the men came up, they saw a mountain lion on a limb above, "as large as a small mule and display[ing] a set of formidable teeth." A shot through the body caused the lion to leap from the tree, but he fought off the dogs and got to another tree. Another shot through the shoulder brought the lion down, and the dogs set upon him. One dog had his skull broken; another had his leg torn off. The dogs finally won, with the help of Givens' rifle. Parker ended his account by saying, "It was a right royal hunt."

Parker may have learned, also, that Givens had been commandant of the small garrison at Fort Phantom Hill when that post was abandoned earlier that year, on April 6, 1854. Phantom Hill is still renowned for the ruins of its stone chimneys. They were all that survived the burning of the picket-house fort by Givens' men as they departed the place they so hated because of bad water, bad food, and boredom.

Soon after Parker was at Fort Belknap, Givens was promoted to captain and placed in command of a company of the 2nd Dragoons. However, his added responsibilities did not deter him from other nonmilitary pursuits. Plans were being made to establish an Indian reservation on the Clear Fork some thirty miles to the west of Fort Belknap and to locate a military post there. The two installations would require a considerable supply of beef. Givens had scouted the Clear Fork country and knew it was an ideal cattle range. He quickly decided to start a ranch just south of the area where the reservation and the post were to be situated and to be in business when the Indians and soldiers arrived. No one can explain how, in addition to his military duties, he managed to bring it off, but he did.

He made contact with the small ranchers to the east for cattle. He employed the freighters who brought to Fort Belknap provisions and materials from such distant points as Jefferson and Indianola. His mother lived in San Antonio, where he presumably had grown up. Through these and other sources, he procured carpenters and stonemasons. He knew there was an abundance of stone in the Clear Fork area. He himself was a good organizer.

He selected a spot for his headquarters on Walnut Creek about eight miles northwest of Clear Fork Crossing, a convenient location for what he had in mind. All he needed to protect the improvements of his headquarters was title to the land they were on. The range in every direction, except for the Comanche reservation, was free. Fortunately for him, getting title for a place for his headquarters turned out to be a quick and easy transaction. A short time before, Cooper Campbell had secured a certificate of title to 640 acres. The tract was half a mile wide and two miles long. It included about three-quarters of a mile of the Clear Fork River and extended slightly southeastward about a mile beyond Walnut Creek. On Walnut Creek was a sizable spring beside which the land was relatively level with just enough pitch to drain well, an ideal protected place to establish his headquarters. Givens bought this tract from Campbell for some undisclosed amount, probably not more than fifty cents an acre. As land was selling at the time, it may have been as little as twenty-five cents an acre. He acquired title to the land July 20, 1855.

No record exists as to how Givens managed to put the stone buildings, corrals, and fences together in so short a time. To utilize the abundant stone in the area for building and fences required a tremendous amount of labor, rough hands to break and carry, and skilled masons to shape and lay. Somehow, Givens assembled a small army of workers. No doubt he himself spent much time overseeing the whole operation. While working out all the preliminary arrangements, he had prepared definitive building plans for his entire layout, and the finished buildings bore witness to his skill and precision. Whether he had professional help in the planning and supervision is not known, but there is little doubt that he was responsible for most, if not all, of the project.

Sallie Reynolds Matthews, who lived at the Stone Ranch with her family in 1866 and 1867, details in *Interwoven* how the buildings, corrals, and fences appeared then. Don Biggers, who was familiar with the site, described the Stone Ranch as it appeared in the early 1890's. In 1958, the artist E. M. ("Buck") Schiwetz drew a reconstruction of the old Stone Ranch as described by Sallie Reynolds Matthews. (Today, the once-famous landmark, still known as the Old Stone Ranch, is marked only by several piles of stones amid the native grasses.)

The Matthews and Biggers descriptions indicate that the main house, when finished, consisted of two large rooms, each sixteen by twenty feet, with a twelve-foot hall between. A heavy oak door opened into each of the large rooms. At the end of each room was a commodious fireplace with a tall chimney. One keystone had the date 1856 chiseled into it. (J. A. Matthews later put the keystone into the chimney of the cookshack at Lambshead headquarters.) The walls were two feet thick, with exceedingly fine masonry work. The woodwork, especially the mantels for the fireplaces, was excellent. One of the large rooms had a plank floor, well made, and the other room had a flagstone floor, beautifully fitted with smooth stones. To the north was a detached building with two rooms, a large chimney in the center, and fireplaces opening into each room. Originally, it was the bunkhouse for the hands. Later, when the Reynoldses lived there, it was used by the boys of the family.

While the houses were under construction, another crew was working on a cattle corral made of rock and as large as the average city block. The walls at the bottom were almost four feet thick and stood five feet high. They sloped in slightly at the top. Some two hundred yards east of the cattle corral was a sheep corral, with walls three feet high and more than four feet thick. Some of the stones weighed a ton.

Captain W. J. Maltby, of Callahan County, told Don Biggers in 1890 that, as a young man, he had assisted in the stone work of the houses and the corrals. Also, he had helped with the rock work at Forts Belknap, Phantom Hill, and Chadbourne. He said he had never seen finer stone work than the houses and corrals at the Stone Ranch.

At the spring was a well house. However, the spring ceased to flow, probably during the severe drought of 1886–1887, and a well was dug by hand just across Walnut Creek. Water was drawn from it with an old-time sweep.

Captain Givens was not allowed to realize his dream of becoming a cattleman with a handsome estate and leisure to ride to the hounds. He was apprised by his superiors that no commissioned officer could sell supplies to the army. This ended his plan of furnishing beef to Fort Belknap and the new garrison at the recently established Camp Cooper, where he was stationed.

Soon he was to become involved with other matters that prevented him from enjoying the life of a sportsman at his Stone Ranch.

6 *Texas Indian Reservations*

ANUMBER OF LITTLE-KNOWN, comparatively small Indian tribes survived in the eastern half of Texas, living under Spanish, French, and Mexican flags for many generations, long before Texas became a state. Due to abundant rainfall, vegetation, timber, and game, they remained fairly sedentary. For two hundred years, however, the nomadic southern Comanche bands followed their total commissary, the buffalo, over the grassy, arid plains of West Texas. The U.S. government took over the handling of these two divergent groups of Indians in 1845 when Texas entered the Union. The federal government had developed a policy of locating Indians from the eastern and southern parts of the nation in Indian Territory, lands set aside for them just west of Arkansas. It would seem logical for the U.S. government to have moved all the Indians in Texas up into Indian Territory, and this might have been done had it not been for U.S. Senator Sam Houston.

From long association with the southern tribes, the Plains Indians, and the other Texas Indians, Houston knew they did not want to leave their home territories. He therefore quickly intervened in their behalf. He and his friend Texas Indian agent Robert S. Neighbors advocated instead the establishment of reservations for the Indians living in the state. Because Texas, like the original thirteen colonies, retained her public lands when she was annexed, the federal government would have to negotiate with the state for Indian reservation lands. This might have been done without delay had not the Whigs won the election of November, 1848. Neighbors was replaced, and the plight of the Texas Indians continued for four years.

Fortunately for the Indians, the election of 1852 returned the Democrats to power. Major Neighbors was then appointed federal Indian superintendent for the Texas Indians in May, 1853. Senator Houston and Neighbors at once renewed their plans for Indian reservations in Texas. Preparing the way, the Texas legislature, on February 16, 1852, had passed a joint resolution, sponsored by Neighbors in the House and by his old friend John S. ("Rip") Ford in the Senate, authorizing the governor to negotiate with the federal government to collect and confine the Texas Indians to reservations within the state. Two years later, on February 6, 1854, the legislature approved another bill setting aside twelve leagues of land for three reservations, each to contain four leagues. The bill specified that the land would revert to the state when no longer used as Indian reservations. In other words, the state was only lending the lands to the federal government; in no event was title to any of it ever to pass to the Indians. The bill also provided that a federal army camp could be located on one of the reservations. The intent of this provision was to enable the army to keep watch on the Indians, especially the Comanches, and prevent their raiding the settlements. As it turned out, the army's function would be also to protect the Indians from the whites.

Immediately after the passage of the Reservation Act, Captain Randolph B. Marcy, 5th U.S. Infantry, accompanied by Major Robert S. Neighbors, was sent to select the reservations and to survey them on unappropriated lands long used by the Comanches in western Texas. Two of the reservation tracts were laid out back to back on the Brazos River in Young County, twelve miles downstream from Fort Belknap and near the present town of Graham. These two were later known collectively as the Brazos Reservation. The third, located in Throckmorton County on the Clear Fork of the Brazos, was called the Clear Fork, Upper, or Comanche, Reservation and was mostly on what later became Lambshead Ranch. It was an oblong block of four leagues just north of Jesse Stem's farm and rancho. About one-fourth of the reservation was on the south side of the Clear Fork and three-fourths on the north and east sides of the river. An arm of the block one and a half miles square extended down on the east side of the stream almost to Clear Fork Crossing. It was in this arm that the commissary and agency buildings were placed, just across the river from the Stem farm. The northwest area of the reservation cornered near Marcy's California Road east of Paint Creek.

The Brazos Reservation was opened in the latter part of 1854. Federal agents were appointed by the commissioner of Indian affairs: George W. Hill, who succeeded agent Jesse Stem, was assigned to the Brazos Agency in August, 1853, and activated the reservation by March 31, 1855, with 734 Indians assembled there; in May, 1853, George T. Howard became special Indian agent when Neighbors became supervising agent and was put in charge of the smaller tribes. Howard resigned April 2, 1855, and John R. Baylor was assigned as agent to the Comanche Reservation on the Clear Fork, September 14, 1855, with 226 Indians there under Tecumseh.

As representatives of the Bureau of Indian Affairs, the agents carried out the policies of the federal government, usually by persuasion rather than by force. After 1853, upon appointment the agents in Texas were responsible to Superintendent Neighbors. Little trouble was encountered in persuading the small agrarian tribes, the Wacos, Tawacanos, Shawnee, Ionies, and others to come to the Brazos Reservation. The offer of government assistance, especially food, was alluring. The Comanches, however, were another matter. Their way of life was conditioned by the horse and the buffalo, and a warrior's status determined largely by the number of horses he owned. Every brave strove to enlarge his herd, mainly by stealing. The northern Comanches preferred to live in Indian Territory, where they had a certain amount of federal protection but could still raid into Texas and Mexico. During the duration of the Texas reservations, these Indian Territory Comanches were often referred to as the "wild" Comanches.

Three sizable Comanche bands known as the southern Comanches stayed in Texas, each with its own chief. The largest band was under Sanaco. Buffalo Hump's band was smaller. A third band was under Tecumseh, the chief who was to play a major role in the short duration of the Comanches' Clear Fork Reservation. His name was spelled differently by several contemporary chroniclers: Katumse, Katumsee, Katemseh, Catumise, Ketumsee, Ketumseah, Ketempseah, Katumpssy, and Ketumesee. The last was used by Marcy, Parker, and Neighbors. However, the chief's name became attached to a creek that flows from the north and enters the Clear Fork just above the site of the agency buildings. Modern maps show it as Tecumseh Creek, the spelling used in this narrative. Tecumseh Ranch, presently incorporated into Tecumseh Pasture on Lambshead, also commemorates the Comanche chief.

Major Neighbors first encountered Tecumseh on the San Saba River on February 10, 1847. The next year, in October, Tecumseh joined Neighbors and Chief Old Owl to visit Santa Anna, camped in Lambshead Valley on the Clear Fork. W. B. Parker, who met Tecumseh on Marcy's 1854 expedition, described him as a fine-looking man, about fifty years old, full six feet high, a dark red-bronze in complexion. A colorful character, he wore a "six-penny" hat, buckskin moccasins, corduroy leggings, and a checkered cotton coat. His horse's bridle was ornamented with "fifty dollars worth of silver."

His wives were about sixteen and eighteen years old. The younger was chubby and dark; the older, lean, tall, and as fair as a quadroon. Both were dressed in dark calico shirts, with leggings and moccasins in one piece like boots. Their garments were dirty, their heads bare, and their hair short, thick, and uncombed. The younger may have been Tecumseh's favorite, for she had about her waist a wide belt studded with silver brooches, very heavy, showy, and costly.

Parker also remarked on Tecumseh's consideration for his women. Major Neighbors invited the chief to go with him on a reconnaissance trip of several days. Tecumseh decided to leave his wives in Marcy's camp so they would not have to make the long ride. This thoughtful regard made considerable impression on Parker and Neighbors. Later they learned that the chief had four other wives.

The smaller tribes moved into and settled on the Brazos Reservation in 1855 without incident. Agent George W. Hill began furnishing them with 100,000 pounds of beef monthly. The Indians, under agricultural supervisors, erected the agency buildings, cleared the land, and planted 395 acres in corn, which did well in the rich bottom lands of the Brazos, seasoned by timely rains.

The Comanches, led by Tecumseh, came riding into the Brazos Reservation in March, 1855. They were skittish, aloof, and skeptical. They watched with misgivings the farming operations of the other bands as they prepared the soil and planted crops of corn, oats, and melons. Major Neighbors and his assistants saw at once that the Comanches would constitute a different problem from that of the smaller, agrarian tribes. Neighbors' solution was to move all the Comanches to the Clear Fork Reservation as soon as possible.

Tecumseh was first of all the Comanche chiefs and subchiefs to understand the reservation program. He was foremost to lead his band to the Clear Fork Reservation on Lambshead. They left the Brazos Reservation on May 31, 1855, accompanied by John Connor, a Delaware scout and Major Neighbors' trusted interpreter. At the Clear Fork, Tecumseh had first choice of land for his village. He laid it out in the most desirable and strategic location. For himself, he built a log house, which indicated he intended to stay. His band preferred to live in their traditional tepees. The village was located on what later became the W. E. Linam Survey.

Neighbors assigned John R. Baylor to the Clear Fork Agency in September. The buildings for the agency, placed downriver from the Comanche village on what was later the C. W. Marquess Survey, included eleven drop-log cabins, among them a house for the agent, one for the laborers, a commissary, and a school.

Late in the fall of 1855, Chief Sanaco came in with his band, swelling the Comanche population to 450. In May, 1856, Chief Buffalo Hump arrived with 43 starving Comanches, and Chief Iron Sides followed soon after with a small group, bringing the total to 507. Ironically, on January 3, 1855, the whole southern Comanche band, 1,200 strong, had been waiting in their Clear Fork winter resort at Lambshead to be colonized. But without Neighbors' knowledge, the military from Fort Chadbourne were unexplainably ordered to attack the Comanches at their Clear Fork camp. Tecumseh heard of it and carried the news to Major

Steen at Fort Belknap. Remembering the Council House Massacre, all but his band scattered like skittish colts. Fewer than half the southern Comanches returned in 1855 to join Tecumseh and his group on the reservation.

During 1855, farming went well at the Brazos Agency, but none was attempted at the Clear Fork. Neighbors managed to supplement the Comanches' native diet with enough beef to keep them on the reservation. In succeeding years, with the introduction and help of interpreters, white farm laborers, sutlers, teachers, and a missionary, he got the Comanches to clear some land and plant corn, albeit their efforts were performed cautiously. Overall, according to reports to the commissioner of Indian affairs by Neighbors and his agents, the Comanche agricultural experiment worked reasonably well.

However, Commissioner Manypenny received continuing communiques from the agents and Neighbors on the raids suffered by the Texas reserve Indians. They still did not have the military protection from the whites and northern Comanches promised them by the U.S. government.

The need for protection was made urgent by Captain Newton C. Givens, still at Fort Belknap, who coldly observed the settlement of the Indians on the reservations. Late in 1854, Givens, who believed the military alone should be responsible for the Indians, began a calculated campaign of subtle harassments to cut the ground from under Neighbors and the entire Indian service. The fact that Agent John R. Baylor subversively harbored the same hostility toward the Indians on the Clear Fork and Brazos reservations as Givens, a friend of the Baylor family in San Antonio, soon brought the two men together.

Baylor and Givens became implicated in events that affected the Lambshead area during the late 1850's. Born in Paris, Kentucky, in 1822, and brought up at a military post in Indian Territory, Baylor came to Texas in 1839 and the next year fought in the Comanche campaigns under Colonel J. H. Moore. This was during Lamar's administration, and the eighteen-year-old Baylor absorbed Lamar's attitude toward Indians; he would spend the next twenty years of his career trying and eventually managing to get them out of Texas.

Baylor was a strikingly handsome man, with a large mouth and a loud, persuasive voice, a rabble-rouser of the first order, a man's man and one whom men would follow. He was a member of the Texas legislature in 1853. In 1855, he replaced Howard as agent to the Comanches, under Neighbors. Later developments showed his purpose was not to help the Indians, but to eliminate them. It was inevitable that he would clash with his superior.

7   *Camp Cooper*

T HE FEDERAL GOVERNMENT was unconscionably slow in establishing an army post on the Comanches' Clear Fork Reservation. The southern Comanches got there almost a year before the soldiers. The Indians were finally alerted they were to receive military help when cavalry and infantry came marching along the Belknap Road on January 2, 1856. Colonel Albert Sidney Johnston, accompanied by his wife and children, arrived at the Clear Fork in a raging blizzard, leading two companies of cavalry and two of foot soldiers. Johnston located his camp on the north side of the river where there were several acres of fairly level ground. Behind was a high, steep, sloping bank protecting the area from the piercing gale winds. The thermometer was barely above zero and the Clear Fork was frozen over. On this protected spot adjacent to the river, Colonel Johnston located Camp Cooper, named after Adjutant General Samuel Cooper. He placed Major William J. Hardee in charge to build and establish the post.

Watt Matthews, who was raised in the vicinity and whose memory goes back for three-quarters of a century, says that Johnston could not have picked a worse place for Camp Cooper. In the summer, it is hot, still, and sultry. The only water is in the river there, and, although reasonably clear, it is slightly brackish, barely palatable for human use. (The clear, delicious springs described by Marcy were farther downstream.) Flies and mosquitoes swarm there the better part of the year. But to Colonel Johnston, his family, and his freezing troops, the place must have seemed a haven in the wilderness. They found shelter, water, and an abundance of wood. Towering trees lined the river banks. No time was lost getting the army tents in place and providing the best shelter possible for the horses.

The next day, the weather now clear but not much above zero, Colonel Johnston left Major Hardee and the troops on the Clear Fork. Using the soldiers to do the work, Major Hardee laid out and constructed the tent post in an "L" shape. One part of the "L" furnished the parade ground, the other part was for the quarters. Here officers and troops alike lived in tents. The hospital, guardhouse, bakery, and arsenal were also in tents. Storehouses were roofed with tarpaulins over frames. The fine cavalry horses were kept on picket lines, as there were no stables.

Hardee scarcely had the camp in order when he was superseded in command by Lieutenant Colonel Robert E. Lee, who arrived April 9, 1856, and for the next nineteen months called Camp Cooper "my Texas home." He was not prepared for what he found there. Born in the aristocratic Tidewater belt of Virginia and a graduate of West Point, he was known as a "gentleman soldier" and the "best-read man in the army." He had been ordered direct from the superintendency of West Point to this frontier outpost. His initiation into the new environment was swift and impressive.

Tecumseh assumed the role of host to all comers to the Clear Fork Reservation, welcoming the military, the agents, and other visitors. The day after Lee arrived, Tecumseh came to call. The chief was dirty, greasy, and smelly. Without hesitation, he walked up and embraced Lee, who was utterly astounded but endured it. Tecumseh then, with an interpreter, "volubly and tediously" explained that the Comanches were the white man's friends and were ready to accept their customs. Lee's reply, in essence, was, "I will meet you as a friend if possible, but as an enemy if necessary." Tecumseh was puzzled by this curt reply.

After Tecumseh went away, Lee pondered his next move. He was aware that the military personnel at Camp Cooper were there to back up Major Neighbors' reservation policy. He and his men would be called on to solve cultural and ethnic problems for which no rules existed in the army manual. After much deliberation, he concluded that common courtesy required him to return Tecumseh's visit. The following day, he went to the Comanche village. In a letter of April 12, 1856, to his wife, Mary Custis, who was at Arlington, the family plantation near the nation's capital in Virginia, Lee wrote that he found his Comanche charges "extremely uninteresting" and remarked that the reservation experiment was ill-advised.

The Comanche village must have appeared poor, primitive, and exceedingly noisy to Lee. Lean, snarling Indian dogs snapped at him as he passed. There were close to a hundred tepees arranged in no particular order, with Tecumseh's prominent among them. Made of buffalo hide, they were furnished with mats and piles of buffalo robes on the dirt floors. Rawhide ropes and leather bags hung from the lodge poles, and smoked meat dried in the sun outside. The camp was filthy; flies swarmed everywhere over bones and other refuse.

From the tents, naked, dirty children looked curiously out. The women stolidly pursued their tasks; the men, arrogant and idle, watched the visitor warily. Tecumseh's six wives, decked out in outlandish paint and ornaments, came and went about the camp.

All this Colonel Lee observed before Tecumseh emerged from

his lodge and hurried to meet his distinguished guest. The chief greeted and embraced him in the same manner as he had done the preceding day at Camp Cooper. Lee, dressed as always in correct attire required of an officer of his rank, made only one gesture of deference to the traditional Comanche greeting cere- mony of disrobing; he loosened his necktie.

Tecumseh was paid thirty dollars a month as head chief of the Clear Fork Reservation, which backed up his authority over his band and also made it possible for him to abstain from hunting so he could devote full time to his duties. Every Indian on the reservation was issued "two pounds of beef, three-fourths of a pound of flour or corn meal, and four quarts of salt for each one hundred rations." It was Tecumseh's job to encourage families to cultivate a plot of land and raise corn, melons, and some veg- etables. Most of this work was done by the women while the braves lay in the shade and sang war songs. Tecumseh required individual families to cultivate a separate plot. In this way, the industrious wives could be set apart from the slovenly ones. In all, Tecumseh did a comparatively good job of encouraging his people to conform to the aims of the reservation system.

Lee's visit to the Comanche village, including the ride there and back, consumed almost a day. The next day was devoted to an impressive and quite different ceremony, with Major Hardee turning over the command of Camp Cooper to Lieutenant Col- onel Lee. According to Carl Coke Rister, this sunny morning the troopers' dress rivaled that of the dragoons, though their uni- forms were trimmed with yellow, not orange, and they wore no gauntlets and shoes instead of boots. Each troop represented a separate state, with one troop being selected from many states. The horses of each company were carefully chosen of one color. Company A of Alabama rode grays; Company E of Missouri had sorrels; Company F of Kentucky had bays; and Company K of

Ohio rode roans. "Each man was furnished a brass-mounted Campbell saddle with wooden stirrups, . . . a spring-movable stock, or Perry carbine; a Colt navy revolver and dragoon saber, carried by saber belt and carbine sling; a gutta-percha cartridge box; and a cape or talma, with loose sleeves extending to the knees. He wore pale blue trousers, a close-fitting dark blue jacket trimmed with yellow braid, a silken sash, a black hat with looped 'eagle at the right side' and trailing ostrich plumes on the left. On his shoulders he had brass scales to turn saber strokes" and Indian arrows.

The four companies of the Second Cavalry, in turn, inspected their new commander. Many already knew Lee—a tall man, nearly six feet in height, with a natural military bearing, brown eyes, graying black hair, and a thick black mustache. The troops would come to realize that their new commander had the qualities of a man who could lead in battle as well as make decisions on every facet of army life.

Lee liked what he saw in the veteran soldiers before him. They would be joined in objectives to see that the government's reservation policy for the Texas Indians was given a fair trial. To this end, Lee would have to cooperate with Superintendent Robert S. Neighbors, who came over from the Brazos Reservation to meet Lee at the Clear Fork agency.

After conferring with Superintendent Neighbors, Lee returned to Camp Cooper deeply impressed with Neighbors' knowledge of both the wild and settled Indians and the soundness of his views on how best to deal with them. Fellow Virginians, the two men quickly established the most cordial relations at this frontier outpost.

Lee learned from Neighbors what lay behind Comanche enmity: disappearance of buffalo and other wild game that was their food supply; hostility rising in proportion to the westward tide of settlement; Comanche hunting grounds claimed as home-sites for farms and ranches by white settlers. Back in 1852, Neighbors' special agent Horace Capron had found Tecumseh's and Sanaco's bands near starvation in their village on the Concho River. The chiefs complained with bitter eloquence: "What encouragement have we to attempt the cultivation of the soil, or raising of cattle so long as we have no permanent home? In every attempt we have ever made to raise crops, we have been driven from them by the encroachment of the white man before they could mature. Over this vast country, where for centuries our ancestors roamed . . . what have we left? The game . . . is killed and driven off, and we are forced into the most sterile and barren portions of it to starve." Now renegade whites were using any means to take cattle and horses, stealing, pillaging, and murdering both white men and red while masquerading as Indians. Lee learned that sturdy, well-meaning whites like Jesse Stem of Ohio and Thomas Lambshead of Devon had already brought virgin lands along the Clear Fork into fruitful production. He realized that a number of conflicting forces were clashing along the entire Texas frontier, especially along the Clear Fork.

Leaving a contingent of troops at Camp Cooper from April to July, 1856, to protect the reservation Indians, Lee led expeditions to deter raids by the northern Comanches on the Texas frontier. The following eight months of his assignment were spent away from Camp Cooper attending courts-martial at other frontier military posts: Ringgold Barracks near Rio Grande City, Fort Brown at Brownsville, and Fort Mason. In all, he journeyed nearly two thousand miles back and forth across Texas with other officers. Most of them were longtime friends. They formed a pleasant "traveling club" as they moved from camp to camp. In his letters to his wife, Lee commented on the positive as well as the negative aspects of the various regions of Texas. He was impressed with the friendly, hospitable people and the spirit of optimism that appeared to pervade the state. In fact, had he stayed longer, he might have caught the "Texas fever" which led men like Sam Houston and Robert Neighbors to dedicate themselves to the welfare of Texas and her people.

When Lee returned to Camp Cooper April 18, 1857, he wrote in his memo book that he was back at his "Texas home" and living in his old tent. However, he found conditions bad. A drought was on, and it continued unabated through the summer. Drinking water was foul and contaminated. Grass was scarce for the horses, and there were no vegetables or fruit for the men and the Indians. Temperatures ran as high as 112 degrees. Dysentery, scurvy, and fever plagued the soldiers, the Indians, and the settlers. The camp physician was at his wit's end. Lee sadly buried several of his troopers and two of their children in the small canyon west of the camp that is today called Graveyard Canyon. The Indians, conditioned through generations to vacillations of the weather, suffered fewer losses than the whites, but exposure to the white man's diseases and whiskey took its toll among them.

In December, 1856, Colonel Albert Sidney Johnston authorized Lee to select a new site for Camp Cooper, to rectify the hasty decision made for the location during the blizzard the previous year. Prior to receiving this order, Lee had already improved the original site by adding a bake house, three company kitchens, and a guard house, all of stone with clapboard or canvas roofs. Also, he constructed forage and quartermaster storehouses, and picket lines were replaced with log stables for the horses.

After receiving Colonel Johnston's order, Lee spent considerable time exploring up and down the Clear Fork environs for a more suitable camp location. Three qualifications were essential for the new post: usable water, accessibility, and elevation. It needed to be high above the river valley to catch the breezes, which were fairly constant except in October, when a general calm prevailed. He must have found such a spot about five miles upriver to the west, where a small draw came from the north. To ascertain the availability of fresh water, he probably had a trial well hand dug in the floor of the draw. The view from this site is magnificent; one can see for miles to the south and west. But as far as Lee or his successors ever got in developing this location apparently was constructing a bake oven. Its crumbled remains are still evident today in a Lambshead pasture named Bake Oven.

Both Rupert N. Richardson and Kenneth Neighbours indicate that Camp Cooper was later moved, at least temporarily, to a more pleasant site. According to Richardson, the post was moved in April, 1858, to the mouth of Paint Creek and returned in February, 1859, to its old site. Neighbours notes that Major Robert S. Neighbors arrived in Washington, D.C., on May 8, 1858, "to present to the commissioner the correspondence of Agent Leeper concerning the moving of Camp Cooper and to suggest that the secretary of interior take up the matter of protection of the agents and Indians with the secretary of war." Such a move could certainly have been made by part, or all, of the troops, with Captain Newton C. Givens encouraging it. The Paint Creek camp would have been conveniently near his Stone Ranch, and with the troops twelve miles from the Indians and agent who needed their protection, such an arrangement would have fit neatly with Givens' and John Baylor's plans for anti-Indian agitation.

The loneliness and tedium of Lee's sojourn at Camp Cooper were relieved by the younger officers who came and went. Most were West Pointers, and some had been there when Lee was superintendent. Never, perhaps, were there assembled so many future high-ranking officers at one remote army station than at

Camp Cooper while Lee was commander. Eight besides Lee and Johnston later became Confederate generals: William J. Hardee, Earl Van Dorn, E. Kirby Smith, N. G. Evans, Charles W. Field, John B. Hood, William P. Chambliss, and Charles W. Phifer. Those who became Union generals were George H. Thomas, "the Rock of Chickamauga"; I. N. Palmer; George Stoneman; R. W. Johnson; and Kenner Garrard.

Lee enjoyed these men and usually took one or more with him on local reconnaissance. Occasionally he gave them some fatherly advice. Lieutenant John B. Hood, who later commanded the Confederate Army at the Battle of Atlanta, wrote of Lee:

Whilst riding with him . . . and enjoying the scenery and balmy air as we passed over undulating prairies of that beautiful region [Lambshead], the conversation turned on matrimony, when he said to me with all the earnestness of a parent: "Never marry unless you can do so into a family which will enable your children to feel proud of both sides of the house." He perhaps thought I might form an attachment for some of the country lasses and therefore imparted to me his correct and, at the same time aristocratic views in regard to this important step in life. His uniform kindness to me whilst I was a cadet, inclined me the more willing to receive and remember this fatherly advice; and from these early relations first sprang my affection and veneration which grew in strength to the end of his eventful career.

This gift for friendship, no doubt, was felt by all the young officers who knew Lee, even those he later fought against during the Civil War.

Lee did not, as we have seen, have time to move Camp Cooper to the new site. He was transferred to San Antonio as the commandant of the Department of Texas, leaving Captain George Stoneman in charge of Camp Cooper. On July 22, 1857, Lee splashed through the crossing on the Clear Fork, where Marcy and Neighbors had parted three years earlier. He took the road south, passing what is now Lambshead Headquarters, and going on by Forts Phantom Hill, Chadbourne, and Mason on his way to San Antonio. While conducting a court-martial at Fort Mason, he received a telegram informing him of the death of his father-in-law, George Washington Parke Custis, which required his return to Virginia. His sojourn in northwest Texas was at an end.

8 *Indian Removal*

THE RESERVATION VENTURE went better than could have been expected, considering that neither nature nor the increasing hostility of the settlers worked in its favor. Population from 1855 to 1859, when the reservations were active, varied between 450 and 600 Indians on the Comanche reserve. Tecumseh and the other chiefs cooperated with the agents and the officers at Camp Cooper, but efforts at farming brought mixed results. About 200 acres of good land were put into cultivation under supervision of the agent and his agricultural assistants. In 1855, the Comanches arrived too late in the season to plant, so there was no crop that year. Planting was delayed until May in 1856 because of late snow and a cold spring. Then, when crops were up and growing, a plague of grasshoppers hit the area, so thick at times that the sun was partly obscured by their numbers. A drought followed, and the corn crop was practically nonexistent, though the Indians did manage to raise some melons and vegetables. John R. Baylor, Clear Fork agent at the time, reported that they had planted melons, corn, beans, peas, and pumpkins, which would have been sufficient for their needs had it not been for the extreme drought.

However, the Comanches could not wait for the melons to mature and ripen. They ate them green when the melons were no larger than a man's fist. Aided by the issue of corn and beef, the Indians made it through the winter. In 1857, a drought during the growing season cut the yield to about one-half. The next year produced a bumper crop, enough corn to last two years. It was fortunate that it happened, for nothing was raised in 1859, due to a drought in the spring and an invasion of the reservation by the whites in the summer.

Stock raising was more successful than farming. By nature, the Comanches were more adaptable to stock raising than to tilling the soil. Warriors, who considered the hoe and the plow as implements for women, were eager to care for herds of ponies and cattle and a few hogs. Under the tutelage of the agent's farm helpers, Indian women learned to milk cows, and a limited amount of milk was added to the Indians' diet.

A teacher, Richard Sloan, was employed to instruct forty children in English and the rudiments of reading and counting, but schooling was cut short by the disturbances in 1859. On the whole, the "civilizing" program was a moderate success. However, forces from outside the reservation over which the Indians had no control were to put an end to the venture.

For better or for worse, John R. Baylor served as agent to the Comanches under Superintendent Robert Neighbors for two years. Baylor was ambitious and, like Jesse Stem, saw in his tenure as Indian agent an opportunity to get ahead. In an April, 1856, letter to his sister, he expressed his hope to stay on for another four years, as he could then afford to quit: "I can have in that time a stock ranch that will support a family." Of course, Baylor had none of Stem's enlightened sense of responsibility toward his charges. He had never been comfortable with Neighbors' Indian policy, and, though he had come to his office highly recommended from a respected family, questions arose about his handling of funds, lack of responsibility, and absence from the agency without leave. On May 14, 1857, he was replaced as agent by Colonel Matthew Leeper. Commissioner Manypenny instructed Neighbors to inform Baylor of his removal, ordering the agent to turn over all government property and money.

Proud by nature, Baylor was bitterly galled by his summary dismissal and laid the blame on Major Neighbors. And Baylor was not a man to have as an enemy. Kenneth F. Neighbours points out that during his troubled career his quarrels with three other men ended in their deaths, and J. Evetts Haley characterizes him as "a fighter who believed the way to win wars was by killing his enemies off, instead of beguiling them with words." After his dismissal, Baylor threw in with Newton Givens' campaign to drive the reserve Indians from Texas. His own particular purpose was to oust Neighbors and his agents, replacing the former with his friend Lieutenant Allison Nelson, who arrived in the area with Captain Rip Ford the following year. Givens, too, was eager to get rid of Neighbors, who had thwarted his plans to raise beef for sale to the military. From that time, troubles between the settlers and the reserve Indians increased, with stolen livestock turning up near Indian lands and an occasional arrow found at the scene of a raid, which seemed to point to the Indians.

The Stone Ranch offered a strategic command post for Givens and Baylor to develop their campaign to rid Texas of all reservation Indians, Givens to foment unrest among the military, and Baylor to stir up the settlers. From there, the conspirators wrote vituperative letters to Commissioner Manypenny, Governor Runnels, President Buchanan, and editors of Texas newspapers, accusing the reservation Indians of theft and murder among the white settlers and painting a black and mostly false picture of the activities of Major Neighbors and his agents. They began gathering allies, and soon Baylor and the other agitators had divided the frontier citizenry into two parties, white man and

Indian. Baylor went back and forth addressing mass meetings, promoting petitions, and sending letters, all aimed at destroying the reservations and discrediting their personnel. Without the promised military protection, Baylor's task was not difficult.

The anti-Indian agitation had considerable justification from the white settlers' point of view. The Plains Indians, especially the northern Comanches, continued to raid white settlements all the way from the Red River to the Rio Grande and into Mexico. Their main purpose was to steal horses and outright slaughter of whites was not their primary intent, but when they found whites alone or in small parties, they usually killed them. Often they took women and children prisoners. During the mid-1850's, scarcely a week passed without an atrocity being reported, and news of such events spread fast. The *Whiteman*, a weekly newspaper published first in Jacksboro and, later, in Weatherford by Baylor, became the source for disseminating the accounts. The following episode, which occurred in 1857 or early 1858, is typical of those recounted in the *Waco Democrat*, the *Dallas Herald*, and the *Whiteman*: "William Holden was staying with his brother, Frank, who then lived on the Clear Fork, nearly twenty miles north of Breckenridge [about thirty miles below the Clear Fork Reservation]. . . . William went out from home in search of some stock and was killed by the Indians. The crime was traced to the Comanches living on the Upper Reservation. A demand was made for the guilty Indian and he was produced by Katumpsy . . ."

Hundreds of similar events were reported by the *Whiteman* during 1858 and 1859. Not often was mention made, as in this instance, that the reservation Indians had cooperated in locating the offenders. No doubt small groups of the northern raiders, under hot pursuit, did take temporary refuge in the reservations, and it was easy for the settlers to assume that they were reservation Indians. Only after it was too late would it be proven that this was seldom the case.

As early as 1856, Major Robert S. Neighbors recognized the dangers of a growing antireservation movement and began to reconsider his position in regard to the Texas Indians. In the spring of 1857, he, with his wife, Elizabeth Ann, went to Washington to confer with his old friend President James Buchanan about moving the Texas Indians into Indian Territory for their own protection. They arrived in time for Buchanan's inauguration on March 4 and attended the ball afterward. Neighbors' removal plan was backed by Senator Sam Houston, and a tentative commitment was made by the Bureau of Indian Affairs, but the wheels of bureaucracy moved slowly.

By early the next year, antireservation officers from Camp Cooper and Fort Belknap were, without the agents' knowledge, sending out inflammatory reports, and the dissidents operating from the Stone Ranch were making headway. Baylor, who emerged as leader of the group, called a mass meeting of the settlers in Clear Fork country for February 1, 1858, ostensibly to discuss protecting themselves, but in fact to push the settlers into action against the Indians and to petition for Neighbors' removal. A petition was drawn up (later declared to be a forgery) and sent to Governor Runnels, Captain Givens, Agent Leeper, and the newspapers, asking that Major Neighbors be replaced as superintendent of the Texas Indians by Lieutenant Allison Nelson. (Nelson himself arrived at the Brazos Agency in March.) Bitter letters full of false accusations were forwarded to officials in Washington and Austin and also published in the *Galveston News*, the *Dallas Herald*, the *Texas Sentinel*, and the *Whiteman*.

Friends of Neighbors and his agents, Colonel Matthew Leeper at the Clear Fork Reservation and Captain Shapley Prince Ross at the Brazos Reservation, urged him to go again to Washington and demand that the Indian Service investigate the charges against them. Neighbors went, carrying with him testimonials as to the falseness of the accusations. One endorsement was by John S. ("Rip") Ford, now captain of the Texas Rangers: "I have never been able to detect the Reserve Indians in the commission of a single depredation, or to trace one to their doors." Secretary of Interior Jacob Thompson appointed Thomas T. Hawkins of Lexington, Kentucky, to go to Texas and investigate the charges against Neighbors and his agents. Hawkins came to Texas and notified twenty of the known members of the Stone Ranch group, including the leaders, Baylor, Givens, and Nelson, that a public hearing on their charges against Neighbors would be held at Camp Cooper on October 1, 1858. Announcements of the hearing were also published in Texas newspapers. But when the day came, not a single one of the trio showed up. Givens had been promoted to captain and had moved to San Antonio. Only three of the twenty accusers notified by letter ever appeared, and their evidence dissolved into vague generalities and could not be substantiated.

Investigator Hawkins requested Captain Rip Ford to make an affidavit as to the outcome of the investigation. Ford reported that the tribunal had failed to show that reservation Indians were guilty of depredations and that their accusers, invited to testify, failed to appear. Ford also commented on Nelson's duplicity and spoke highly of the Brazos Reservation Indians' progress. He praised Agent Ross and remarked that his own former prejudices against Leeper had been dispelled by a visit to the Comanche Reservation. He further declared, "The ordeal through which Major Neighbors has passed endorses him. He needs no commendation from any quarter."

Officially vindicated by Hawkins' investigation and responsible public opinion, Major Neighbors enjoyed Christmas of 1858 in San Antonio with his wife and their two children, Mary Beatrice and Robert Barnard. This was to be their last Christmas together. The happy, brief holiday season was the lull before the storm.

In January, 1858, Agent S. P. Ross ordered out an Indian scouting party led by a Waco chief; they captured eighty horses and four captives from a northern Comanche camp. Some of the horses were later claimed by settlers, and Ross, who knew that new settlers were being turned against the reserve Indians by "designing men," thought this episode had worked in the Indians' favor.

But in April, the horribly brutal massacre of the Mason and Cameron families twenty-five miles northeast of Belknap and the sweeping raid through the entire Belknap area led to near panic among the settlers, many of whom, hearing rumors of the army's departure, prepared to leave themselves. Baylor was quick to blame the atrocities on the reserve Indians. However, the Indians had ridden off to the north after the horse-stealing raid, and young Mary Cameron, one of two survivors, said that four white men had accompanied the Indians. Although the white men were pursued, captured, and identified, it did little to calm the excitement on the frontier.

According to Kenneth F. Neighbours, Captain Rip Ford was convinced that a ring of renegade whites was "operating with the Indians to dispose of stolen horses." The *Dallas Herald* reported that "the horse stealing and other depredations on the frontier cannot be attributed to the Indians. The existence of a band of robbers in this State, extending across it and into Mexico, on the one side and the United States on the other, is doubted by few. . . . They find where the horses are, and the Indians, under their guidance and assistance, steal them."

A letter written in December, 1858, or January, 1859, found

by troopers from Camp Cooper on the body of the man Page, confirms that such a ring was operating on a large scale in the area and strongly suggests that Baylor had dealings with them.

Yours of the 25th ult., has been duly received and we are happy to know that your part succeeded so well in getting the last drove of horses, etc. from Belknap and that you so completely fixed the affair on the Indians; but I am now becoming apprehensive, as the animals or the proceeds have not come to hand. . . . I think our friend near Camp Cooper is asking too much compensation for the burning down of his stable, particularly as he has not succeeded in making that haul on Camp Cooper; let me know if they have moved to the Stone Ranch above the latter place yet. . . . Also inform me if the Captain has yet got back from Austin, and what he has done towards raising the Reg,t. of Rangers which is of all importance to us. Should he succeed in getting them up, you will of course instruct him when we are likely to pass, that he may know in what quarter to scout with his rangers. . . . Tell our friend of the *Whiteman* [obviously Baylor] above all things, to keep up the Indian excitement, as it must be kept up until spring for there cannot be much done this bad weather; also acquaint our friends of Belknap particularly that it will be necessary to keep the matter up; even if we have to kill or shoot at some fellow there; there are a great many emigrants passing through here on their way to Texas, It will be well to keep them scared out of the upper part of the state as much as possible; but such as do come, keep your eye on them, as they have some excellent mules and horses; . . . Everything is quiet here at present except some little grumbling about the last division as some you know got too much, but this was policy, as for the others, we can scare them into terms.

How deeply Baylor or others of his group were involved must remain a matter of speculation, but there is no doubt that such activities served his purposes well.

Captain Ford, with grim foreboding, reported on April 12, 1859, to Governor H. R. Runnels: "The frontier is in a bad way. The feeling of insecurity, of hostility to the Reserve Indians, . . . render the frontier people violent and, in many respects, unreasonable. . . . We have had the cooperation of the Reserve Indians.

... [but] let an infuriated mass of men attack the Reserves, break them up, interfere with the United States Government in the consummation of a settled Indian policy, and we may apprehend danger, trouble and bloodshed from Red River to the Rio Grande."

Neighbors had already recommended to the commissioner of Indian affairs that the reservation Indians be moved to the new reservations located east of the North Fork of the Red River. In February, 1859, he again strongly stated the move was imperative. Finally, on April 19, 1859, he was authorized to abandon the Clear Fork and Brazos Indian reservations. It had taken him nearly as long to convince the government the reservations should be abandoned as it had to persuade them that they be established.

In the meantime, Baylor, blaming the two Texas reservations for all Indian depredations and the agents for condoning the raiding and killings, was offering a bounty for the scalps of Neighbors and Ross and whipping up passions to a point of mob hysteria. He was backed up in his campaign not only by Givens and Nelson, but also by Peter Garland, another Indian-hater of the first order. Garland believed that Indians, like rattlesnakes, should be killed on sight. In fact, he personally led the move to exterminate Indians, regardless of who or where they were.

An example was the case of Choctaw Tom, a respected, long-time friend and interpreter for Sam Houston and Major Neighbors, one of the most trustworthy Indians on the Brazos Reservation. He was given permission by Captain Ross, the agent, to hunt bear, as he did every year, in Palo Pinto County. Choctaw Tom and his party camped near Golconda (close to the present town of Palo Pinto) on December 26, 1858. Garland, with about twenty men, appeared in Golconda and announced they were going to wipe out Choctaw Tom and his party.

Local settlers who knew the trustworthy old Indian, so long a friend to the whites, tried to dissuade him. Garland stalled, saying he and his men would return next day and discuss the matter further. Instead, next morning at daybreak, they attacked the sleeping Indians, killing four men and three women and wounding several more. The Indians gave such fierce resistance that Garland's group rode away without finishing the slaughter. Charles Goodnight called this affair "a dirty piece of business. They just wanted to be killing some Indians." Neighbors, who was spending Christmas with his family in San Antonio, received word of the massacre from Ross, who urged his immediate return to the Brazos Agency, the home of the murdered Indians. Neighbors took the stage at once, going by way of Austin to lay matters before the governor and on to Waco to see other officials and urge action. At Waco, Neighbors made affidavits for the arrest of Garland's party, and writs were issued by Judge N. W. Battle to Captain Ford for the arrest. Neighbors traced the sources of the atrocity straight to Allison Nelson and John R. Baylor; some of their accomplices and tools were in Garland's party. "They have concocted and carried out the whole of this diabolical murder," he wrote.

Ross also reported the affair to Governor Runnels, who ordered warants issued for the arrest of Garland and his men. Warrants were sent out, but the feeling against the Indians was running so high that no frontier sheriff dared serve them. Ranger Captain Rip Ford offered his assistance to any lawman or other civil officer in making the arrest, but he refused to take the initiative since the orders came from a civil authority.

Throughout the winter, Baylor and Garland went from county to county on the frontier proclaiming long and loud their intent to exterminate all Indians in Texas, whether on reservations or elsewhere. Baylor now threatened to hang Ross and Neighbors, given the opportunity. In January, Allison Nelson gathered 200 men from five frontier counties to attack the Brazos Reservation, but Major Thomas sent troops to the agency, and the planned attack did not take place. In March, Baylor called for a mass meeting of settlers to assemble in Jacksboro and plan an assault on both the reservations. No record exists as to how many settlers attended; however, the purpose was accomplished. Word then was sent up and down the frontier for all red-blooded men to meet on Rock Creek on May 21, 1859.

Rock Creek runs from north to south near the western edge of Jack County, two or three miles from the east line of the Brazos Reservation, which was in Young County. On the date set, about 500 men showed up. They were a motley bunch. Many of them were honest, sincere, and respected settlers and stockraisers, bearing such names as Jowell, Slaughter, Millsap, Cowden, Barber, Fauntleroy, and so on. Some were just ordinary dirt farmers. Others were horse thieves, who stole from each other and the Indians. They came from Montague, Denton, Cooke, Wise, Parker, Jack, Palo Pinto, Erath, Bosque, Comanche, Coryell, and Collin counties and a few from counties farther south. May 22 was spent getting the group organized on a branch of Rock Creek, now known as Filibuster Branch (Baylor referred to the men assembled there as "filibusters"). Baylor was elected commander and designated colonel, with Peter Garland as his first assistant. The men were armed with every kind of shooting weapon in use at the time. Charles Goodnight had a shotgun and so did many others. Rifles were of every make and gauge. Some had only pistols, most of the one-shot variety. Colt revolvers were just coming into use, but few frontiersmen had them. Ammunition for the various weapons was what the men could carry in their pockets.

No time was lost in drilling or tactics. One basic decision was made: to attack the two reservations simultaneously, if possible. In that way, the army could not combine their troops from Camp Cooper and Fort Belknap at one place. Garland was to leave at once for the Clear Fork Reservation with 250 men, and Baylor would hit the Brazos Reservation next day, May 23, with the other 250 volunteers. Because of the forty miles' distance to the Clear Fork, Garland could not strike until May 24 or May 25.

The military, however, knew well what was planned and were prepared. Troops from Fort Belknap had already been moved to the agency at the Brazos Reservation and temporary fortifications provided. Ross had all his Indians collected behind the troops. The same precaution was taken at the Clear Fork Agency. Only a guard was left at Camp Cooper.

Early in the morning of May 23, Baylor loose-herded his 250 men over the eight miles to the Brazos Agency, which was just southeast of the present town of Graham. What happened when they approached the agency is described in a report to Major Neighbors by Captain J. B. Plummer, who was in command of the military:

Sir, I have the honor to inform you that information was brought to me this morning at about half past ten o'clock, that Captain Baylor, with about two hundred and fifty men, had marched upon the reservation to attack the Indians, and was then about one mile distant and approaching the agency where my command and the Indians were encamped. I immediately dispatched Captain Gilbert with his company to meet Captain Baylor, and to demand of him "for what purpose he had come upon the reservation with an armed body of men?" To that demand, he replied, that "he had come to assail certain Indians of this reserve, but not to attack any whites, but should the troops fire upon his men during the fight, he would attack them also, or any other whites who did the same thing, and treat all alike." He desired my reply, and would wait for it three quarters of an hour.

As soon as I received the above message, I sent Lieutenant Burnet to Captain Baylor, with instructions to say to him that my orders were to protect the Indians on this reserve from the attacks of armed bands of citizens and that I would do so to the best of my ability, and with the arms in my possession; and that I warned him in the name of the government of the United States to leave this reservation.

Captain Baylor rejoined, that this message did not alter his determination of attacking the Indians on the reserve, and that he would attend to leading it himself; that he regretted the necessity of coming in collision with the United States troops, but that he had determined to destroy the Indians on this and the upper reserve, if it cost the life of every man in his command.

The Indians, in the meantime, as well as the troops, prepared for action, and some of the former, who were mounted, were hovering near Captain Baylor and his men, watching their movements. By friendly signs, they [Baylor's men] induced a very old Indian to approach them, when they tied a rope around his neck, and then moved off in a westerly direction, but before going far, killed and scalped their prisoner. They were followed by fifty or sixty Indians, constantly exchanging shots with them; and eight miles from the agency, and about one and a half miles from the limits of the reserve, they came to stand, taking possession of a farmer's house and outbuildings; there the Indians fought them until dark, when they returned to their reservation. They killed, they state, five of Captain Baylor's men, and had one of their own number killed besides the one I have already mentioned, and several wounded.

I am, very respectfully, your obedient servant,

J. B. Plummer
Captain 1st Infantry
Commanding

Here, we have the U.S. Army protecting the Indians from the whites. What happened when Baylor's raw collection of farmers and small stockmen found themselves face to face with a well-armed, disciplined army contingent, with some field pieces loaded with shrapnel and backed by mounted Indian defenders? They lost their zeal for taking Indian scalps and, like sensible men, began to drift off toward the east in groups. Colonel Baylor found himself unable to make good his threat "to destroy the Indians if it cost the life of every man in [his] command." The only other Indians killed were by some of the stragglers among his departing followers, who shot one old woman who was working in her little vegetable garden and one old man who was away from the village looking for a pony.

When Garland approached Camp Cooper, where he was to capture any pieces of artillery that could be used in destroying the Indians on the Clear Fork Reservation, some soldiers at the camp, who also hated the Indians, told him of the strength and preparedness at the agency. When the news spread among Garland's "troops," they lost interest in the annihilation project. Some, disenchanted, headed home, but a large group returned to Rock Creek or at least remained in the area, continuing to stir up trouble.

In April, 1859, Major Neighbors had gone to Austin to confer with the governor about the desperate state of affairs on the frontier. He then went to San Antonio for a brief visit with his wife and young children. On May 17, he started back to Camp Cooper, going by the military road connecting Forts Mason, Chadbourne, Phantom Hill, and Cooper. Arriving at Camp Cooper on May 25, he was told immediately of the turmoil there and of the battle at the Brazos Reservation two days before.

The citizens' attack on the Indian reservations received much publicity over the settled parts of Texas. Opinion was divided during May as to whom to blame. It became a political issue in Governor Runnels' race for reelection. There was little doubt his sympathy was with the Baylor element, as he appointed a partisan commission to investigate the causes of the attacks on the reservations. Runnels was opposed by Sam Houston, who was staunchly pro-Indian and pro-Neighbors. Several investigations exonerated the reservations of wrongdoing, but no one had the courage to take official action against the perpetrators of the attacks.

After his return to the Clear Fork Reservation, Neighbors quickly resumed plans for removing the Indians to Indian Territory, more urgent now than ever. Neighbors was authorized to make arrangements with Elias Rector, superintendent of the Plains Indians in Indian Territory. On June 26, 1859, he set out with Tecumseh, José María, and the other chiefs of the six Indian tribes on the two Texas reservations. At Fort Arbuckle, July 1, 1859, Neighbors, with Elias Rector, held a council with chiefs of the Texas Indians and those Indians north of Red River. The chiefs were told that, as they must live together thereafter, it behooved them to get acquainted. This they did in their own formal, dignified manner, with speeches of eloquence by chiefs of both groups. The occasion ended amicably.

August 1, 1859, was the date Neighbors set for the removal of the Texas Indians from the tumultuous and constant dangers of the Clear Fork and Brazos agencies. They were to go to the relative safety of the Wichita Agency, on the Washita River in present Caddo County, Oklahoma, four miles east of Anadarko. But much had to be done before the departure.

At the Clear Fork Agency, Neighbors inventoried all the Comanche property that would be left behind, buildings and livestock for which Indian ownership could not be established. He anticipated that the white cattlemen would be sure to cut the herd for stray animals. (The livestock the Comanches rode or drove with them was estimated to be worth $9,550.00 but what had been lost, stolen, or left behind was valued at $14,922.50.) The Comanches had many hogs. Neighbors sold all of these that could be rounded up, but since the hogs ran wild, he did not get them all. There are wild hogs on Lambshead today, some perhaps descended from those left behind over a hundred years ago.

The logistics of moving more than fourteen hundred people, even with scant possessions, were considerable. Supplies of corn, flour, and salt, enough to last a month, had to be obtained and hauled. A contract was made with Peter F. Ross, son of Agent Shapley Prince Ross, to furnish eighty wagons and a number of Mexican carts drawn by oxen. C. E. Barnard, sutler for the reservations, was engaged to drive a herd of beeves to be slaughtered along the way. A blacksmith was hired to mend breakdowns that might occur. An army surgeon was secured to make the trip, since the expedition might well be bushwhacked by irate citizens.

After the Baylor-Garland episode in May, Governor Runnels asked John Henry Brown to raise a hundred "volunteer" Rangers and take up a position near the Brazos Reservation to "keep the peace." It was not clear whether he was to protect the Indians from the whites or the whites from the Indians, but his ninety recruits were almost entirely from among the Baylor-Garland forces. Brown took a position at Caddo Spring on the extreme eastern edge of the Brazos Reservation. His main activity, as it turned out, was to prevent the Indians from going off the reservation to look for their horses and cattle and to ensure the right of the settlers to go onto the reservation to search for their livestock. There were no fences, and livestock intermingled on the open range. The federal officers at Fort Belknap felt they should not interfere with the state troops unless they attacked the Indian villages. So, while preparations for the removal went on, the Brazos Indians lost many of their horses and cattle, which Brown's men drove to Jacksboro and sold at auction.

Under the direction of S. P. Ross, the Brazos Reservation was also preparing for the move. Superintendent Neighbors rode back and forth, coordinating the two operations. One of Neighbors' most important decisions was to determine the routes of the two groups. Three possibilities existed: take the Comanches to the Brazos Reservation and start north from there, or vice-versa. The third alternative was to start each group toward the Red River and converge at the river. He decided on the third plan, as it would save a forty-mile march for one group or the other.

Next, Neighbors arranged with the army for a military escort. On July 18, 1859, Major George H. Thomas received orders at Camp Cooper to take two companies of cavalry and two of infantry to get the Indians safely into Indian Territory. Thomas was commander of the escort, with Companies G and H of the Second Cavalry Regiment directly under him. Captain J. B. Plummer commanded one company of the First Infantry Regiment, which Thomas took with him to accompany the Brazos Indian contingent. Neighbors deemed three companies necessary to protect the Brazos entourage because the vast majority of the aroused settlers lived east of the Brazos Reserve, and John Henry Brown and his anti-Indian troops were also there. The other company of the First Infantry, commanded by Captain Charles C. Gilbert, was to escort the Comanches from their Clear Fork Reservation.

Resolutely, Major Neighbors left his log office late in the afternoon, July 31, 1859, thankful he had determined the future of the Texas Indians in 1857.

Early next morning, at trumpet call, Neighbors led the cavalcade of 1,051 Indians from the assembly point three miles north of the Brazos Reservation, accompanied by horse and foot soldiers, their agent, Captain S. P. Ross, and other personnel. Mexican *carretas*, ambulances and wagons, shouting teamsters, cattle, oxen, mules, horses, and Indian dogs completed the procession that wound across the prairie.

The Comanches, 370 strong, left their traditional camping grounds and reservation in Clear Fork Valley led by their agent, Colonel Matthew Leeper, and guarded by Captain Gilbert's

Indian exodus from the Comanche Reserva-tion.

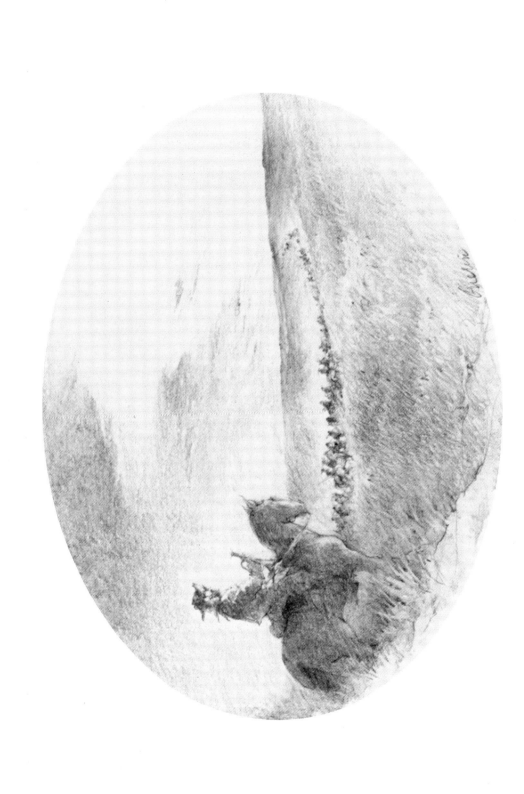

company of the First Infantry from Camp Cooper. Leeper's daughter gave an eyewitness report. The departure was

... accompanied by a perfect babel of noise, Indians galloping hither and and thither and shouting to each other; pappooses [*sic*] shrieking and wailing from fright at the sight of so many strange faces and such undue excitement; dogs howling, barking and fighting the intruding canine contingent; army mules, having dire presentment of arduous labors in store for them, brayed out dismal protests, while the blasts of the cavalry bugle, the shrill notes of the fife and the roll of the infantry drum all contributed to the din and pandemonium of the exodus. ...

Sometimes the camps were extremely picturesque, being pleasantly shaded and cool after a long day's march through dust and heat. With the timber which fringed the creek channel as a background, there stood out in bold relief the long line of white tents of the military escort and the hooded wagons of the commissary and sutler, and then up and down the valley, on either flank, the hundreds of Indian tepees and campfires, which sent up their flickering flames as night closed down on the scene, making it seem like a vision of enchantment. As darkness thickened, the thumping of the Indian tom-toms, accompanied by the droning, monotonous songs of the Indians, the barking of an army of dogs and the weird howling of hungry coyotes, constituted a peculiar medley which lulled tired travelers into restful slumber.

Moving across the prairie in line, not column, with the soldiers in the middle, the caravan stretched out for nearly three miles. Startled game was pursued by countless dogs, and some of the Indians joined them, on horseback and afoot. The dogs tired quickly in the heat, and one arrived in Indian Territory carried by a squaw on her back like a papoose.

The route passed about five miles east of the present town of Throckmorton, to the northeast corner of Throckmorton County, then diagonally across Archer County to its northeast corner, and, from there, to the mouth of the Big Wichita River on the Red River. Miraculously, they arrived the same day as the Brazos

Indians. They had made better time than the Brazos bands despite having traveled about twenty miles farther.

The Brazos contingent had had several interruptions. John Henry Brown's company followed close on their heels, backing up cattlemen who demanded the right to cut the Indian horse and cattle herds to see if any of their animals could be found among them. On these occasions, Major Thomas and his troops stood by to see that no Indian animals were cut from the herds. The route of the Brazos group was almost due north. From the Red River on August 8, Neighbors wrote to his wife about the departure: "If you want to hear a full description of our Exodus out of Texas read the 'Bible' where the children of Israel crossed the Red Sea. We have had about the same show, only our enemies did not follow us to Red River. If they had—the Indians would have in all probability sent them back without the interposition of Divine Providence."

After a successful crossing of the Red River on August 8, 1859, the combined parties of Indians and their military escorts continued north for seven days toward the Washita River. Before they reached the valley of the Washita, however, an express from General Twiggs in San Antonio caught up with them with orders for Major Thomas and his two companies of cavalry to return immediately to Camp Cooper and for the two companies of infantry to return as soon as their destination was reached. Major Thomas and his cavalry left the Indian cavalcade on August 15, 1859, arriving at Camp Cooper on August 21.

On August 17, Neighbors found a pleasant valley with good grass and excellent water, where he camped to await the arrival of Superintendent Elias Rector, into whose charge he was to deliver the Texas Indians. Captains Plummer and Gilbert headed back toward Camp Cooper with the two companies of infantry on August 20, arriving there on September 3. Plummer was then ordered to return with his infantry to assist in establishing Fort Cobb to protect the Texas Indians and adjacent tribes, and he left Camp Cooper again for Indian Territory on September 16.

Neighbors, Captain Ross, and Colonel Leeper, left without military protection, quickly explored the surrounding country that Indian Agent Samuel A. Blain had located for them and from which the various Indian tribes could choose good locations that pleased them. Neighbors, Ross, and Leeper were tremendously impressed with what they saw along the valley. Neighbors wrote, describing the country enthusiastically:

This is, in my judgment, truly a splendid country. Valleys are one to five miles wide on alternate sides of the Washita. Soil, to judge from the heavy coat of grass and weeds, is very rich, and similar in appearance to the valley lands of Red River and will, in my judgment, prove a superior farming country. The adjacent hills are covered with post oak of the very best quality for building and fencing, and the timbered bottoms of the river and creeks afford a good supply of black walnut, over-cup or burr oak, and red cedar. I also noticed in the hills good quarries of stone, but had no means of testing its qualities. The whole country also abounds in good springs of the coldest freestone water and to judge from the unusual height of the timber, and the luxuriant growth of grass, it must be sufficiently seasonable to produce good crops.

The favorable sites selected were approved upon arrival of Agent Blain, acting for Superintendent Rector. On September 1, 1859, Neighbors released to Blain 1,420 Indians. Six had died on the trip and one had been born; four were unaccounted for.

The tremendous responsibilities and constant harassment of the previous months caused Major Neighbors to resign from the Indian Service upon safe delivery of his charges to their new location. However, once freed of responsibility, the relief was so great and the country so enticing that he began to have second thoughts.

9 *Death of a Martyr*

AFTER NEIGHBORS CROSSED the Red River into Indian Territory, the galling tensions of the past few years began to drop away. John Henry Brown and his volunteers had turned back. The Indians were safely out of Texas. Ironically, although John R. Baylor was taking full credit for driving them out, Neighbors could put aside the vicissitudes of the previous two years as he contemplated how pleasant it would be to live quietly with his Indians as teacher, shepherd, and friend.

On September 4, 1859, he wrote Elizabeth Ann, who had just given him another son, of the beauty of the country and the possibility of asking for appointment as agricultural instructor to his former Indian charges, expressing his wish to "go to work in real earnest and make these people . . . self-sustaining." If that materialized, he planned to take his family and slaves with him to the Washita area.

Neighbors' leave-taking from his Indians was poignant and emotional. He wrote his wife:

I made my last talk yesterday—old Placedo [the Tonkawa Chief] cried like a child at the thought of my leaving, and if it was put to a vote there is not one that would agree for me to leave. . . .

There were a thousand Indians present, and I shook hands with each of them. Some of the old warriors, whom I have known ever since I have been Agent among them, clung to me and refused to let me go. When I rode off from them, they threw themselves upon the ground, yelling, in the wildest grief, so that it required all my fortitude to leave them. I have labored hard for them, trying to discharge my duty in sight of God and man.

Captain Ross, too, resigned his position as Indian agent and parted with sadness and regret from the Indians of the Brazos Agency whose loyal friendship, confidence, and respect he had won through his concern for their best interests.

All the Texas tribes, along with the Wichita tribe brought up from Fort Arbuckle, were banded together under the jurisdiction of Colonel Leeper, who became agent for the Washita Agency headquartered near the new military post of Fort Cobb, where the First Infantry Regiment was to be stationed. Many civilian helpers who had made the trip remained to work with Agent Samuel Blain. Last to leave, on September 6, was Major Neighbors' party: Captain Ross, Colonel Leeper, who was returning on official business, and a dozen white employees. Two days later they were set upon by northern Indians and several renegade whites. After a short, spirited battle, the Indians made off with three horses, leaving Colonel Leeper afoot and severely wounded. He made the remainder of the journey in Major Neighbors' ambulance.

The group found the Red River on a rampage but managed to cross the flood by using a raft. Eventually, just north of Fort Belknap, they came to the Brazos, also in dangerous flood. They spent the night on the north side, and by the next morning, the muddy waters had receded sufficiently for them to cross. Neighbors' destination was Camp Cooper, but first he needed to go by the courthouse in the village of Belknap. When he stopped by the fort early the next morning, September 14, 1859, Major

Thomas told him that animosity was still running high against him there. Although the Indians were now gone, the people still held him responsible for the loss of lives, livestock, and scalps. Major Thomas suggested a guard go with him into the village. Neighbors refused.

He went alone into Belknap. There, he spent two hours with the county and district clerk, William Burkett, writing up his final report as an official in the Indian Service. As he stepped out of the courthouse door, he met a Mr. McKay, an old acquaintance from New York. The two talked a few minutes and then decided to visit Colonel Leeper in the post hospital. They had taken but a few steps when a man named Patrick Murphy, gun in hand and backed up by another armed man, confronted Neighbors. "I hear you called me a horse thief. Is that so?" Murphy shouted.

Neighbors, placing his hand on his Colt six-shooter, replied, "No, sir, I did not . . ." He never finished the sentence. His words were cut off by a blast of twelve buckshot from a shotgun held so close it burned Neighbors' coat. Edward Cornett, a man he never saw or knew, had shot Neighbors in the back. He gasped, "Oh, Lord," and collapsed. Sheriff Edward Wolfforth ran from the courthouse. He raised Neighbors' head, but the major died in the sheriff's arms without speaking. Burkett also rushed from the courthouse, took in the situation, and assembled several witnesses who had seen the murder and immediately testified that Neighbors had been killed by Edward Cornett.

This appears to have ended the legal proceedings for the murder. There is no evidence that Cornett was arrested by Sheriff Wolfforth or that he was ever brought to trial, which probably attests to how bitter public sentiment was against the Indians and the man who tried to help them.

Burkett took from the dead man's body his six-shooter, gold watch, spectacles, a pencil case, a bunch of keys, a box of cartridges, and $116. Later Colonel Leeper took possession of Neighbors' ambulance, four mules with harness, and other items.

What happened after the "cause of death inquest" is a matter of legend. Various versions persist. According to one account, the assassins had instilled such fear into the people of Belknap by threatening death to anyone who approached Neighbors' body that "although it is probable that death was instantaneous, the body of Major Neighbors lay untouched in the sandy street, from morning until late afternoon, when it was taken by Colonel Leeper's Negro servant, who digged a grave and buried it." Another legend has it that "a poor, decrepit, old warrior, fast tottering down the declivity of life," saw the shooting. "As soon as Major Neighbors fell, the old savage began to yell and scream in most piteous tones of lamentation; and refused to be comforted, continued his wailing the entire day." This version seems scarcely credible. If public sentiment was so biased and poisoned that the murder of an outstanding citizen went unpunished, an old Indian would scarcely have been left alive to mourn.

One authentic reference to Neighbors' burial does exist in a letter William Burkett wrote to Mrs. Neighbors the afternoon of the murder, stating, "The body will be buried tomorrow, accompanied by the [coroner's] jury." No account of the actual burial is extant. It is not positively known whether Neighbors was buried in the Belknap civilian cemetery or the military cemetery, which are some distance apart. In 1936, before extensive research had been done on Major Neighbors, a Texas Centennial monument to his memory was placed in the military cemetery. In 1975, Dr. Kenneth F. Neighbours, historian and foremost authority on Robert S. Neighbors, wrote, "The weight of evidence seems to indicate that Neighbors was not buried in the military cemetery." Neighbors' family believe he was buried in the civilian cemetery one-half mile east of Belknap. Henry Williams, an old settler, pointed out a vault twenty-one feet north of the vault of Charlie and Conrad Newhouse as Neighbors', and Newhouse descendants have done the same. In 1962 the Texas State Centennial marker of 1936 was moved to this vault, where Caddo Indians from near Anadarko, Oklahoma, come each Memorial Day to place wreaths and perform tribal ceremonies.

Little information exists as to the effect Neighbors' death had on his wife, Elizabeth Ann, but it must have been devastating. The tenderness and affection expressed in their frequent letters to each other indicate a devotion seldom encountered. Their youngest son, whom her husband never saw, was only a few weeks old. When William Burkett's letter arrived, she had doubtless been counting the days until her husband's return. One can only imagine the effect the dreadful news had upon her. She died three years later.

Neighbors' virtues and accomplishments were quickly proclaimed from beyond the confines of the inflamed frontier. News stories were carried by leading papers throughout the nation, with eulogies by prominent Texans and others in Washington, Austin, and San Antonio. One journal remarked: "Man's inhumanity to man is found in many a chapter of the history of the American frontier, but in none do the deeds of true heroism and fidelity shine brighter by reason of such a dark background than do those of Major Robert S. Neighbors. . . . If other men acquired fame in war, let it be remembered also that [he] wrought mightily for peace."

Old friends and comrades Sam Houston and Captain Randolph B. Marcy both bitterly condemned the "lawless and base assassination of Major Neighbors." Houston added, "The recollection of these things is too painful to dwell upon, and had a competent Executive ruled Texas, they would not have occurred. . . ."

Secretary of Interior Jacob Thompson wrote Sam Houston,

now governor of Texas, indignantly condemning the murder. Lieutenant William E. Burnet wrote his father, first president of the Republic of Texas: "The 'Baylor Party' have murdered Major Neighbors, and I suppose would like to get others. The assassination of Major Neighbors was a most foul and cowardly murder, but in good keeping with the other acts of the same party. . . ." Just why Neighbors was assassinated remains unclear, though the author of the letter carried by Page might have shed some light. Neighbors did not know who shot him, and had never met the man or even known of his existence. Edward Cornett was known as a "drinking, blustering, dissolute desperado, and [one who] has before murdered his man." Parker Johnson, a Texas Ranger, thought Neighbors was killed before he could call to account the men responsible for the recent disturbances.

When the news of Neighbors' death reached the reservation Indians, they mourned for days and threatened vengeance. It was well for Cornett that Indian justice did not prevail. Instead, on May 25, 1860, Sheriff Wolfforth, with a posse, shot Edward Cornett in the hills near Belknap while trying to arrest him for attempted murder of Dennis Murphy, a kinsman. According to tradition, the Rangers were along, too. As an old settler told it, "Son, Ed Cornett was indicted, tried and executed by a band of Rangers without the help of judge or jury; but you won't find no record of that in the court house."

All accusations against Neighbors were cleared once and for all when E. B. Grayson arrived from Washington to settle Neighbors' financial affairs and check his reports. Summoned to San Antonio, Ross and Leeper assisted him and also settled their own accounts. Neighbors' reputation for exceptional care in dealing with contracts and claims was well deserved, Grayson discovered; the final balance showed a credit of $37,985.02. Major Neighbors' faithful friend, John S. ("Rip") Ford, learning of this amazing record, declared it "incontrovertible proof of his honesty in the administration of financial affairs."

Baylor and his contingent of reckless men had promised the settlers on the frontier that peace and tranquility would descend upon their land with the removal of the Indians and the murder of Neighbors. Instead, they were harassed as never before. After Neighbors' assassination, J. M. Smith, a former member of Governor Runnels' peace commission, expressed his forebodings: "And woe to the frontier now, it will have less sympathy and protection than ever from the Genl. Government, as Neighbors was one of the few officials that was known to be strictly honest, and always had the entire confidence of the authorities at Washington."

Later in life, John R. Baylor's son declared: "Personally, I think the killing of Major Neighbors was about the greatest misfortune that could have befallen our northern frontier. I think he could have, by his influence over the Indians, prevented largely the horrible murders of men, women and children along our northern frontier for many years after his untimely death."

J. M. Smith's prediction of woe for the frontier proved true. The removal of the reservation Indians by no means diminished the raiding of the frontier. Whether any of the Texas Indians later participated in marauding parties in retaliation for having been expelled is uncertain. But harassment by the horse Indians, mostly Comanches, went on until 1875, when Colonel Ranald S. Mackenzie rounded them up and forced them to live on their reservations in Indian Territory.

And what of the men who had so diligently fanned the flames against Neighbors and the Indians? Of the three Stone Ranch plotters, only John R. Baylor remained on the frontier. He retreated from the turmoil he had helped create in northwest Texas to his ranch near Weatherford, but not for long. In 1861, he joined other hot-blooded southerners as a delegate to the Secession Convention and then went into the Confederate Army. Commissioned lieutenant colonel of the Second Regiment of Texas Mounted Rifles, he was sent to El Paso. From there, he helped drive the Union forces out of New Mexico. As provisional governor of Arizona Territory, he once more vented his hatred of the Indians. On March 20, 1862, he ordered "the extermination of all hostile Indians." This time, however, he was called to account and dismissed from both his command and the Confederate Army. Back in Texas, he served in the Confederate Congress from 1863 to 1865, when he was again on the frontier, having raised five battalions of Texas volunteers. This was his last exploit. He later lived for a while in San Antonio, and then in Montell, where he died February 6, 1894, remembered more for his misdeeds than for other aspects of his career.

Lieutenant Allison Nelson apparently moved off the frontier scene after his aborted raid on the Brazos Agency in January, 1859. With the Indians gone, there was no office of superintendent for him to occupy, so he turned to politics. He was elected to the Texas legislature in 1860, and he joined Baylor in the Secession Convention. Commissioned brigadier general in the Confederate Army, he was later promoted to major general. Nelson died in October, 1862, and was buried in Little Rock, Arkansas.

Captain Newton C. Givens, transferred in 1858 to duty in San Antonio, died as the result of an accident while hunting with Captain E. Kirby Smith, who had been among the Second Cavalry stationed at Camp Cooper with Major Hardee. Givens died March 9, 1858, in a San Antonio hospital. It was said that his effects were turned over to his mother, who was present at the time of his death. He may never have realized the magnitude of the destructive forces he loosed in Clear Fork country.

10   *The War Years*

C AMP COOPER, surrounded by the reservation, remained for a period a center of order and military support for new arrivals and those who stayed on the frontier. Among the first to come to the vacated reservation lands in September, 1859, was the family of First Sergeant John G. Irwin, U.S. Dragoons, from Fort Chadbourne. Lieutenant I. F. Minter, federal officer in charge of the military post and the Comanche Reservation, welcomed the Irwins. John Chadbourne, Sergeant Irwin's son born at and named for Fort Chadbourne in 1855, recalled many years afterward that his family lived in a house they built downriver from the fort. Later, when Camp Cooper was abandoned, Lieutenant Minter gave his father permission to take charge of the Indian agency quarters. They moved into the house formerly occupied by the agent, where they lived until "forting up" at Fort Davis in 1865. In an interview with J. R. Webb in 1936, Irwin described the remoteness of the country when his family arrived. When they came to Camp Cooper, he said, there were no ranches in their area except those of Judge J. C. Lynch and George Greer, about forty miles south on Hubbard Creek, and Bob Sloan's on Deep Creek.

There were others in the area, however, like the W. H. Led-

88

betters and the Reynolds and Matthews families, whom the Irwins did not yet know.

The Irwins were typical of the better element of people attracted to the still virgin prairie lands of the western frontier—young, sturdy, determined to make a good life there for themselves and their families. Others were the Joseph Beck Matthews and Barber Watkins Reynolds families, who arrived in 1858 and 1859, respectively, to settle in Clear Fork country. Originally from Georgia and Alabama, they became neighbors on adjoining ranches near present Breckenridge, about thirty-five miles southeast of the Irwins. Soon, these two families and the Irwins lived closer together. First, the Reynoldses and Irwins "forted up" in Fort Davis in 1865, then all three families moved to live along the Clear Fork in the 1860's and 1870's. They continued as neighbors there for over seventy years, and the Matthews and Irwin families still live close by.

Sergeant Irwin did what most frontiersmen came to do—made a living and took advantage of opportunities open to him. He established a ranch and put in a crop on the Indian reservation. Stem's farm was just across the river and may have served Irwin as well as it probably did Thomas Lambshead until he left the Clear Fork the previous September to operate the Butterfield Stage stands to the southwest.

John C. Irwin recalled that his father kept the Butterfield Stage stand on the Clear Fork and that it was located where Judge Stribling's ranch house later stood. They dug the well, now abandoned but still to be seen there. All that is left of the station are a few buried rocks, part of the chimney. Stage Line Creek is named after the old stage line. The Clear Fork Crossing may still be seen, Irwin noted, and the rutted road can be traced north of the station in the Stribling pasture. The stage drove four to six horses or, sometimes, mules. Henry McCluskey herded the horses kept at the Clear Fork station for stage changes. It is likely that McCluskey had followed his friend John G. Irwin from Fort Chadbourne, and also that he took care of the remount station across the Clear Fork from the stage stand on Lambshead Creek.

By 1860, John G. Irwin had a beef contract to supply Camp Cooper. It was countersigned by Colonel Robert E. Lee, who had returned to San Antonio as commander of the Department of Texas. Joseph Carroll McConnell says in his *West Texas Frontier* that John G. Irwin also bought and ran Jonathan Lee's post store.

But national events were soon to affect settlement on the frontier. Secession had been hotly debated in Texas and, despite the opposition of Sam Houston and his followers, in late January, 1861, by act of convention, Texas left the Union and joined the Confederacy. At Camp Cooper, Captain S. D. Carpenter commanded 250 federal troops. Had things gone a little differently, the first shot of the Civil War might have been fired on the Clear Fork on February 18, 1861, instead of two months later at Fort Sumter.

Three days after Brevet Major General W. A. Twiggs, federal commander of the Department of Texas, had agreed to surrender all federal military posts in the state to Texas troops and sent orders to the respective commanders, Camp Cooper was surrounded by armed men on the hills. Up and down the Clear Fork were posted both state troops and citizen soldiery from the vicinity of Weatherford. Colonel W. C. Dalrymple, commander of Texas troops, called for surrender. Captain Carpenter at first refused and prepared to defend his military post, but before the Texans could open fire on Camp Cooper, Carpenter received Twiggs' message. Aware of the agitated political condition of the country and the serious consequences for the whole nation if he opposed, Carpenter acceded to terms: within twenty-four hours to surrender the post "with all arms, munitions, animals and other property heretofore belonging to the Government of the United States."

The troops marched out of Camp Cooper, February 21, 1861. Officers and men alike, upon surrender, were allowed to write letters and to keep their arms. Many soldiers returned to their homes in the north or south. Most of them later found themselves in either the Confederate or Union armies.

At Camp Cooper, citizens present at the official transfer of the post reported that public storehouses "had been opened and the regular soldiery as well as other persons were permitted to take what they wanted to use or destroy, and that several tents with their contents comprising the quarters of a portion of the troops were burned as well as a good deal of other property, by the regular troops or others before evacuation of the post, and that the doors of all public storehouses as well as officers' and men's quarters were open and the whole post filled with persons when the State Troops entered."

Colonel W. C. Dalrymple left the post in command of Captain E. W. Rogers. Colonel Henry E. McCulloch, commissioned by the Convention at Austin to take by force or to receive the surrender of all federal posts in northwest Texas, arrived at Camp Cooper March 6, 1861, demanding that Captain Rogers turn the post over to him, which he did. McCulloch reported to the Committee of Public Safety that property had been destroyed and the commissary houses looted either by federal troops as they left Camp Cooper or by state troops and civilian personnel who came in as soon as the federal forces were gone. As a result, his troops took less in the way of goods and supplies than they had anticipated.

McCulloch put Texas Ranger Captain J. B. ("Buck") Barry in

command of the post. Scouting out as far as the Red River with his command of Texas Mounted Rifles, Barry stayed until April, 1862, when Camp Cooper was permanently abandoned. John and Bill Hitson and family moved into some of the buildings and operated their cattle business on the adjoining free range along the Clear Fork.

After the surrender of the federal forts on the Texas frontier in February, 1861, there was no organized military protection for the region during the remainder of the year. Removal of the troops produced a surge in raids from the Indian Territory. On December 21, the state legislature authorized the creation of the Frontier Regiment of ten companies of state troops under Colonel James M. Norris. A new line of defense was established, with posts from the Red River to the Rio Grande. Each company was divided into two sections and stationed in separate camps. On the north was Camp Cureton on the west prong of the Trinity River in Archer County. The other station for Company A was at Fort Belknap. One-half of Company B was at Breckenridge and the other at Camp Pecan on Hubbard Creek in Callahan County. The other companies were spaced about twenty-five miles apart down to the border at Eagle Pass.

The routine of the regiment was to patrol daily between the camps to see if any Indians had passed through into the settlements. The Indians quickly caught on to this procedure and managed to slip through without leaving a trace. On the whole, however, the presence of the regiment along the frontier acted as a deterrent.

Troops were enlisted for one year. On March 6, 1863, the continuation of the regiment was authorized by the legislature for another year, but only two-thirds of the men stayed in service. The second year, Colonel Norris was replaced by Colonel J. E. McCord, a more able commander who abandoned the patrol system, consolidated the companies, and established a search-and-follow procedure.

Indian troubles were coming thick and fast to the settlers sticking it out in Clear Fork country, some thirty miles west of McCord's line of defense. Many families abandoned their homes and left for the relative safety of interior settlements. Several northern counties were virtually deserted. The Elm Creek raid of October, 1864, in Young County, was the final blow. In one of the worst raids to occur in northwest Texas, perhaps as many as a thousand Indians, broken up into smaller bands, swept through the area, killing and plundering. Many whites were captured, killed, or wounded. News of the attacks spread quickly, and settlers seeking a way to save their families from similar savage assaults decided to move together for protection.

Stockades were proposed in different sections. As B. W. Reynolds' youngest son, Phin, described them in an interview with J. R. Webb, families came together and

. . . built their houses in close proximity so that they would be gathered in groups, thus providing larger forces of men to repel Indian raids. . . . these communities of houses were termed forts, though they were forts in no literal sense as they had neither soldiers nor artillery. They did have men who were called upon for guard duty and scouting purposes. The settlers who occupied these forts or communities spoke of having "forted up" during the War and it is so spoken of until this day. In our section were several such forts, one known as Fort Davis being the largest. . . . Other forts in the section were Pickettville, near the site of Breckenridge, Owls Head, Clark, Mugginsville and Hubbard, also known as Lynch's Ranch.

Our family moved to Fort Davis which was built in the form of a square, and a picket stockade was started but never completed. It was to be constructed around all the houses, but as the scare died down somewhat work upon it ceased. . . . Our house was on the southwest corner of the hollow square; next door to the north was that of John Hittson who was the wealthiest man in the country; next was the home of Jim Thorpe; and next to his was the house of Matt Franz. He had been the stage line agent at Clear Fork Station of the Butterfield Stage Line until the stage line was abandoned at the outbreak of the Civil War. . . . then the school house which was the northeast corner of the square. Sam Newcomb, my brother-in-law, who taught the school and kept a diary of events at the fort, occupied a house within the square. John G. Irwin who had a meat contract at Camp Cooper before the war also lived within the square. . . . John Selman (pronounced Silman) with his mother occupied the house on the east side of the square next to the school house. His mother gave me, while we were living at the fort, the first apple I ever saw. . . .

The Hitson family was still at Camp Cooper after most of the settlers had "forted up." While out cow hunting on the north side of the Clear Fork, the two Hitson men, John's son, Press Mc-Carty, and a Negro boy were attacked by a band of Comanches. The Negro was killed, but the others, though wounded, made it to a bluff on Tecumseh Creek and fought off the Indians. Sam Newcomb describes the action in his diary and tells how the Hitsons, having survived, immediately moved their family to the protection of Fort Davis, several miles down the Clear Fork. All the men, however, did not stay with their families in the stockade. The Hitsons, the Irwins, the Reynoldses, and most of the other men in Fort Davis continued to return to their Clear Fork range to cow hunt, horse hunt, and generally look after their stock-raising business. The young people sometimes rode over to Camp Cooper to picnic, but not during the light of the moon.

Sam Newcomb describes stock-raising operations in his diary entries for Friday, January 5, and Saturday, January 6, 1866:

The people of this country do not have much to do in the winter season, not like the farmer in a farming country who is never through with his work. The busy time of a year with stock raisers is spring, summer and fall; though during the winter they have their years supply of bread stuff to get laid in, which is a pretty big job as they have to go one or two hundred miles after it.

This country has some peculiarities that are very disagreeable. The principle ones are, the sand stormes in spring, the northers in winter, the traveling grasshoppers in the fall and the long, severe and parching drouts in the summer and all other seasons of the year. This is a good grazing country and answers very well for stock raising, which is the only occupation followed by the people of this country. But the cold northers in winter scatter the cattle very badly. Men in this country gathering their stocks, often hunt over scopes of country seventy-five miles in diameter. The cow-hunter of this country starts out upon his one or two weeks with his wallet of provision and camping blanket tied to his saddle, and his cow whip, which is from ten to sixteen feet long and then his gun lashed to the bow of his saddle to protect himself from the Indians. Thus equiped he travels over a large scope of country, driving in his stock to mark and brand the calves, and wherever night overtakes him if there is plenty of water and grass he camps, hopples his horse, eats his supper of bread, dried beef and cold water, then lies down upon his blanket with his saddle for a pillow and sleeps as soundly as a king in his palace on a bed of down.

In 1865 and 1866, after the war, conditions were ripe for making honest gains or plucking ill-gotten ones. Cattle were roaming the free range of the Clear Fork and Brazos River valleys. Enterprising men who knew cattle and were alert to potential new markets for beef began to trail cattle to New Orleans, Mexico, and Santa Fe. Later, they pushed herds west halfway across the continent to Colorado, Salt Lake, and San Francisco; north up to Montana and the Dakotas; and northeast to Saint Louis and Kansas City. Among those determined to seek a market for their beef cattle and new ranges to settle on were George T. and William D. Reynolds, Charles Goodnight, and Oliver Loving. They drove herds from Clear Fork country along the old Butterfield Trail to Horsehead Crossing on the Pecos and up the river into New Mexico. Some sold in Santa Fe, others found a market at the military post at Fort Sumner for the Navajo Indians removed there. Later, they drove to Indian reservations in Oklahoma and other states, then to the mining camps of Colorado, Nevada, and California.

George T. Reynolds, son of B. W. Reynolds, had come with the family to Palo Pinto County in 1859 and at fifteen, carried the mail from Golconda to Weatherford. In 1861, he joined Company E, 19th Texas Cavalry, under command of Nat Buford, participating in his quota of battles. It was unusual for a boy of seventeen to leave the unprotected frontier and join the Confederate Army. He contracted measles, relapsed, and was discharged in 1863, returning to his home, which was then near Breckenridge. He helped with the livestock, "forted up" with the family at Fort Davis, and sought a way to broaden his range. He found it, according to Sam Newcomb, whose diary entry of October 16, 1865, notes: "George Reynolds and W. R. St. John talleyed out their beef steers this morning; they have about eighty, and intend to start to Mexico with them to-morrow. [S. I. Huff also went on the drive.]" Newcomb also describes their return to Fort Davis, where the Reynolds family welcomed them January 14, 1866:

We were agreeably surprised this morning by the arival of G. T. Reynolds and S. C. [*sic*] Huff into this place. They have been gone with a drove of beef steers, three months with the exception of three days. When they left here they expected to drive to old Mexico, but after getting down upon the Concho they heard that beef steers were not selling very well in old Mexico, so they changed their notions and course for New Mexico. There were only three of them and they must have had a hard time of it, guarding their cattle every night one at a time, one third of the night each. They say that they met a croud of men upon the plains that asked them where they were from and if three men was all there was along; and when told that it was they expressed themselves surprised and said, that they gloried in their courage but did not go much on their judgement. But they made it through without meeting any very bad luck or Indians, though they ran some very narrow riskes. They sold their beef steers in New Mexico near the head of the Reo Pecos (at Santa Fe). After they sold out, W. R. St. John, who it appears had owned a claim in the mining regions at Pikes Peak, heared of his partner selling out their claim for a large sum of money, and as the other two boys said they thought they could make it back, alone, he left them and went on to Denver City to receive his share of the profit. . . .

In 1866, hearing of George Reynolds' successful drive to New Mexico, Charles Goodnight continued preparations to gather cattle to be moved along the old trails beaten out before the Civil War. He determined to go west for two reasons: the mining areas would have more money, and there was good cattle country and grass in the region, "so if [you] could not sell, [you] could hold." Goodnight gave his hands top consideration, his horses second, and cow-hunted for more than a thousand head. When Oliver Loving joined him on this first drive, he pointed the herd west. Goodnight scouted ahead, and Loving led the herd, first by the Comanche Reservation and Camp Cooper on the Lambshead range, thence to Fort Phantom Hill, Buffalo Gap, Fort Chadbourne, and across the North Concho, following the ruts of the Butterfield Trail as George Reynolds and his outfit had done the year before. They made it from the headwaters of the Middle Concho, following Centralia Draw, through Castle Gap to Horsehead Crossing on the briny Pecos. They grazed their herds up the Pecos Valley north to Fort Sumner, forging the route that history records as the Goodnight-Loving Trail.

But everyone interested in cattle was not of the caliber of Reynolds and Goodnight. On the western frontier of the Confederacy, during the last two years of the Civil War, the Cross Timbers of Texas, extending intermittently from Jack County to Bandera, was the refuge of draft dodgers and deserters from the Confederate Army. Their number has been estimated at more than a thousand. Some of them may have been conscientious objectors, but most were simply men of bad character. They lived by their wits and off the land, which abounded with game and untended cattle. They helped themselves to both. When the war was over, many of these fugitives drifted back to their homes, but many of the roughest and toughest stayed and became seasoned rustlers. Throughout the chaotic period from 1865 to 1867, they competed with the marauding Indians at preying on the livestock and possessions of honest settlers. Painted, befeathered, and moccasined as Comanches, renegades not only stole from, but often scalped their own people.

Such men clearly constituted a criminal element. In these violent and unsettled times, however, there was often a fine line between "good" and "bad," and near the Clear Fork men of both sorts would soon gather on the Flat, below the fort to be located on Government Hill. Both places would be called Griffin.

II   *Fort Griffin*

THE FEDERAL COMMANDER of the Department of Texas was ordered by the military authorities in Washington to locate Fort Griffin in the post–Civil War line of defense to protect the hardy settlers along the farthermost frontier. On July 31, 1867, Colonel Samuel Davis Sturgis, accompanied by four companies of the Sixth Cavalry, mostly blacks, arrived at the site of Fort Griffin, located earlier by Lieutenant H. B. Mellen, whom Sturgis had sent out from the post at Fort Belknap. Mellen sought and found the highest, best-protected, coolest, and best-watered point near the Clear Fork, below which all frontier trails crossed. Sturgis approved the choice. For fourteen years, Fort Griffin operated there.

The soldiers were to concentrate on apprehending marauding Indians from Indian Territory and white outlaw bands. However, they largely dedicated themselves to pursuing the Indian depredators, leaving the cattle rustlers, outlaws, and horse thieves to state and local authorities.

Between the mesa-like hill on which the fort was located and the Clear Fork River to the north was a stretch of level land about a half-mile wide, which became known as the Flat. Here, within rifle shot of the troops on Government Hill, as the post was called, a town inevitably emerged. Protected on the south by the Hill,

99

the Flat was bounded on the west by Collins Creek, whose towering trees had some good limbs for hanging undesirables. On the
north was the Clear Fork River. Toward the east, extending for
miles along the river, were level grasslands, ideal for accommodating cavalry horse herds, cattle herds, and freighting and buffalo outfits with their oxen or mule teams. A fairly straight road
from the west side of the fort almost due north across the Flat
to a natural rock bottom crossing on the river became the main,
and only, street in the town. On either side the town grew and
sprawled without order.

With the coming of the soldiers, settlers who had fled during
the war and its aftermath began returning to their claims. Along
with them were newcomers looking for land. This increase in
population created a demand for supplies. Frank E. Conrad and
Charley Rath were quick to fill this need. Rath was originally a
buffalo hunter in western Kansas, where the buffalo slaughter
for hides began in 1870. As the movement got underway, he
shifted from hunting to merchandising, supplying hunters and
buying hides at his hastily built store south of Dodge City. A
treaty between the federal government and the Indians put a stop
to killing what was left of the buffalo herds in Kansas, so Rath
shifted his business to Fort Griffin, where he formed a partnership with Conrad. They had a completely stocked store for pro-
visioning settlers, buffalo hunters, and trail outfits, including an
enormous safe out of which Conrad ran a banking business on
the side.

Many hunting outfits followed Rath to Texas and operated out
of Griffin, as the Flat was also called. A typical outfit consisted of
a hunter, two skinners, two wagons, four mules or work horses,
and one saddle horse used by the hunter to scout for herds. The
Mooar brothers, John W. and J. Wright, in Kansas, had twelve

wagons and six skinners. They too followed the herds to Texas, via Fort Griffin to the Snyder area.

The great Texas buffalo slaughter began in 1873. For six years, Griffin was the outfitting post and collecting center for buffalo hides brought in by the hunters, who ranged as far west as New Mexico. However, the predominant range of the buffalo was between the Cross Timbers and the eastern edge of the High Plains. They seldom ventured on the Plains, where there was no water when the playa lakes dried up.

Millions of hides passed through Griffin and were handled by Conrad and Rath. Acres of ground in the Flat were covered with huge ricks of them. Getting the hides to a railroad terminal required a small army of professional freighters, each with a wagon and a trail wagon, drawn by mules, horses, or oxen. The nearest terminal in 1873 was Denison. The distance was reduced in December, 1874, when the Texas and Pacific Railroad reached Eagle Ford, seven miles west of Dallas. By September, 1876, the T. and P. was completed to Weatherford, which shortened the freighters' haul even more. This was fortunate, because the peak of the slaughter lasted for two more years. The freighters hauled hides to the terminal and returned with provisions not only for the hunters, but also for the cattlemen and settlers. Conrad and Rath were doing an enormous two-way business, and Griffin, which had been slow beginning, was a boom town.

By 1874, out on the prairies, buffalo hunting, cattle trailing, and cattle thieving were occupying hunters, stockmen, and rustlers. Down in Griffin, a "crime wave" was sweeping the Flat. Fort Griffin's commander, Major W. H. Wood, declared the Flat and its environs to be under government control and ordered the gamblers, outlaws, and prostitutes to leave, which they promptly did. However, with the organization of Shackelford County in

1874, the government relinquished control over the Flat. The news spread and the unsavory characters were back in the Flat by 1875, increasing the size of the town twofold. The height of activity in Griffin was from 1874 to 1878, when the saloon keepers and merchants had money from the cattle drovers, the buffalo hunters, and the military.

By 1875, the main cattle trail to Kansas had shifted from Fort Worth over a hundred miles west to Griffin. South Texas drovers brought scores of herds through each spring and summer. Occasionally, two herds arrived the same day. Most stopped for a day or two at Griffin to let the cattle rest and to restock supplies. There was no other place until the herds reached Doan's Store on the Red River. The cowboys were allowed to relax, which they did, all day and all night, joining the buffalo hunters, freighters, soldiers, professional gamblers, con men, and ladies of pleasure in the saloons, bordellos, and gambling houses.

Both sides of the street were lined with saloons, hotels, gambling halls, dance halls, small businesses, and lawyers' and doctors' offices. Scattered about behind these establishments was the "red light" district, the palaces of sin where the madams and their girls displayed and dispensed their charms. Some were only one room, where an independent operator plied her trade, but most were larger establishments supervised by a madam. The Flat clearly offered antidotes to the monotony of the trail.

According to historian Carl Coke Rister, the Flat had one thousand permanent residents and twice that many transients between 1875 and 1880, with the "revolver settling more differences between men than the judge." Formidable characters came to this remote part of Texas. William Martin, former Indian scout, gunman, outlaw leader, and "slick rascal" from Arizona and Kansas, a "high roller, travelling . . . the whirlwind of crime so fast and furious" that he became known as "Hurricane Bill," ar-

The town of Fort Griffin on the Flat, viewed from the military fort on the hill.

rived at Griffin in 1875. "Hurricane Minnie" was his paramour. Both were mixed up in most of the questionable affairs at Griffin, Albany, and on the Lambshead range. Irish opportunist and Griffin saloon keeper Dick Shaughnessey, whose mistress was the mysterious lady gambler Lottie Deno, served as informant and go-between for lawmen like Wyatt Earp who came to search for the notorious outlaw Dave Rudabaugh. Pat Garrett and Doc Holliday were there at times, and scores of questionable characters passed through the Flat and its environs.

J. Evetts Haley, who knows well the lawmen and badmen of this period, says: "There were also gangs, groups and bands, just loose confederations, who rendezvoused there or merely passed through Griffin. The country was full of them. The bands, not really organized groups, just men who always worked together, were in no way so organized as the Mafia. Griffin served as a gathering place, the worst of all, for bad men."

Among these were the McBride-Henderson gang, about thirty desperadoes led by Bill Henderson during the early 1870's, who, from their stronghold in the Wichita Mountains in Indian Territory, openly and ruthlessly robbed, stole, rustled, and killed, terrorizing the Clear Fork country until 1876. Twice their number of sympathizers lived off their pickings and provided information that allowed the gang to operate successfully and to cover their tracks.

John C. Irwin, describing the establishment of both the fort and the Flat, which he first saw in 1867 as a boy of twelve, said: "It looked to me like all of the bad characters from everywhere were swarming around there. It got so tough there that I was afraid to ride down the streets. During the buffalo and trail herd days it looked like the civil authorities were either helpless or controlled by the lawless elements and out of this condition sprung the Vigilantes."

Wild and wicked as Griffin no doubt was, a considerable number of stable, honest people lived and worked there, too, and a tremendous amount of business was transacted. The Hank Smiths (known as Aunt and Uncle Hank) built and from 1875 to 1878 operated the Occidental Hotel in Griffin before taking over the Rock House Ranch in Blanco Canyon near Crosbyton. Of the Griffin days, Aunt Hank said:

> We made lots of money those days. . . . Everybody had plenty of gold, twenty-dollar gold pieces; the government post was still there. . . .
>
> Fort Griffin was a pretty tough place. . . . There were bad men there from everywhere. There were buffalo hunters, both good and bad, and there were adventurers and bad women and gamblers. Most of the places of business were saloons, and murder was common. My boarders used to say, "Mrs. Smith, we have another man for breakfast hanging down yonder in a tree." Of course, I didn't want to see them. The better citizens of the town organized a vigilance committee, who generally did the hanging. . . .
>
> It wasn't all bad at Griffin. We used to have camp meetings and carry our dinner; had lots of fried chicken and chicken pie, and just plenty good things to eat. . . . Fort Griffin was occupied by the Tenth Cavalry [*sic*]. . . . the officers took part in many of our social functions. . . . There were lots of educated people in Fort Griffin. . . . plenty of them who didn't drink or gamble.

There were good hotels, like the Occidental, a church, a school, an opera house, and a Masonic lodge with its stone building. Professional men came to Griffin, lawyers like County Judge C. K. Stribling, Judge M. D. Kent, Judge J. W. Wray, and County Attorney J. N. Browning, son of W. L. Browning who, with Thomas Lambshead, had been named commissioner for Throckmorton County in 1858. Dr. M. W. Powell and Dr. I. J. Culver practiced medicine there. Dr. Culver, who was the Matthews family physician, and his associates also ran sheep on property they owned on Lambshead. J. A. Matthews purchased that land from them in 1885, and it was known thereafter as Culver Pasture. Members of both the Matthews and Reynolds families also lived in or near Griffin during its brief existence.

Like other boom towns, Griffin flourished and faded with the conditions that brought it into being. The southern herd of Texas buffalo had been exterminated by the time the railroad built west from Weatherford in 1880. With the decline of Indian raids, the coming of the railroads, and the rapid advancement of settlement, the need for the military on the frontier dwindled. In the early 1880's, several forts were abandoned, among them Fort Griffin, whose flag was lowered for the last time on May 31, 1881. That same year the Texas Central Railroad reached Albany, a growing settlement to the south. By 1882, the once-crowded street of Griffin lay empty and still.

A T THE SAME TIME that Griffin was enjoying its unruly heyday, responsible, law-abiding folk continued to settle or to expand their holdings in the Clear Fork country. There they built their houses, enclosed their fields, and ranged their livestock. By 1877, the old Comanche Reservation land was already parceled out in 160-acre units. In addition to the John Irwins and the John Hittsons, H. R., J. H., and David Treadwell held land there, as did A. J. Lancaster and other small stockmen and farmers, often referred to as Grangers. John Selman, old family friend of the Reynoldses, and John Larn, ambitious newcomer from Alabama and husband of young Mary Jane Matthews, had places along the river and were well into the cattle business. And the extended, intermarried Matthews and Reynolds families had located their homesteads and other patented lands on both sides of the Clear Fork and were reaping the benefits of their expanding cattle interests.

Those who tried farming on the Clear Fork did not often make a go of it. The experience of John C. Jacobs, a tenderfoot from Kentucky who arrived in Clear Fork country in 1872, is probably typical.

Jacobs described his venture into agriculture to J. Evetts Haley, February 27, 1932: "I wanted to come hunt buffalo and fight Indians. I went direct to Fort Griffin, to the outside house. I was broke, of course, like all young men, and got work on Joe Matthews' ranch the first thing. Mrs. Matthews was the finest woman I ever saw. She mothered me. I worked from May to September, 1872, for him on the Clear Fork of the Brazos."

Matthews himself loved to farm, though family and friends often chided him that it took the ranch to keep up the farm (the ranch was at Pleasant View, which had good bottom land with productive fields). Matthews must have encouraged Jacobs to put in a crop for himself.

In any event, Jacobs did try farming in partnership with John William Poe. A young farmer also from Kentucky, strong, energetic, and ingenious, Poe had just arrived at Fort Griffin, looked up his fellow Kentuckian, and, after being shown the farm, propositioned Jacobs to take him in as a partner. He pointed out that Jacobs had the land, an ox team, and was already well along toward getting the corn put in. He offered to contribute his horse, Pete, and eighty dollars, suggesting that with the "two . . . working, the crop [would] go in faster and it [would not] be so lonesome, either." Shaking hands, they cemented the beginning of a partnership and lifelong friendship.

John Jacobs and John Poe became "masters of makeshift." To plant more quickly, they rigged single harness for Jacobs' oxen. John Poe could plow with the one-sweep walking plow while John Jacobs harrowed behind him with the other ox. The corn grew quickly. One day, when it was just tasseling out, John Poe suggested going hunting for fresh meat, but John Jacobs was looking "at a strange haze in the east, swiftly moving across the sky"; a vast green cloud of grasshoppers, "with a metallic buzzing," descended upon their corn field. As Jacobs described it,

They actually darkened the sun. They stripped all the trees, and the water in the Clear Fork ran black with their excrement. When they flew, a peculiar haze, or cloud, floated over the ground. They came in one morning. That night, the corn was eaten down and into the ground, and the furrows were level with grasshoppers. The next day, they kept passing overhead. This was my first year in Texas and I lost all I had.

They were completely wiped out, their promising farm now as barren as a desert. "There goes my wedding to that golden-haired girl back in Kentucky," John Jacobs said. "If you want to go hunting, here's our chance. I'll sell the oxen and buy a horse." They did, and the two friends teamed up with Joe McCombs as a buffalo-hunting outfit, following the southern herd for six years. All three men were to figure in later events at Griffin.

The land was far better suited to ranching, and those who ran cattle met with much greater success. By 1865, the Reynolds family was already into the cattle and trail-driving business, which their oldest son, George, as we have seen, launched that year, starting from Fort Davis with the small drive he led into New Mexico when he was twenty-one. In 1867, the second son, Will, then twenty-one, left from the Stone Ranch, where the family was living at the time, to trail into New Mexico with Charles Goodnight and Oliver Loving. He returned from that ill-fated drive as escort to the body of Oliver Loving, who had died in Fort Sumner from Indian-inflicted wounds.

Pushing ever farther west, George was twenty-four in 1868 and his bride of a year, Bettie Matthews Reynolds, was only seventeen when they took Ben Reynolds, then sixteen, on a cattle drive to Colorado. They stopped at Hole-in-the-Rock Ranch in Colorado before trailing the herd on to San Francisco, where they profited from a fine cattle market and enjoyed the new and exciting refinements of city life. The trail-driving Reynolds men always returned to home base, their family place in Parker County near Weatherford, until the fall of 1872. Then, B. W. and Anne Maria Reynolds were enticed by their sons to sell out in Parker

County and move to the Point of Rocks Ranch, which George and Will had established in a rich, well-watered valley in south-eastern Colorado. With them came their younger children, Phin, fourteen, and Sallie, eleven. The summer before the Reynoldses left their Parker County place, their widowed daughter Susan Reynolds Newcomb married Nathan L. Bartholomew, a Connecticut Yankee, in a double ceremony with her brother Will and his bride Mary Byrd. Susan and Nathan Bartholomew moved to a ranch in Eastland County and Will took Mary to Colorado, where, unfortunately, she died within six months.

In the spring of 1872, Ben Reynolds, now twenty, and his boyhood friend John Alexander ("Bud") Matthews, nineteen, drove separate herds from the Colorado ranch to deliver them on the Humboldt River in Nevada. The two young drovers traveled on to San Francisco, lured by Ben's memories of the "Golden City" from his travels four years before with George and Bettie Reynolds. Bud returned to Texas late in 1872, but not in time for the wedding of his younger sister Mary to John Larn. The Reynolds family stayed on in Colorado, though the men often made trips back and forth to Texas. Then, in 1875, the entire Reynolds family moved back to Texas, settling like a flock of homing pigeons along the Clear Fork in the Lambshead region. Ben drove a small herd of Durham cattle to a bend in the Clear Fork, and that winter he and his father located a ranch there and planned a headquarters and house, which were built the next year. The site became known as Reynolds Bend.

B. W. Reynolds' old friend Joe B. Matthews was now his neighbor, eighteen miles down the Clear Fork from Reynolds Bend and six miles east of Fort Griffin. In 1871, Matthews had settled on the Home Ranch, also known as Pleasant View. He had discovered it during Civil War times, when he had become well acquainted with every bend and valley in the river while cow hunting. There he built a commodious stone barn with seven portholes in the west wall, as Indian raiders were still abroad in the land. The family's first home, built of pickets, burned in 1874. Joe Matthews replaced it in 1875 with a sizable one-and-a-half-story cut-stone house of gracious proportions.

Housebuilding boomed in 1875 and 1876 up and down the Clear Fork. Cattle sales had been good, but, even better, Colonel Ranald S. Mackenzie had rounded up the marauding Comanches, Kiowas, and Cheyennes, unhorsed them in Tule Canyon, on September 28, 1874, and put them on the reservations in Indian Territory.

Mackenzie began his first campaign in the fall of 1871, using Griffin for a supply base, with Joe Matthews furnishing him beef. He made the Mackenzie Trail at that time, rutting the prairie across the south side of Lambshead with his wagon trains from Fort Concho to Griffin, and, later, Camp Cooper. Mackenzie used Camp Cooper, before John Larn homesteaded there in 1872, as an operational base for his successful forays into northwest Texas. He was helped, of course, when the buffalo hunters began killing off the Indians' food supply in 1873. With the Indian menace gone, at last it was possible to build a house without making it into a fort. And many families did.

Most of the new houses erected in the Lambshead area at this time were built of stone, as were the fences surrounding them. Stonecutters, masons, and woodworkers were in great demand, and their craftsmanship is still evident in these family houses, which were considered mansions in their day. Both the Matthews and the Reynolds families had run the gamut in frontier housing: from dugout to picket house, log cabin to adobe, then to stone. The only type they missed living in was box-and-strip, available only after the railroads brought lumber to the frontier. But they later lived mostly in lumber houses in town.

John Larn was the first of the group to locate on the Clear Fork in Lambshead. He built his three-room "Honeymoon Cottage" on the flat parade ground of Camp Cooper, and here he brought his bride in 1872. It is said he used some of the rough stones from the small storage buildings and assistant surgeon's quarters to build it. The sophisticated taste of this young stockman is revealed in the stone borders of four flower beds in the front yard, which cleverly outline designs of hearts, spades, clubs, and diamonds, still discernible among the ruins.

In 1875, Larn built an impressive and unusual stone house near the cottage, locating it above the Clear Fork on a high bank, which commanded the cooling breezes and a sweeping view. The same year John Selman had his one-story, three-room rock house constructed to replace his original picket house on Tecumseh Creek, which flowed into the Clear Fork a long mile northeast of the Larn place. He named his place, homesteaded in 1872, the Rock Ranch.

Joe Matthews, no doubt, started his cut-stone house in early 1875, before son-in-law Mart V. Hoover finished his late in the same year. Mart and Martha Matthews lived in the old Stone Ranch while building their attractive story-and-a-half stone house to the north, a few miles downriver from the Stone Ranch. They set up housekeeping there in December, 1875.

Two Reynolds family houses were built in Reynolds Bend in 1876. First, Barber Watkins Reynolds' modest one-and-a-half-story rock house, encircled, with its barn, by a stone wall, was begun in January, 1876. The workmen then moved nearby to construct Susan and Nathan Bartholomew's story-and-a-half stone home in the summer of 1876. It was surrounded with stone fences and revealed the influence of Bartholomew's Connecticut upbringing in the intricate interior and exterior architectural details. Sallie Reynolds Matthews tells how the lumber had to be hauled more than 150 miles from Eagle Ford, just west of Dallas, the end of the Texas and Pacific Railroad, to build stairways, window frames, mantels, and other items for both these houses. Lumber for the floor joists and lintels over the windows of the B. W. Reynolds house was cut from trees along the river.

In 1877, George and Bettie Reynolds built their story-and-a-half stone house across the river west from the B. W. Reynolds place. It had an elegant bay window, dormers, and an upstairs porch, ideas probably gleaned in their travels, perhaps from the Centennial Exposition in Philadelphia, which they visited in 1876. A wooden barn was built as a smaller edition of the house, with its own dormer windows from which hay could be tossed to the horses and cows waiting in the corrals and lots on either side of the barn.

Will Reynolds and D. C. Campbell followed suit downriver from the Bend, erecting houses with lumber hauled from Eagle Ford. Each had fine stone fireplaces. Only the stone foundations now remain at the D. C. Campbell house, built in 1877. A crumbling rock chimney marks the homestead where Will Reynolds built a home for Susie Matthews, whom he married January 1, 1879, at the Joe Matthews' new rock house. Will moved his bride in with his wedding gift to her—a handsome square piano, the first in Throckmorton County.

Glenn Reynolds, who had remained in Colorado to try his luck in the mining districts, soon came back to Texas, but not for long. On March 2, 1876, he married Gustie Russell in Rocky Ford, Colorado, and they stayed on there at the Point of Rocks Ranch to help Will and Phin close it out. The four of them returned to Texas for sister Sallie and Bud Matthews' wedding in the B. W. Reynolds' new home in the bend of the Clear Fork on Lambshead, Christmas Day of 1876. George brought his sister a spanking new Miller buggy as a wedding gift.

On a map showing the original grantees and patentees of the Lambshead region, to the west, north, and south and within the Comanche reservation, the name of Reynolds, father B. W. and sons George, Will, Glenn, and Phin, are well scattered across the area. Relatives' and in-laws' names stand out also on patented lands—D. C. Campbell, Mart V. Hoover, M. F. Barber, Frank E. Conrad, N. L. Bartholomew—as does the name of J. A. Matthews and of John Matthews, a cousin. John Larn patented two 160-acre plots contained in Camp Cooper—one in 1876 and the other, obtained from M. F. Barber, a Reynolds relative, in 1878.

The two oldest Reynolds sons formed a partnership in 1874 for their free-range cattle operations in the west, calling it the Reynolds Brothers. They were also running cattle together in Haskell County with their boyhood friend and new brother-in-law Bud Matthews, who, with bride Sallie, began housekeeping the spring of 1877 in a long, low rock house on California Creek, a tributary of Paint Creek. First, George and Bettie stayed with them in the California Ranch house. Later that year, Glenn and Gustie, Sallie's friend from Colorado days, came to live with Sallie and Bud. Glenn injected variety into the family ranching enterprises in 1878 by going into the sheep business. He homesteaded 160 acres and built a small stone house for Gustie and their two sons. It was located about two-thirds of the way between Reynolds Bend and Camp Cooper, down the river.

Brought together on Lambshead, the Matthews and Reynolds families not only occupied common territory, but also shared common origins and experiences. Both originated in England, Wales, and the highlands of Scotland. Both were firmly grounded on the bedrock precepts of Presbyterian ethics, which they brought with them to the eastern seaboard of the United States, on to Alabama, to Louisiana, and thence into Texas and the Clear Fork frontier. Probably unable to own extensive landholdings in the old country, they were land hungry and persevered until they pushed on to fertile valleys along the Clear Fork. Here was a promised land for the taking, and the men had the will, the courage, and the prowess to make it their own. Their women were the sort who "stuck by the stuff," loyally standing by their men when the going got hard. It was the women who provided a good religious upbringing and insisted on the best possible educations for sons, daughters, and extended family, and their men supported them.

By 1877, the newly married Reynolds-Matthews couples locating on the Lambshead range were well traveled, reasonably educated, informed, and experienced young men and women; the youngest, Sallie, was sixteen, and the oldest, George, was twenty-seven. B. W. Reynolds was fifty-eight and Joe B. Matthews was fifty-three; they had now been in Clear Fork country for eighteen and nineteen years, respectively.

John Larn was a relative newcomer, with a different background. Still in his teens, he had left home in Alabama, running away as a newsboy on a train ending up in Colorado, and thence by way of Kansas and New Mexico to the Texas frontier. In 1870, now twenty-one, he was living in the Newcomb household and perhaps working for Joe Matthews. Like his future in-laws, he discovered a prospective cattle empire in Clear Fork country. Although he had the cultivated tastes and demeanor of the Old South, he lacked the moral fiber of the family into which he married, as later events proved. He appeared to have been influenced for both good and bad during his travels. He arrived early enough to pick one of the most choice sites on Lambshead, to build one of the most impressive houses, and to launch himself by his wits into the cattle business. He also had the good judgment to fall in love with and marry Joe Matthews' lovely daughter Mary, who brought a dowry of several hundred head of cattle with her. In addition, he teamed up with John Selman, who knew the Clear Fork country and its people well.

In November, 1872, Larn brought his bride to his ranch home, the Honeymoon Cottage. Just before their wedding, quite a little stir had occurred, but it was kept closely guarded within the families. Barber Watkins Reynolds, "Uncle Watt," as he was called, came over from Palo Pinto to have a private talk with "Uncle Joe" Matthews about rumors concerning the questionable character of John Larn. George, Will, and Glenn Reynolds, his boys, had just returned from Kansas and Colorado trail drives with stories, hearsay information about John Larn's character, no proof but something that might bear investigation.

The Reynoldses' friendly concern had no effect on Mary Matthews, a pretty brunette with curly brown hair, large blue eyes, a lovely figure, and a strong will. Neither her parents nor Uncle Watt Reynolds could persuade her to postpone the wedding. She loved the dashing young cowboy, she was determined to marry him, and she did.

John and Mary began their family the year after they settled in the Honeymoon Cottage. Their first son, Will, was born on December 17, 1873. Another son was born in the spring of 1875, but lived for only six short months. The Larns, known to have made a love match, led an exemplary home life. John was as devoted to his young wife as she was to him, "a kind, considerate, . . . and loving husband." The only known photograph of John Larn, a daguerreotype made in 1878, shows a well-dressed, attractive man with broad shoulders, thick black hair, high cheek bones, dark intelligent eyes, an aristocratic nose, a wide mouth, and a trim moustache and tidy goatee. With his good looks and good manners, John Larn won many friends in the area. He had a reputation as "a leader of men and a charmer of women," and was described as "fine looking, of good address, good nerve and a splendid marksman. On account of these traits, he soon became popular on the frontier." Life on Lambshead looked promising for the young couple.

Things seemed to be going well on the Lambshead range, but events lay ahead that would bring violence and tragedy to its occupants. The Indians were no longer such a problem, but rustlers and outlaws continued to harass the settlers and stockmen. Fort Griffin, a virtual haven for such characters after 1874, was only a few miles distant.

During the decade and a half after the Civil War, no legal organization existed capable of dealing with outlawry. In the absence of legal law-enforcing machinery, the most fearless and daring of the honest citizens of necessity banded together to protect themselves and their property. This group was known in the early 1870's as the Old Law Mob, or OLM. By 1874, it was called the Tin Hat Brigade, for what reason, no one exactly knows. By 1876, it had emerged as the vigilantes, or the Fort Griffin Vigilance Committee. Membership was secret, yet most of the stable citizens had an idea who belonged. The band did not banish outlawry from the land, but it did much to deter it. The methods of the vigilantes were swift and drastic. As Aunt Hank mentioned, it was not unusual for the people in the Flat to get up in the morning and see one or more bodies hanging from the elm or cottonwood trees along the Clear Fork. Sallie Reynolds wrote in *Interwoven*, "The times called for drastic measures and they were used to put down lawlessness of all kinds." As Mrs. Ethel Matthews Casey has said, "It was the only way the honest, law-abiding people could survive." The vigilantes were mostly citizens of means, with something to lose. The Grangers, small landholders trying to eke out a living on their little plots of land, were destined to get caught in the middle of the struggle between the vigilantes and the rustlers.

During the turmoil that engulfed the Lambshead area during the 1870's, four basic groups were involved. First were the honest citizens of substance: merchants, professional men, and most cattlemen, to whom the first settlers eventually sold, as they could not make a living on small tracts of land. (The usual homestead was 160 acres, with 20 acres necessary to support each cow-calf unit.)

The second category was the Grangers, small farmers, poor in worldly possessions, who filed on many of the 160-acre tracts of the old Comanche Indian Reservation when it reverted to the state. The average settler had two or three horses, and a wagon in which he hauled his few belongings and his family. A boy or a girl on a horse perhaps drove two or three milk cows behind the wagon. These were usually honest, God-fearing people, but they had little in common with the more substantial ranching families. Most Grangers suffered severely, trying to survive and protect their lives and property.

The third group was made up of those who undertook to get ahead by dishonest methods, such as cheating, robbing, rustling, and stealing. Theft of horses and cattle was a crime of the first order, more serious even than manslaughter.

The fourth group was composed of the flotsam and jetsam of humankind in the Flat at Fort Griffin. These were people who lived by their wits. Some were gamblers, who learned from professionals and who came and went. Others were thieves, who stole anything available, including cattle and horses. Some were killers. Those in the third group had much in common with the fourth, though the third faction generally operated in the country and the fourth mainly in the Flat.

The distinction between those who lived within the law and those who were bent on getting ahead outside the law, however, was not always clear. Changing hats as it suited their purposes, some men became involved in enterprises that moved them from one group to another. Two men, in particular, became notorious two-hat men—John Selman and John Larn.

13   *The Two-Hat Men*

N
O ONE EVER KNEW for sure John Larn's real name or who his family was. Variations of his name were used by a number of people from many states. Some knew Larn in Griffin as John Laren or John M. Laren. John William Poe, who was a buffalo hunter from 1872 to 1878 and knew Larn in Griffin, called him John Laren. Henry and James Comstock, brothers from Wisconsin, came to Griffin in 1872 and knew him as John Laren. They joined him in a cattle drive to Colorado, returning to live in the Griffin area until 1874. Edgar Rye, also from Kentucky, who was newspaper editor, justice of the peace, and county attorney in Shackelford County from his arrival in 1876 on, referred to him as John Laren. Lieutenant G. W. Campbell, Company B, Frontier Battalion, Texas Rangers, used the abbreviation Jno. M. Laren in reports to his commanding officer concerning events in Clear Fork country in 1877 and 1878. J. K. Duke speaks of Johnny Laren in his article "Bad Men and Peace Officers of the Southwest." Emmett Roberts, a stockman on the Clear Fork in 1873, tells how he got his stolen cattle back from John Laurens. Charles A. Siringo calls him Johnny Larn. John R. Cook, a buffalo hunter, tells of his encounter with Johnny Lorin, sheriff at Fort Griffin. The majority of these men knew Larn firsthand. The only woman to mention him was Aunt

Hank Smith of Griffin, who refers to "John Lawrens from Kansas."

John Larn, or John M. Larn, is the name others used, as did Larn himself. He signed "John Larn" to a receipt for "one bay mare," written in his own hand at Fort Griffin, September 11, 1872. The Matthews and Reynolds family members naturally said John Larn, as Phin Reynolds states in his reminiscences. John Meadows, also originally from Alabama, called him John Larn in interviews with various people, including J. Evetts Haley, the historian. Newton Josephus Jones, Millet Ranch hand and later a member of Texas Ranger Company B, sent in his reports on John Larn. John C. Irwin, Larn's close neighbor down the Clear Fork, Henry Herron, a deputy of Shackelford County in 1878, and Joe McCombs, buffalo hunter at Griffin from 1874 to 1878, called him John Larn. The final statement is chiseled on his tombstone, "John M. Larn."

John Selman, well known in Clear Fork country since 1864 and a close friend of the Reynolds family, received equal variations in the spelling of his name. Edgar Rye called him "Sillman, an all-round sport, horse trader, gambler and three-card man." Sophie Poe, wife of John William Poe, writes of John Sellman, one of John Laren's "closest friends." Charles A. Siringo said that "Mr. George H. Tucker, formerly of Ft. Griffin, told him John Sillman had a bad record as killer of men, as a cattle thief in Ft. Griffin, and that he was in partnership in cattle stealing with Johnny Larn." Other persons who knew John Selman spelled it "Silman" or "Silliaman." However, Phin Reynolds and John C. Irwin, both of whom knew him at Fort Davis in 1865 when the Selmans first came to the frontier, specifically speak of "John Selman (pronounced Silman)" in their interviews with J. R. Webb. He signed himself "John Selman."

Nothing clouds the Selman name for the first thirty years of his life. John Henry Selman was born in Madison County, Arkansas, on November 16, 1839. The census records of 1840 show his father to have been Jeremiah Selman, a Kentucky schoolteacher who owned five or six slaves. John's mother was an Underwood from somewhere in the Carolinas. The Selman family moved to Grayson County, Texas, in 1858.

After his father's death, John Selman "moved west" in the typical tradition of the frontier. He was twenty-five when he came to Clear Fork country in 1864, bringing his widowed mother, brother Tom, and three sisters. John Selman brought the family to a "lower fort," probably Picketville, near Breckenridge, early in the year. They supposedly located there because Jasper N. deGraffenreid, a friend from Sherman, lived nearby at the T. L. Stockton Ranch. Soon, the Selmans and deGraffenreid moved twelve miles to "fort up" at Fort Davis with the B. W. Reynoldses, John Hitsons, J. G. Irwins, and Sam Newcombs, along with some hundred other people determined to stick out the Civil War on the frontier. Sam Newcomb, schoolteacher and son-in-law of B. W. Reynolds, noted in his diary for March 8, 1865, that "John Selman has some of his pickets hauled for his mother's house." On March 14, 1865, he wrote, "There was a house raised in this place today for Mrs. Selman by her son John who is at home from the army on furlough." Sam Newcomb refers several times to Selman's being back home "on furlough." His military record shows he was in and out of service from December 15, 1861, until he finally deserted April 25, 1863. Selman was, doubtless, one of many such "deserters" who came to Clear Fork country during the war.

Selman had a strange quirk that surfaced at this time. He wanted to become a peace officer, an attraction that continued throughout his life. Right away, he offered for sheriff of Stephens County, riding with several other candidates into Fort Davis on

February 18, 1865, to electioneer. He did not become sheriff, likely because he was already in the state militia, having enlisted in the Stephens County Company of Texas State Troops on February 4, 1864. He was made lieutenant under Captain J. W. Curtis. Shrewd Sam Newcomb observed in his diary that "a little office would keep a person out of the service."

The Confederate Army finally caught up with Selman. Newcomb recounts that on April 29, 1865, "four soldiers from Fort Belknap came into this place and arrested John Selman for desertion." The next day he added, ". . . it is hard to tell what punishment they will put upon him." On June 5, 1865, Newcomb noted: "John Selman got back home alive and well today. . . . It has been little more than a month since he was taken off." Newcomb explained that news of Robert E. Lee's surrender must have reached Selman below Waco. There he also encountered his old company, who were disbanded and heading home, so he returned, too. Sam Newcomb also recorded that in August, 1865, Selman went back to East Texas, married Miss Edna deGraffenreid, Jasper's sister, and brought her back to Fort Davis.

Susan Reynolds Newcomb made frequent mention in her diary of John Selman, the widow Selman, and Jasper deGraffenreid. The diary covered the period from August 1, 1865, to May 16, 1869. On February 17, 1866, Susan wrote:

There were three families left the place today. the widow Selman, John Selman and I. Willet. They moved down to the old lady Dodson's ranch on the Clear fork. The old lady Selman has not gone yet. . . .

February 20, 1866: Ma [Anne Maria Reynolds] has not been well for a long time and to day she is scarcely able to be out of bed. . . .

February 21, 1866: Ma is worse to day she has not set up any   she is salivated very bad and her mouth is very sore, she has had a fever all day. I have been making soap to day and I tell you it has kept me busy to wait on Ma nurse a cross baby and tend to the soap. I dont recon I could have done as much as I did if it has not been for the old lady Selman   she is a faithful hand to wait on the sick, it looks like she never tires, it makes no difference what is to be done she is always there ready.

January 20, 1867: After dinner we went down to Tom L. Stocktons. We found all well but the old lady Selman. She is quite feeble with the chills and fever.

January 21, 1867: Tom Stockton and John Selman have been killing hogs for some time. They have ten fine large ones to kill today. . . .

April 4, 1867: John Selman and Jasper deGraffenreid came here [the Stone Ranch], late this evening after a yoke of oxen. John says that his mother has been failing very fast for the last week or two, he don't think she can live much longer. . . . I dressed John's arm for him after he had taken a long nap of sleep. I had to rip his sleeves to get them up. He had not washed his arm since it was shot, the blood was dry and his under sleeve stuck fast to his arm. I know it must have hurt him while I was working to get it loose, but he did not flinch; he said it was very sore. It being the first wound I ever dressed I expect I was a little awkward. . . . He said that it felt a great deal better after the blood was washed off.

April 5, 1867: John Selman found the oxen very easy and they left early this morning.

Susan's account indicates that Jasper deGraffenreid had moved back to the Stockton Ranch and that the Selman family had also moved back there, with John learning the butcher's trade from Tom Stockton. Susan also mentioned John Selman's coming to the Stone Ranch to hunt hogs and on other neighborly business, bearing out the information passed down to present-day members of the Matthews-Reynolds family that "our family always liked old John Selman."

The Selman family early had a reputation as God-fearing, sturdy, frontier citizens. While at Fort Davis, the family was baptized by missionary Baptist preacher Parson W. B. Slaughter, all but John and brother Tom. The widow Selman was well respected and a good friend to Mrs. B. W. Reynolds, the old lady

Dodson, and other families of the Fort. When Mrs. Selman was on her deathbed, she sent for Mrs. Reynolds on a May day in 1867. According to Sallie, Mrs. Reynolds' youngest daughter, her mother, past fifty, mounted a horse at the Stone Ranch and galloped twenty miles over and back, with son George and Si Hough as armed escorts. Her dying friend held Mrs. Reynolds' hand and whispered a fervent "God bless you." Mrs. Selman was buried "in a small cemetery near the Clear Fork on what was then the Shaw Ranch." The last mention Susan makes of John Selman is in her diary of May 18, 1867, when she notes that John Selman rode with her and others from the Stockton Ranch back to Fort Davis.

The Selmans and deGraffenreids continued living unobtrusively at the Stockton Ranch until 1869, when, for some reason, the John Selman and the deGraffenreid families pulled stakes and crossed the Llano Estacado to Colfax County in the wildest, northernmost corner of New Mexico. John Selman took his wife and infant son into this gang-infested region. No doubt, brother Tom came along, since their sisters had married and had their own homes. The 1870 United States census shows John Selman there with "real estate worth $200 and personal property valued at $1,000." He was listed as a laborer by the census and described in a later account by the deGraffenreids as nearly destitute after losing his horses and cattle in an Indian raid; one wonders how he managed to tough it out, who his associates were, what his exploits were, and what events determined his return to Texas.

As mysteriously as he left, John Selman with his family suddenly appeared back on the Clear Fork in 1872 to discover a new world was opening up there. As a run-of-the-mill frontiersman, good to his mother, brother, sisters, his wife and children, and accommodating to friends, he had never distinguished himself or ever experienced much of life beyond the frontier.

He was astonished, therefore, that Fort Griffin, the small outpost he had left on top of a mesa, had become Government Hill, expanding not only into a respectable fort but spilling over onto the half-mile-wide valley below.

Selman was fascinated with the activity he found in the robustious village called the Flat. Among the colorful characters parading the boardwalks, Selman met John Larn, a natural young leader possessed of attributes the older man lacked but intensely admired. A friendship grew up between Larn and Selman and soon evolved into a loose partnership in which Selman acted as Larn's segundo.

When he arrived in Griffin, Selman was in his early thirties, several inches under six feet tall, and compactly built. He had light blue eyes, black hair and mustache, and a dark complexion. Though he did not often look people in the eye, he was known as a persuasive and plausible talker and a good gambler and bluffer both at the card table and away. He was reputed to be deadly with a six-shooter, fearless, but with little principle.

Inhabitants of the Flat saw John Selman there more and more often. The inducements offered by gamblers, outlaws, and prostitutes residing in and passing through Griffin evidently attracted Selman and fired his ambition. Parson Slaughter's and his mother's religious influence apparently was ignored after he returned and established his family north of the Clear Fork on Tecumseh Creek, eight miles upstream from the Flat.

Drawn into the rough life of the Flat, Selman became known as a "two-gun, three-card man" and made his first killing in Griffin in 1876. Selman's associates in the Flat were said to be gamblers, renegades, cattle rustlers, murderers, and the notorious McBride-Henderson gang. Up to this time, Selman had reputedly been a good husband and father, but he now took up with Minnie Martin, a prostitute in the Flat also known as "Hurricane Minnie." It was touted about in the late seventies that "wherever a whore by the name of 'Hurricane Minnie' is around, there will John Selman be." Minnie was the woman of Hurricane Bill Martin, a Kansas gunman who had a long criminal record and with whom Selman had dealings from time to time.

John Selman's deep-seated desire to become a peace officer surfaced again, but the delicate balance between his being a "law man" or a "bad man" in the town of Griffin swung back and forth like the shadow of a noose against a picket wall. According to some accounts, Selman did achieve his ambition. He became involved with the vigilantes, as a leader for law and order. There is a report that he was appointed deputy sheriff, though no official records exist in Shackelford County to this effect; perhaps he was temporarily deputized. Selman was ambitious and undoubtedly had the experience, ruthlessness, and endurance required to direct other tough frontiersmen, though usually from behind-the-scenes.

In the meantime, John Selman's name became attached to what had been Chief Tecumseh's land, known now as the Tecumseh Pasture on Lambshead: 2,400 acres divided into approximately equal areas east and west by Tecumseh Creek. Selman, as the original grantee, located his homestead in 1872 on 160 acres in the eastern portion of the Tecumseh Pasture on the old Comanche Reservation. On the west bank of Tecumseh Creek, four miles from the mouth, he built a one-room picket house for his wife and sons, Henry and William. Seeing the good corn and oat crops in Lambshead Valley as he rode past the old Stem farm on his way to and from the Flat, he may have tried to farm. No one knows when Selman got into the cattle business, though his first brand was registered in Shackelford County on February 11, 1876.

In the meantime, other families were settling on the quarter-section tracts of the old Comanche Reservation. They tried to farm and raise a few cattle but found the going hard. As Sam Newcomb remarked in January, 1866, agriculture suffered because of sandstorms, northers, grasshoppers, and drought. Some gave up and went back to more tillable lands to the east, moved west to grow apples in the state of Washington, or, like John Jacobs and John Poe, found other ways to make a living.

The Selmans, however, settled in to stay. Their first year on Tecumseh Creek, John and Edna had a daughter, Margaretta, and, in 1875, another son, John, Jr. The one-room picket house was then forsaken for the rock house Selman built in 1875 across Tecumseh Creek on the east side, and he began calling his homestead, now lived out, the Rock Ranch. It was a good, well-built stone house Selman planned, three large rooms with two stone fireplaces, constructed in the traditional "L" shape of the better homes along the Clear Fork. Later, the public road from Albany to Throckmorton went past the house and the name was changed from Rock Ranch to Tecumseh Ranch.

Whether by coincidence or design, while John Selman was building on Tecumseh Creek, John Larn was erecting his large stone house above old Camp Cooper. The distance as the crow flies from John Larn's to Selman's place was only four miles. This close proximity may have had some influence upon the subsequent relationship of the two men.

Remarkably little is known for certain about John Larn, though we probably know more about him now than his in-laws did at the time. All available accounts paint him as one of the most colorful and controversial figures in Clear Fork country during the 1870's. The first official record of John M. Larn appears in the 1870 United States census for Fort Griffin. There, he is listed as stockraiser, from Alabama, male, white, twenty-one, no personal property, living in the household of Mrs. Susan E. Newcomb on Cedar Creek. Susan Reynolds Newcomb is listed as keeping house, female, white, twenty-one, with $10,000 in real estate. Also listed in the household were Carlos Augustus, Susan's four-year-old son by husband Sam Newcomb (who had died that April during an epidemic of measles), and Benjamin Reynolds, her brother, who is listed as stockraiser, male, white, nineteen, with $500 in real estate. Newcomb had located a ranch in 1870 on a creek later named for him, northeast of Albany, still shown on contemporary maps of the region. Ben was helping there with the ranch work, but who was John Larn, what had lured him to Clear Fork country, and what was he doing in the Newcomb household? No clues are to be found.

Sophie Poe writes that

John Laren had come to Fort Griffin from Dodge City, Kansas. He was a man of strong and pleasant personality—a typical cowboy. He rode for a rancher named Matheson [Joseph Beck Matthews] and presently married one of the boss's daughters.

His father-in-law helped him start a brand of his own, and John Laren seemed to be on the way to success as a cowman. Everybody liked him, and he was particularly popular with the sporting element of "The Flat" in Fort Griffin.

One of his closest friends was a man named John Selman. . . .

Selman and Larn, as we shall see, became deeply involved with "the sporting element of the Flat" during the heyday of Griffin town.

Many years later, in 1945, Phin W. Reynolds recalled:

John Larn told me that he was a newsboy on a train out of Mobile, Alabama, that he ran away from home when a boy and went to Colorado. He told me this when we [the B. W. Reynolds family] were living in Parker County about 1871. Larn was down there hunting horses. He told me that he came to Griffin from Trinidad, Colorado. Said that a fellow for whom he worked would not pay him, so he took a horse and left. The man followed him on a mule to the Patterson Bottom above Rocky Ford, Colorado, and rode up to him with a gun in hand and said, "I've got you." Larn said that he then drew his gun and killed him.

Shaughnessy, saloon keeper at Fort Griffin, told me a different tale about this. He said that Larn stole the horse and, when overtaken by the horse's owner, that Larn shot and killed him. Larn was a bad man but most likeable.

John P. Meadows came to Griffin on March 1, 1876, and worked for John Larn and John Selman until June 7, 1877, when a late frost killed everything in the ground. In a 1935 interview with J. Evetts Haley, John Meadows recalled:

[John Larn] was originally from Alabama, where all the damn rascals come from. I didn't know him before he come here. . . . That Larn was a funny man. He didn't know what whiskey tasted like. . . . I never heard him use a vulgar word nor I never heard him use a profane word. "Dadgummit" was the worst word I ever heard him use. He married Mary Matthews, old Bud's sister. . . . Larn had a little principle. But Selman had none at all whatever. He was close to a six-shooter. I believe I'd rather fight Larn twice than Selman once. He took the advantage every time.

The women in Clear Fork country described John Larn as "a handsome, dashing young man, a good dancer, who didn't smoke, cuss, or drink," and they loved him. "He had everything," the men said later, "except he was a killer and a thief."

In the 1950's, a manuscript came to light that confirmed, seventy-nine years later, the rumors the Reynolds brothers had heard in 1872. Henry Griswold Comstock, who came to the Clear Fork from Wisconsin with his younger brother, James, in the summer of 1871, chronicled the exploits of John Laren, trail boss for a cattle drive from Fort Griffin to Colorado for Bill Hayes in July, 1871. Comstock's account is herewith summarized.

Hayes's outfit, with Larn (Comstock calls him "Laren") in

charge, gathered cattle up the Clear Fork until September 10, 1871, when Hayes tallied the herd, supposedly recording it at some county seat. Larn rode point as the herd moved out for Fort Concho with destination Trinidad, Colorado. He bypassed Fort Concho and cattle-brand inspectors there, "getting lost" far to the west.

He took the old Goodnight-Loving Trail to Horsehead Crossing on the Pecos River. Arriving at Horsehead Crossing, he murdered two young, well-dressed Mexican horsemen, who were passing by on the other side of the river, and threw their bodies into the river to feed the catfish. He returned to camp with two good horses, saddles, and bridles.

The next afternoon, Larn discovered they were being followed by a detail of twelve cavalry troopers, all blacks, armed with re-peating Spencer carbines and well mounted on fine, grain-fed horses. By the next morning, Larn decided they had been sent from Fort Concho to bring the herd back for inspection. Larn and the hands surprised the cavalry at noon; the corporal took in the situation quickly and denied wanting the men or the cattle, asking only for fresh meat, which Larn gave him. Larn then led his crew back to camp in good spirits after succeeding with his bluff. The cavalry, however, reported that they had come out best in the scrape, but that the cattle had scattered and could not be brought in.

Larn kept his first name and place of origin to himself, but he admitted to having killed a sheriff one year before in the area of Fort Union, or Santa Fe. Larn was at the entrance to a "hurdy-gurdy house," when the lawman pressed the muzzle of his re-volver to Larn's chest and said, "Your name is Laren, I believe; you are my prisoner!" Larn, remaining calm, pretended to look back at something going on behind the sheriff, who also looked back. Taking advantage of his momentary distraction, Larn drew and killed the officer. Larn said, "If a man was to shoot me through the heart, I would kill that man before I died."

Late in October, as the herd wound through the prairie about eighty miles southeast of Las Vegas, Larn and a man named Bush who rode point with him, committed another murder. A Mexican youth looking after a flock of sheep, presumably on the famous Maxwell land grant, saw the two men riding after him and, as he was better mounted than the trail drivers, was getting away when one of them shot and broke his horse's leg. They killed the youth and the injured horse, leaving both where they fell for the wolves and buzzards. They left the sheep to their fate. No reason has ever been ascribed for the murder other than that "Laren did not like Mexicans."

Hayes met the herd about fifty miles south of Trinidad, Colorado. He decided to count the herd. This was done by letting the animals string out and driving them between Hayes and Larn, who counted them as they passed. No other count of the herd was made. This tally came to 1,700 head of cattle, but Hayes probably had no right to more than 400 head. Hayes was pleased with the count and knew that the good number was due to Larn's "nerve and management."

These events led to another violent episode that was known about at the time, though the version accepted at Fort Griffin was probably not altogether accurate. In November, the Hayes herd was moved into the Trinchera Peak region near Trinidad, Colorado, to winter, with Larn still in charge. Hayes's luck had run out, however, as he had not been able to get a good price for his cattle and had to borrow money to pay off the hands. In February, 1872, with branding time approaching, Hayes gave Larn the power of attorney over his cattle interests in Texas, and Larn, Bush, and another hand took the trail back to Clear Fork country. In Colorado, Hayes eventually lost most of his cattle to moneylenders. By the summer of 1873, he had just enough money to get back to Texas. At Griffin, he was met by Larn and more trouble. The two men were claiming rights to the same brands. Bush and Larn had been closely associated during 1872 after their return to Clear Fork country, but Bush now cast his lot with Hayes in another cattle drive. In midsummer, 1873, Bill Hayes, a brother, John Hayes, Bill Bush, and six other men gathered a small herd and headed them toward Fort Sill in the Indian Territory, hoping to sell them to the government beef contractor for the Kiowa and Comanches.

Larn swore out a warrant against Hayes and Bush and the others, charging them with stealing cattle. The acting sheriff, a man named Carter, was called on to serve it. Carter, his posse, and a squad of black cavalry from Fort Griffin detailed to deal with what had been represented as "a dangerous bunch of desperadoes" were led by Larn. They caught up with Hayes at noon, about thirty or forty miles from Griffin. The report came back that four men were killed and five taken prisoner. The latter were killed the next night "while trying to escape."

In later years, Phin Reynolds recounted the mobbing of the Hayes outfit:

At the time the Hays outfit were mobbed at Bush Knob in Throckmorton County, Texas, they were gathering a bunch of cattle to take to Fort Sill. John Larn, Riley Carter, Lieutenant Turner and thirteen negro soldiers went there to arrest them. They had an unenviable reputation, the Hays outfit did. George Reynolds told me about this. I was in the Panhandle at the time it occurred but George was at Griffin. John Larn was in command of the posse. The names of the men with the Hays outfit at the time who were killed were: John and Bill Hays, George Snow, Bill Bush, "Gov" James, Charlie "Nosey" Wilson and a man whose name I cannot now recall.

John C. Irwin also remembered the episode:

. . . the Hays outfit were wiped out . . . at what is now known as Bush Knob in Throckmorton County. There were seven in the outfit. . . . All of them were killed. . . . The killing was done by soldiers from Griffin and settlers or ranch men who were with them. John Larn and two men named Carter and possibly a cattle inspector named Beard went over there with the soldiers at the time the killing took place. The Hays outfit were accused by Larn of rustling cattle. Nothing was ever done about this—it was during the reconstruction days after the War.

The Bush Knob incident appeared plausible at the time. Larn used due process of law on the rustlers and led the posse after them. But Comstock, who was at Fort Griffin, believed that Larn cold-bloodedly killed Bush first as the most dangerous one, Hayes next, then the others; he had heard Larn say many times, "Dead men tell no tales." The Hayes herd, in any case, most likely helped to set Larn up in the cattle business.

There were other episodes. A newcomer to Clear Fork country, Emmett Roberts, encountered Larn out on the prairies in 1873 when he was bringing cattle up from Stephens County to his headquarters near Nugent:

I believed Laurens was driving away some of my cattle, and I followed the trail of a herd he was driving and overtook his party. He would "burn out" brands, and brand them with his brand, and also mark them. But my brand J.P.B. with the "B" lying up against the other two letters was hard to burn out. Also, as it happened, part of the cows he had branded out of my herd were old gentle milk cows, and I knew them anyway. Laurens was not with the herd when I came up, but a fellow named Wilson was watching the herd. I rode up and told him that he had some of my cattle and that I wanted to get them. He told me to go see Laurens, who was away about a half-mile shoeing his horse. I insisted that I knew the cattle and that I wanted to get my own stuff, that we didn't need Laurens. . . . when I began to work the herd . . . [Wilson] began following me up trying to undo what I was doing, and protesting all the time . . . to go get Laurens—he was the man who had branded them. But I continued, and as I glanced over my shoulder I thought I saw him raise his rifle as though fixing to fire. I had no chance to protect myself and work the cattle also (we were heavily armed with pistol and Winchester, and Wilson was carrying his rifle across the pommel of his saddle), so I called in George Outlaw, who was with me, and who was working for the C. J. outfit, and told him to cut the cattle out while I watched Wilson. Before this I had asked Wilson if he wanted to scrap me over the matter, and he said he did not, but that he wanted me to see Laurens before I cut out the cattle. Now there were several of the Laurens gang around besides Wilson. In a fight they would have had us badly outnumbered, and Outlaw refused to cut out the cattle. I was vexed with Outlaw . . . but . . . now I know it was the sensible thing to do. They would have had all the advantage of us in a fight, and they would have taken any advantage they might have had. There was nothing for me to do, but go down to Laurens' camp and see him. He treated me cordially. I went down and ate a meal with him and his outfit. He came back to the herd with me, and said he would give up any cattle that were fresh branded. He insisted that in order to determine this I would have to ride into the herd and rope and throw the cattle I claimed. I told him there was no sense in doing this, that I knew the cattle, that he knew them, and knew that he had lately burned out my brand and placed his own on them. He kept insisting, and I was just as determined that I was not going to do that, and I told him to give up the cattle without further ado. I do not know where matters would have drifted to; it looked like a fight with odds against me. But just then up rode a bunch of men from Fort Belknap . . . out for the same purpose I was after—that is, to get some of their cattle which Laurens had branded and was driving away. Among these men were Archie Medlin, B. Williams, and there were eight men in the outfit. We had it on Laurens then, and he knew it. I set in and cut my cattle out, and asked Medlin if he needed any help in getting his. When he replied that he did not, I moved on.

There may have been rumors at the time about the kinds of activities just described, but both Larn and Selman were well connected, well liked, and well established in the region. That they were probably given much benefit of doubt allowed them to change their hats with ease.

By 1876, Larn had built his fine house and put together the Camp Cooper Ranch, embracing the site of the military camp.

Honeymoon Cottage and the Larn house from the bluff above Camp Cooper.

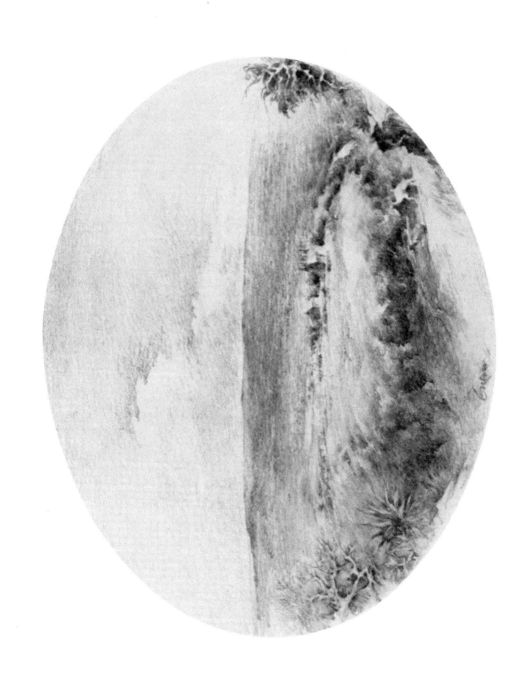

He acquired title from the state to the quarter-section containing the west half of the camp. Then negotiations with M. F. Barber gave Larn the quarter-section to the east, making a total of 320 acres. The range was still open, affording him free access to all the land and water he needed.

Visitors today to the Larn House agree that John Larn must have been something of an architect. He brought in skilled stone-masons and craftsmen to construct one of the largest and most handsome mellow gray limestone homes in Clear Fork country at the time. The house, with a facade of ante-bellum overtones, faces south on a high bluff some distance above Camp Cooper and the cottage, south of the river. With its five towering chimneys and high-pitched roof, it dominates the landscape. Atop the roof, between the double row of stone chimneys, was once a square cupola or widow's walk. Massive stone walls still enclose six large rooms: a parlor and three bedrooms with stone fireplaces, a dining room, and a kitchen, also with a stone fireplace. Wide, spacious porches front and back are connected by an enormous hallway. The beaded, wooden ceiling in the dining room is ornamented with an octagonal mosaic medallion of walnut or mahogany. Instead of candle-lighted crystal, John Larn hung a brass, gas-lighted lantern from a hook in the center of the medallion.

A visitor riding up to the house from the southwest would be intrigued by the elegant windows of beveled glass topped with oval white casings in the south and west walls. No windows are on the north or east, as seems to have been common in early Clear Fork houses.

Some distance east of the house is the barn with corrals and milk pen on its east side. North of the house is a stone smoke-house with a rock spring house below. Larn's establishment—

handsome, impressive, and unusually functional for its day—looks today, despite some alterations, much as it did in 1878, when Larn last saw it.

Fields and the horse pasture on the Camp Cooper Ranch were enclosed by miles of stone fences so solidly put up that they still stand over a hundred years later. The stonemasons, said to be Jones and Wilks, who built the dry-wall fences in the spring of 1877, knew what they were doing. Their handiwork may also survive in other fences standing on Lambshead today, examples of irreplaceable, prideful craft knowledge.

John Larn seemed ambitious to get ahead in a hurry. His fine new home was evidence that he had done so, to a point, but the question was beginning to be whispered about, "Where did the money come from?"

14   *End of an Era*

JOHN LARN'S POPULARITY in the Flat and his leadership ability among the free-range Clear Fork stockmen placed him in a money-making position. Opportunities were available, both legitimate and otherwise. Larn had married into a prosperous ranching family and had a herd of his own. He also had connections in the Flat, from reliable citizens like merchant and banker Frank Conrad to wheeler-dealers like saloon keeper Dick Shaughnessey. Through Selman, he was also acquainted with those who followed six-shooter rule with no regard for property, human rights, or human life. Neither the Sixth Cavalry nor, after 1874, any local enforcement agency, offered much resistance to such desperadoes, who were bringing more ruin to the countryside than had the Comanches. Both cattlemen and Grangers lost livestock and property and learned to live in fear for their lives. "It was as tough as a sow's snoot," John Meadows said of the Flat.

As we have seen, frontier citizens were therefore forced to protect themselves and their property, and the vigilantes came into being. At the outset, both John Larn and John Selman joined up.

Some division of opinion existed over the role of the vigilantes in enforcing the law. Phin Reynolds said of their activities: "All of the men killed by the Vigilance Committee, to the best of my information, were killed for stealing. None of them were killed for having murdered anyone. Work of the Vigilance Committee had good effect in putting down lawlessness. The hangings and killing of the ones accused of stealing had good effect in stopping thieving in this country. After this time there was less stealing here than anywhere I know of."

A present-day historian, Bob Green of Albany, agrees: "Iron-willed frontiersmen had the drive to overcome lawlessness and they just did it with the gun and whatever it took—the rope. It was done by people, not by Rangers, nor by the Government. They had to be pretty tough men, like Charles Goodnight, who thought when a man needed shooting, he should be shot. They thought no more of it than we would about Dillinger, Pretty Boy Floyd, or others, like Charles Manson."

Henry Herron, who was Sheriff Cruger's deputy, opposed mob law, but even he admitted that "it did look at times as if the law abiding people were helpless to obtain relief from the lawless conditions which prevailed. Oftentimes when a man was indicted and the officers worked hard to get the evidence, there would be alibis, witnesses would fail to appear, false evidence would be given, and the juries would fail to convict. As a result, many good men determined to control a bad situation and joined and supported the Vigilance Committee."

According to Sophie Poe, whose husband John William was U.S. marshal at Griffin in 1878:

There were two factions in the community. One side believed sincerely that the machinery of law was not competent in the face of such widespread lawlessness as West Texas knew; and that only vigilantes could check the criminals at the time. The other faction—and John William was of this party—believed with equal conviction that the regular processes of law, even if imperfect, were better than the summary measures of a vigilance organization. The two factions came to a crisis in what was known as "the Larn Case."

A chief in the Fort Griffin Vigilance Committee, John Larn, by February 15, 1876, had won sufficient confidence and respect to be elected the second sheriff of Shackelford County. He succeeded Henry C. Jacobs, who was not satisfying everyone, especially in the Flat. The people who elected John Larn believed he had the stuff to clean out the ruthless McBride-Henderson gang, pestiferous cattle and horse thieves and killers who had moved in on them from Indian Territory.

John Poe thought that Larn was a sheriff who did satisfy everyone, that he enforced the law "fearlessly and intelligently." Edgar Rye remarked, "During the first six months of his term, Laren did more to quell lawlessness than any man who served the people as sheriff, before or since his time." W. R. Cruger, who had been Sheriff Jacob's deputy, continued on under Larn. Between the election and his swearing-in April 18, 1876, Larn had rounded up a gang of women prostitutes and bad men from the Flat who were making their getaway with twenty-six stolen horses. By April 14, he had flushed the McBride-Henderson gang. Undoubtedly, his unofficial deputy, John Selman, served as decoy and helped Larn considerably through his close association with these thieves and rustlers. All but Bill Henderson and two others were caught and taken care of. Then Charlie ("Doc") McBride was lured from hiding and hanged near Judge Ledbetter's place on the Clear Fork. On April 27, Larn obtained a warrant for Henderson and Floyd and left for Dodge City. On arrival, he telegraphed William Gilson, city marshal at Fort Griffin, that he had the two men and was returning with them. They were put in the Griffin jail, from which they were taken June 2 and hanged by the vigilantes.

The Griffin jail was not a safe place for prisoners. On December 28, 1876, the Austin *Weekly Statesman* reported that eleven men were hanged in Griffin. The governor reprimanded the elected officials and directed the Texas Rangers to take charge of three prisoners then in the jail.

Griffin town, with its one thousand residents and an equal number of transients, at first supported its popular sheriff for his effective execution of the duties of his office. Later, they became somewhat skeptical of John Larn. They were especially suspicious of his cohort, John Selman. Larn's popularity was tested when he was suspected by several of the ranchers, including some of his own in-laws, of increasing his herd at their expense. John C. Irwin had seen Larn driving away a herd of cattle not his own. Larn tried to bribe Irwin, offering him $100 not to talk. However, Larn's father-in-law, Joe Matthews, loyally stood by him in the face of mounting suspicions and the differences were settled, at least temporarily.

Sheriff Larn continued to be backed by friends who had put him into office to fight fire with fire. He was a true shot, a quick draw, coldly courageous, and he knew the mind of an outlaw. They respected his ability to clean up the gangs and individuals engaged in horse-thieving, cattle-stealing, and killings at Griffin and throughout the countryside. Larn was equally backed by some of his enemies, who thought he could be more easily killed off in office.

From fall, 1876, until spring, 1877, was a time of obvious transition for Sheriff Larn and his friend, partner, and surrogate deputy, John Selman. Larn's double life—as sheriff and vigilante chief and as cattle and horse thief—was no longer completely secret, but he continued with some success to play both ends against the middle, relying on his cunning and his intimate knowledge of activities of persons on both sides. However, more of his one-time friends and supporters began to suspect he wore two hats. Certainly the white hat of the lawman was more frequently being replaced by the dark slouch of the cattle-rustler and killer.

In the fall of 1876 Larn and Selman went to the old Stone Ranch and threw in with the Millet cow outfit, which had taken up temporary quarters there in September of 1876 and the spring of 1877. The Millet brothers had widespread ranching interests from South Texas to Kansas, Idaho, the Dakotas, and Colorado. One of their toughest outfits was called the Millet and Irwin Salt Fork Ranch, headquartered on Miller Creek near Seymour. Alonzo Millet was the oldest of four brothers, and he had a reputation for being a hard-driving, enterprising cattleman who hired tough men to run his ranches. The local cattlemen concluded that the Millets were moving in on their territory.

Newton Jones, a Millet hand, described Millet's trail boss, Billy Bland, as "a desperate character but a good man in a way." After driving up from South Texas with a herd of 2,929 cattle, most of which were lost from stampedes on Miller Creek, Bland went off hunting a new location for the ranch. He returned and "said we could go in camp for winter at the old Stone Ranch . . . on Walnut Creek." In addition to Bland, Larn, and Selman, the outfit included Charlie Reed, Billy Gray, Jack Lyons, and Selman's brother, "Tom Cat." They used the Stone Ranch headquarters for manipulating cattle herds to their advantage.

John Meadows told J. Evetts Haley June 13, 1935, that in the winter of 1876–1877, Larn and Selman drove a herd of cattle to Flat Top Mountain in Stonewall County, where they changed the brands on stolen cattle to their own. They said they had bought the herd from some boys who had driven them from Indian Territory. Meadows said that Larn and Selman had killed the boys and thrown their bodies into what was called the Bottomless Wells, on the right prong of Tecumseh Creek. One of the bodies came up; Meadows said he saw it, and it had a rock tied to it.

On a cold January night in 1877, the Millet hands went into the Flat on a spree and shot up the town. In the shooting scrape, foreman Billy Bland, the instigator and Larn's confederate, was killed by Larn's deputy, William Cruger.

Newt Jones described the aftermath of this episode: "Soon after [Bland's] killing, John Larn, the Sheriff of Shackelford County, resigned his office [March 7, 1877], and it was generally believed in the community that he was in sympathy with Bland in this fight, resented the killing, and resigned in protest over the killing." Larn and Selman were convinced that Deputy Cruger's killing of Bland was completely unjustified, but in spite of Larn's sentiments, the county commissioners' court appointed Cruger to succeed Larn as sheriff.

A report leaked out, Jones says, that the surviving Millet hands and Larn and Selman were planning to avenge Bland's death, to perpetrate more raids on Larn's and Selman's neighbors, the Throckmorton and Haskell County Grangers, to "burn" more cattle, and to continue their gambling, drinking, and carousing.

According to Jones, a Captain Young took Bland's place as foreman of the Millet herd; Young was a good man who had no use for men of the Bland type. "Alonzo Millet and Young came to these men . . . and told them that the Vigilance Committee had agreed with them that if they would quit getting drunk and doing as they were, they wouldn't bother them. As Bland was dead and Reed had left after that, Lyons and Billie Gray left the country too as they knew Young had no use for them." Newt Jones helped move the Millet cattle in two herds to the Baylor County ranch, leaving the Lambshead range to Larn and Selman.

But trouble continued to crop up. Conflicting rumors began floating around as to the fate of the two stonemasons who built

Larn's stone fence in the spring of 1877. One story had it that Larn offered them five hundred dollars to erect a mile of rock fence near his new Camp Cooper house, with one hundred dollars in advance. They built the fence but never received the remainder of the money. They just disappeared, along with the old carpenter, possibly Peter Bendenger, who worked on both the Larn and the Selman houses.

John Meadows, who was working for Larn and Selman at the time, reported the facts as follows:

[John Larn] hired two brothers to build a rock fence a mile and a half long. . . . They built the fence, and they was pulled out of this Clear Fork of the Brazos dead—shot and throwed into that Brazos. John Selman and John Larn done it to keep from paying for it. They owed me three-hundred-and-twenty-some-odd dollars for labor [they had promised to pay Meadows as soon as they sold their steers, and they had sold to Dutch Nance the week before], and the reason that I escaped was on account of Uncle Hunt Kelley. . . . [He] says, "John, I'll tell you, if I was in your place, I'd get up and leave here. . . ." I wanted to kill them men. But old John Selman was the one I wanted. He was the meanest of the two. He was the meanest man that ever lived. . . . [Uncle Hunt] says, "You've got a right to be mad, but you're going too far with it." . . . the 7th day of June, '77, . . . that was the day I left there. I went off and went to work for Millet up on the Brazos.

Them brothers that he had killed was the Williamses. The old carpenter—old Chips is what we called him. His name was Bendenger. He was a Frenchman. They pulled him out of that water, too, out of that Clear Fork. He built both their houses. He disappeared and they got him out of the Clear Fork.

A year later, at the time of Larn's death, the Galveston *News* reported (July 13, 1878):

There were two mechanics who had a contract to build a rock fence for Larn, for which they were to get $500. After the completion of the fence they reported that Larn owed them $400. They suddenly disappeared and some two weeks afterward, one dead body too much decayed for recognition, was brought down from a rise in the river to Fort Griffin. A friend thought he recognized it as his partner's body. Another body was taken out of the river in Stephens County. . . .

Two witnesses have affirmed that the two rock masons were thrown in the river by Larn and Selman to their knowledge.

On July 2, 1878, the Fort Worth *Democrat* also recounted the story: ". . . it was reported two men who had been in Larn's employ were missing and that two dead bodies (which were not recovered) had been seen floating in the Clear Fork of the Brazos. Your correspondent is not advised of what circumstances, if any there were, connecting Larn and others for whose warrants were issued, with the disappearance of the two young men; or them with the dead bodies found in the river."

Some present-day writers and historians who have looked into circumstances dealing with the fate of these stonemasons agree that the story is murky, but the consensus seems to be that John Larn was not responsible for the men's disappearance. They say he was too smart a man, living in the midst of family and friends, to have killed someone who built his rock fence. These were stories that got out to paint him blacker than he was, they have concluded.

Phin Reynolds, who was with Will Reynolds and a trail herd south of the Canadian River at Adobe Walls in the spring of 1877, gave his opinion to J. R. Webb: "I never believed the story about Larn killing the two men who built his rock fence and then disappeared. I have heard that one of them was seen after that was supposed to have occurred. Although Larn was a pretty hard character, I do not believe he did that. I always liked John Larn personally."

Factions in the Flat and on the range split during the spring of 1877. Larn's ranching neighbors became openly suspicious. The vigilantes were breathing down the collar of ex-Sheriff Larn,

Reynolds Bend.

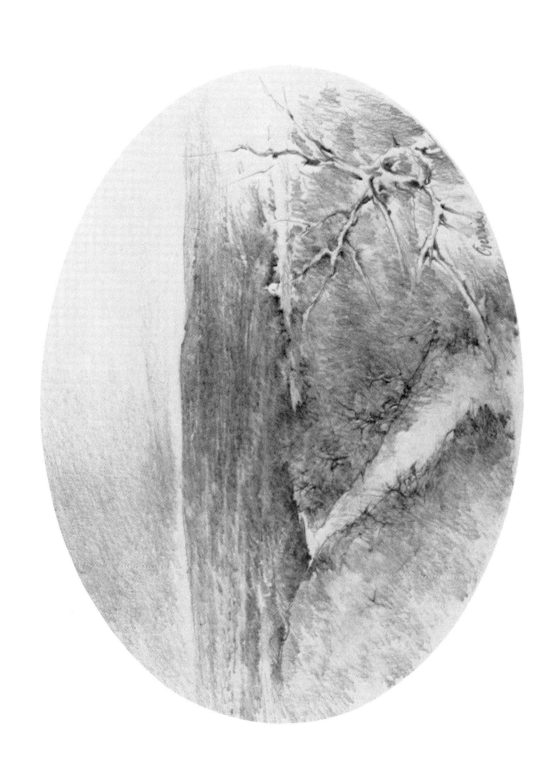

but he ran their bluff and could still count on staunch friends and backers among them. And his supporters evidently prevailed. Instead of closing in on Larn and Selman, the group decided to give the men another chance, hoping that their better natures would win out, that they would abandon their illegal activities and become upright citizens again.

John Larn and John Selman were appointed to positions of public trust on April 28, 1877. As deputy inspectors of hides for Shackelford County, they were bonded at $1,000 each, the bonds signed by Joe B. Matthews and Frank E. Conrad. Conrad, reputedly "the largest, best-known merchant on the Texas frontier," later married the youngest Matthews daughter, Ella.

For more than a year, Larn and Selman had every opportunity to prove themselves. Their duties of office were to inspect cattle herds entering or leaving the country and to receive reports from butchers listing the number of beeves butchered and furnishing hides as proof. They were to supervise the butchers, as this was a very strict requirement and came under the commissioners' court.

The two men also received a contract to furnish beef to the army post of Fort Griffin and the Tonkawa Indians there. This was an ideal set-up to show how they would handle their business, with honest profits to be made. However, every opportunity for wrongdoing was also present: the government contract could be filled by rustling and inspector's fees could be named at random, with no check on what was pocketed. There was little expense, and illegal profits could be handsome.

According to John Meadows, the temptations proved too strong.

[Larn] give him [Selman] every opportunity he could to make a few dollars. Selman got to be hide and animal inspector, inspecting the big herds that come along the trail. . . . he'd get seventy-five to a hundred dollars off of some of them herds. That went into Selman's pockets. Larn put him where he could pull off his dirty work, and he done it. [Selman had earlier learned the butcher's trade at the Stockton Ranch in the late 1860's.] Larn just depended on downright stealing, and that is all there was to it. He had a contract to feed them Tonkawa Indians at Fort Griffin. . . . And, by God, he stole so damn many of his neighbors' cattle that they just couldn't stand it longer. These are facts. You can go and trace it back.

John Selman's alliance with Hurricane Bill Martin inflicted a financial setback on October 10, 1877, when the State of Texas filed suit against Selman and another defendant for recovery of $1,000 forfeited bond cost. They paid on October 10, 1877. Hurricane Bill Martin had been indicted for assault with intent to murder the year before, on October 19, 1876, with J. H. Kelly and Selman as sureties for his bond. Larn's name did not appear in the court records. Even as sheriff, he usually had had Deputy Sheriff Cruger sign for him. The defendants, Kelly and Selman, "appeared before the court in person with Attorneys and having answered Judgment heretofore rendered against them, and the Court being satisfied that the reasons set forth in said answer were sufficient, it was considered by the Court that the Judgment be set aside and case dismissed upon the defendants paying the costs incurred." This was only one of numerous and typical court cases in which Hurricane Bill was arraigned but not jailed.

It is questionable if Larn and Selman continued as hide inspectors at this time, though there is no record of their resigning or being dismissed. They must have retained their beef contract with Fort Griffin, for public opinion against them was growing daily over their stepped-up cattle stealing. The victimized Grangers remaining in the country desperately began supplementing the vigilantes' work against rustling. They, too, dedicated themselves to eliminating the cattle and horse thieves who were frightening the citizens, running the Grangers out of the region, and generally throwing Clear Fork country into a state of confusion and lawless disorder.

Don Biggers summarizes the Griffin vigilantes' efforts: "Within a period of twelve years of this town's history thirty-five men were 'publicly killed,' eight or ten more were found dead and no further questions asked, . . . It was these and kindred offences that brought into existence and possibly made necessary the most famous vigilance committee that ever operated in Texas, a committee that did its quota of good and its share of mischief."

Newt Jones left cowboying and joined the Texas Rangers, Company B, in June of 1877. He came to Camp Sibley early in 1878, near Fort Griffin, with Lieutenant G. W. Campbell and four other Rangers. They had been sent to investigate the turmoil in Shackelford County, where the Fort Griffin Vigilance Committee was the most active in the state.

Fresh rumors circulated in February, 1878, concerning a cache of hides in a waterhole in the Clear Fork near Larn's Camp Cooper Ranch. Newt Jones reported that a posse of civilians got a warrant to search the river hole for hides. Lieutenant Campbell and R. A. Hutchinson were the Rangers and John C. Irwin was in the civilian posse deputized to arrest Larn on charges of cattle rustling, slaughtering the cattle for beef he was furnishing Fort Griffin, and then throwing the hides into the river. When Larn was told they had a search warrant, he offered to surrender his pistol to Campbell, but the lieutenant did not take his gun, saying, "I don't need to disarm you; I just came to see this place searched and, if you don't refuse that, I don't need to disarm you." John and Tom Selman were present when grappling hooks brought the hides to light.

Lieutenant Campbell's official report of February 26, 1878, details the outcome:

Have had a big excitement in the settlements over making arrests on Jno. M. Laren and Jno. Sillman, charged with stealing cattle and selling them for beef. They have been furnishing Fort Griffin for some time. The citizens swore out a search warrant and I served it, and found six beef hides in the bed of the Clear Fork, not in their own brands [Larn and Selman's], brands claimed by different citizens of the country . . . taken them [the hides] to Griffin and turned them over to the officers. . . . a compromise was made and the parties released. . . . there has been a miscarriage of justice.

Questions arise, of course. What did Larn and Selman do with the hundreds of hides of those beeves (of their own or the brands of others) their contract required them to furnish the military for more than a year? Did the river or ravines contain them, or were they hauled away? No evidence has surfaced to solve this riddle.

The lawlessness and violence continued unabated, as Ranger Sergeant J. E. Van Riper's report to Major John Jones, commander of the Frontier Battalion, on June 15, 1878, makes clear.

. . . I am induced to report . . . a just and true state of affairs in this section of the country, which are in a terrible stage—armed parties of men are continually riding the country—riding at midnight into the door yards of peaceable citizens and discharging their firearms, frightening women and children, citizens are being run out of the country, leaving their property; Mr. Treadwell and others living in the neighborhood of Jno. M. Lauren and Jno. H. Sellman are continually finding their horses and cattle shot down on the prairies. Milch cows and calves are shot down on the premises after night fall. They [Grangers] have recently lost several hundred dollars worth of stock in this manner, and they have now taken up arms in defense of their lives and property, as a last resort, having received no redress nor encouragement by law, both parties going in squads. Serious trouble is hourly expected. Men are mysteriously disappearing . . . under very suspicious circumstances. . . . at the Coroners inquest [a verdict was found] and passed . . . over as a "Coleman case of drowning" . . . Heavy threats have been made by Jno. M. Lauren, who swears to have the lives of five certain men . . . two of his intended victims [to be] Lieutenant Campbell and myself. . . . Local citizens . . . are praying for aid and protection from the dreadful crisis which is . . . not far distant—something will have to be done or this country will ere long be the scene of blackening crimes horrible to think of. . . . [Some of our missing monthly reports] were taken out of the Fort Griffin Post Office by parties who are closely connected by Oaths and ties to these same parties, principals in this present trouble . . . etc.

Harassed citizens were driven to write Major Jones and other authorities pleading for relief and more assistance to prevent bloodshed and civil war.

By mid-June, records of the fast-moving, chaotic, events became confused and, to an extent, contradictory. Larn, though a man with no conscience, was both intelligent and shrewd. He and Selman had many friends and strong supporters in the Flat, although they no longer had the allegiance of the full Vigilance Committee. Foremost associate was Hurricane Bill Martin, a smooth, crafty, and lawless man. Larn used him to build a back-fire against the vigilantes. The plan was for Martin and Selman to cooperate with the Texas Rangers for protection, to turn state's evidence and reveal the identity of the vigilantes and get them tried for the many hangings for which they were responsible. Technically, each such case was equivalent to manslaughter. Larn and Selman, until recently members of the vigilantes, knew every man on the roster. Hurricane Bill had been paid by the Vigilance Committee to slip the nooses and cut down the victims. Hurricane Bill lost no time in spreading counter-rumors— that the hides in the river had been planted by the vigilantes, who were themselves bent on running honest cattlemen out of the country in order to take over their ranges.

The Rangers apparently did not swallow these reports, but it was their duty to see that every man had his day in court. The possibility of disclosure of the identities of the vigilantes was a serious matter. The plan was leaked. The vigilantes took counsel and decided that the best and quickest way to head off exposure was to have Judge J. R. Fleming, who was one of them, write to Governor Hubbard to disband the Ranger Company in their midst. Citizens requested Judge C. K. Stribling to write the governor, also. It worked.

Lieutenant Campbell was perplexed when he received an order to disband his company. He wrote to Major Jones on June 16, 1878:

I would like to have seen and talked to you here before I left . . . things was in a bad state of affairs before the company was disbanded, but they are in much worse [condition] now. I had the matter worked up so . . . you would see how it was, and take hold of it, and bring the guilty parties to justice. There is now two parties in arms, one the Lauren and Sellman and the other the Granger party. The Lauren and Sellman party have been in arms ever since the search warrant was executed and the beef hides found in their river, also since the company has been disbanded there has been about three hundred dollars worth of stock killed and run off by unknown parties. . . . two men working for Mr. Lauren missing. . . . [their bodies] found in the Clear Fork and both of their horses floating in the River. . . . this week another man nearest neighbor of Mr. Lauren has very mysteriously disappeared . . . scarcely a day passes without there being stock of some kind killed . . . the Grangers as they are called by the Lauren party have taken up arms in self defense for the protection of lives and property. . . .

. . . in regards to the company, some parties have circulated the news over the country that this company was *Dishonorably Discharged* from the service: I would much rather have stayed until you came up *without Pay* than as it is, on account of bringing these parties to justice. . . . I only ask that you have published in the Galveston News the cause of Company 'Bs' being disbanded. And oblige.

The episode of the cache of hides in the river, the rumors of the drownings of the carpenter and stonemasons, followed by the disbanding of the Ranger Company, which thwarted his plan against the vigilantes, aroused in Larn every psychopathic instinct in his being. He could sense that his dream of building an empire on the Clear Fork at the expense of the Grangers and of other cattlemen, including his own wife's family and relatives, was in jeopardy. Now was the time for a showdown. The truce with the vigilantes was broken.

Larn and Selman gathered sixteen or more desperate, outlaw characters and went on a rampage of cattle-rustling, horse-stealing, and killing forays, exceeding even the McBride-Henderson Gang. Larn's night riders terrorized Grangers and ranch people in their homes at night. No one dared show a light or answer a call of "hello-the-house." One of the Treadwells was ambushed and his horse shot out from under him. Families with two-story houses slept upstairs. In addition to the crimes Larn and his gang were perpetrating, there was still the chance that he would reveal the members of the Vigilance Committee. Drastic action was imperative.

Though terrified for his life and those of his family, A. J. Lancaster, a Granger whom Larn and Selman had attempted to bushwhack, agreed to go to Albany and swear out warrants for the arrest of the two, charging them with assault with intent to murder. The warrants were issued by Justice of the Peace Edgar Rye on June 22, 1878.

Iron-willed men had made a tight, confidential plan, and that night of Saturday, June 22, Sheriff Cruger, with warrants in hand, put it into effect. At the head of a carefully selected posse, Cruger and his men slipped in to encircle the Camp Cooper home of Mary and John Larn. They wanted to be sure no one entered or left the premises. No one did. At early light, Larn went to his cow pen adjacent to the barn to milk. He was caught completely unaware, as Sheriff Cruger, Deputy Dave Barker, and Ben Reynolds had intended. They held the warrant accusing Larn of attempted murder. When told, Larn quietly unbuckled his belt and, with shaking hand, offered his gun to Cruger. He looked at the warrant, scowling in disbelief when he saw it was from Albany, so confident was he that it would be from Griffin, where he had strong backers. He told Cruger he never would have surrendered had he known the warrant was from the Albany court.

Realizing the seriousness of the situation when he saw the other men who were in the posse, Larn called to Mary and his young son Will. He held his son tight, advising him to look closely and remember well the men he saw there. Embracing Mary fiercely, he told her to follow quickly in the buggy with Will and their farm hand behind the posse; to get a young lawyer, John W. Wray, in Griffin, to come with her to Albany; to try to arrange his release or a jury trial as soon as possible, a delaying action that could help to save his life. All this Mary did, then took a room at the Shields Rooming House on the square north of the little picket house used as the temporary jail, which was down on Hubbard Creek just east of the bridge. Here John Wray came to tell her that John Larn's bail and release had been denied. Mary probably sensed that her husband's doom was already sealed.

Another part of the plan to capture Larn and Selman was for Glenn Reynolds, with Bill Howsley and another posse, to surround Selman's house at the same time that Cruger and his men closed in on Larn's house. This they did, but Hurricane Minnie, who had learned of the plan, rode wildly to Selman's place and warned him. Selman got away. He raced to Larn's ranch, hoping to alert him, but was only in time to watch Larn being taken away, his legs tied securely beneath his horse. Glenn Reynolds' posse returned as planned to the Treadwell house near the Camp Cooper Ranch. Soon other vigilantes assembled. The risks of Selman's getting his party together to rescue Larn were evaluated, and the decision made to go to the jail to circumvent Selman.

The Rangers arrived, as Sheriff Cruger had sent for them after Larn's arrest to meet him at Treadwell's "as soon as God would let us come," according to Newt Jones. All six Rangers went to Treadwell's place and found the vigilantes arguing over Larn's fate. Cruger wanted the Rangers to go after John Selman, but Sergeant Van Riper refused, hurt that the Rangers had not been called on in regard to Larn. He returned to camp, and Rangers Newt Jones and Jack Smith went by to see Mrs. Selman, who gave them news that shocked them: that Larn would be killed that night and that he would have surrendered to the Rangers. Her husband John, his brother Tom, and John Gross had left together.

Fearing that Selman might collect a party large enough to rescue Larn, Glenn Reynolds, with Bill Howsley and his posse, started to Albany, making the trip in less than three hours. Here they joined the vigilante chief, the sheriff, his deputies, and other members of the posse that had brought in Larn. Around midnight, nine men left the rendezvous, quietly approaching the jail from behind, unseen by Mary, who kept watch from the second-floor window of the rooming house. The men crept up to the picket house in which twelve men were chained through their manacles from wall to wall, with iron shackles on their ankles, lying on blanket pallets, side by side. Hurricane Bill, strangely enough, lay next to John Larn. Alert to the familiar tramp of approaching vigilantes and afraid it was he who would be shot, he turned his face to the wall, as did the man on Larn's other side. The nine vigilantes chosen to enter the jail (one had cast a dissenting vote but nonetheless went in) had placed bandanas over the lower part of their faces and wore long, yellow range slickers so as not to be recognized by the other prisoners or by the four guards, whom they disarmed and sent away. They strode through the door, and John Larn stood up to face them.

The masked leader, very tall and straight, said, "In recognition of your better qualities, we are not going to hang you." Larn called them cowards and lifted his chin in defiance. A fusillade rang out and Larn fell to the floor. (It is said one gun contained a blank cartridge, so no one would know for sure who killed him.)

Galvanized by the dreaded burst of gunfire, with a piercing scream Mary ran through the shadows toward her dead husband. She saw the body carried in a blanket and laid out on the guard-house mess board.

Early the next morning, Justice of the Peace Edgar Rye rendered a verdict that the deceased met death by gunshot wounds inflicted by parties unknown. Then Mary, the distraught, twenty-three-year-old widow, was told of events leading up to the tragedy she had witnessed the night before.

At the Matthews' Pleasant View home, father, mother, and daughter stood in front of the fireplace and cried together, while the old wooden Sessions clock on the mantel ticked away their grief-filled moments. Her family went with Mary to take her husband's body to the Camp Cooper Ranch, where they buried him beside the second Larn child. The two graves are still there on the river's bank about two hundred yards northwest of the front of their elegant home. A tall, handsomely carved stone marks Larn's grave: "John M. Larn—Born March 1, 1849—Died June 24, 1878." A four-foot rock wall surrounds the sixteen-foot-square plot.

The identities of the men who appeared at the jail are not known, though it is reasonable to assume that most of them, at least, had been with the posses who seized Larn and went after Selman. Bill Howsley, a Reynolds hand, admitted to Phin Reynolds that he was there and hinted as to the identity of the leader. "Bill Howsley told me that there were nine men in the bunch that killed Larn and that he was with them. He said they wore slickers and bandanas around their foreheads. He said the leader was a tall man, and I said, 'I guess that he was Tom Merrill, who worked for the Horse Shoes on the Double Mountain Fork.' He said, 'No, it was not him,' and left the impression it was one of my brothers." John Meadows told J. Evetts Haley that two of Larn's brothers-in-law were there, or at least approved of the action taken. But it is still said in Albany that not even the women knew who fired the fatal shots.

John Selman supposedly was rounding up a party to rescue Larn. However, according to Phin Reynolds, Selman rode down-river to the Tom Lanier Ranch in Stephens County, there showed himself to throw the posse off the trail, then doubled back and that night took Larn's $300 chestnut sorrel stallion Old Bab and rode a hot trail with brother Tom Cat, Tom Curtis, and two other men toward New Mexico.

John Meadows was at the head of Seymour Creek with the Millet outfit when foreman Tom Peeler told him about Larn's killing and Selman's escape. Meadows told Peeler: "I'd like to get in on that trail. I'll trail him to hell or find him, one of the two."

Meadows encountered Sheriff Cruger and Glenn Reynolds' posse trailing Selman. They followed Selman's bunch to Spring Lake, on the plains near present-day Muleshoe. When they got there, Meadows said that Selman's bunch "captured a buffalo hunter's outfit and swapped horses with them and got fresh horses and got away from us. . . . We found Larn's old stud horse, old Bab . . . at the buffalo camp. . . . Luke McCabe . . . took charge of old Bab and carried him back and give him back to Mrs. Larn." And what of Selman? "He come over here in New Mexico, and I come right behind him, and goddam, I might as well tell it like it is. I come here to kill him, that's what I did, and if I'd of met him, one of us would have hit the ground."

John Selman ended up in Fort Davis, Texas, with Hurricane

Minnie. He was arrested there on June 22, 1880. A telegram to Major John Jones, Texas Ranger, indicated that Selman was ready to turn state's evidence and help clear out the other cow thieves in the Lambshead region. Sheriff Cruger, however, replied that he could not answer for Selman's life if he was brought back. Cruger feared that the arrival would trigger a renewal of what they had been through.

Phin Reynolds told J. R. Webb in 1944 what happened: "Selman was brought to Fort Griffin later and was being guarded by Bill Jeffries, Bill Howsley and George Shields. Bill Howsley said they took him back of Conrad's store and gave him a horse and saddle, shook hands and told him to go. The guards shot off their pistols as he escaped. He started out on John Sauer's flea-bitten horse, but George Reynolds, who was Sauer's boss, gave Selman another good horse to ride." Selman returned to the Trans-Pecos region, and, for several years led a checkered career, in and out of the law. He finally achieved his desire for fame by killing John Wesley Hardin in El Paso in 1895.

Opinions vary as to the characters of the two men. As his remarks reveal, John Meadows had a deep-seated hatred for Selman, who had cheated and perhaps threatened him. Certainly Selman earned a reputation as a sharp and violent man. But the Reynolds brothers, who had known him since the days of "forting up," still held him in sufficient regard toward the end to prevent the possibility of his being taken by the vigilantes when he was brought back to Griffin from Fort Davis.

Larn also inspired strong feelings in those who knew him. His wife Mary, at least some of her family, and others remained loyal to the end. Joe McCombs, a buffalo hunter from Griffin, wept when he recalled Larn's death for Ben O. Grant in 1934: "My God! If I had been there! He was one of the best friends I ever had; he saved my life once and, if I could, I would have done as

much for him." But John A. Matthews felt otherwise: "John Selman was a dangerous man, but compared to John Larn, he was
a gentleman. Larn was the meanest man I ever knew." Rupert N.
Richardson has remarked that "John Larn was morally dead."
Watt R. Matthews probably has the most accurate characterization of Larn: "He was a charmer with many attributes of a gentleman, but he was an outlaw, a cow thief, and a killer."

Certainly both men were amoral, ambitious, with a penchant
for violence. That they both also could command loyalty from
sometimes surprising sources simply confirms the deep division
in their characters that led them to become two-hat men.

The Larn affair ended an era. The vigilantes faded away. Killings continued, but on a diminishing scale, as criminal law, maintained by the courts, supplanted lynch law. Slowly tranquility
returned to the land.

Epilogue

T HE CONFLICT between cattlemen in the Clear Fork area and cattle thieves in Shackelford, Throckmorton, Stephens, and Haskell counties was typical of freebooting elsewhere along the Texas frontier from the Rio Grande to the Red River. In northwest Texas the violence reached its apex during the late 1870's and early 1880's. To the south, an unusually serious outbreak culminated in the Mason County War. The basic cause of the struggle was the same: where civil authority for law enforcement, not yet well established, could not adequately protect life and property, outlawry flourished and citizens organized to stamp it out.

Vigilance committees sprang up at the local level, but another early and more far-reaching solution was the organization of the Stock-Raisers Association of North-West Texas at Graham in Stephens County in 1877 by frontier stockmen who had long suffered pillaging of their property. It took a little time for the group to become effective, but eventually the association emerged as a potent force in the protection of life and property. It established a corps of cattle inspectors, men of the same caliber as the Texas Rangers. Unlike county sheriffs, whose authority stopped at county lines, the inspectors could go anywhere and follow any trail, wherever duty led them. The organization later became the Texas and Southwestern Cattle Raisers Association, with headquarters in Fort Worth.

The invention of barbed wire made it possible to enclose pastures, and the handling and protection of livestock was consequently much easier. Enclosed ranches became, in a measure, self-protected units. Between 1881 and 1885, the rolling plains between the Cross Timbers and the high plains, an area larger than all of New England, became a vast network of enclosed ranches varying in size from a few thousand to a million acres, not counting the three-million-acre XIT Ranch on the high plains. Living on each ranch was its owner or manager who controlled a crew of cowhands. These owners or managers were most often bold men who, with their hands, enforced the rights of ownership. Cow thieving was discouraged and drastically reduced.

With ranches enclosed, the Reynolds brothers decided to go west where they could acquire larger layouts in Texas than were available in the Clear Fork area. The partnership they had formed earlier with their brother-in-law John A. Matthews was amicably dissolved and the Reynolds Land and Cattle Company formed to consolidate their extensive holdings. They then took cattle and capital to expand west of the Pecos, later acquiring part of the XIT Ranch in the Texas Panhandle and other ranching properties. John A. Matthews decided to stay in Clear Fork country. In Throckmorton and Shackelford counties, he and his wife, Sallie Reynolds Matthews, put together Lambshead Ranch and raised their large family. How this came about is recounted in *Interwoven*.

ADDENDA

GEOLOGY OF LAMBSHEAD RANCH

By GLEN L. EVANS

EARTH FEATURES, like people, have character and individuality that distinguish them from all others of their kind. No two hills, no two valleys, are ever exactly alike, and when they appear so the resemblance is superficial. They, like ourselves, come into being and, after an appropriate time span, pass out of being. They too have a history; they are, in appearance and substance, the result of a succession of preceding events.

Astonishing as it may seem, the pleasant hills and valleys and lesser land features that together make up that piece of earth now known as Lambshead Ranch were shaped into their present forms by a series of geological events and processes that began some 250 million years ago, and the beginning event was a major one. A great arm of the Permian Sea invaded the continent through a broad down-warping of the earth's crust that extended for a thousand miles across Mexico northward through western Texas, Oklahoma, and Kansas, and, at least in its early stages, eastward across and a little beyond our area. In that sea were born the layered rocks from which the landforms of Lambshead Ranch were sculpted.

If you were standing today on one of the ranch's hilltop limestone ledges that offer an advantageous view to the west, you would notice that the rock strata there are not perfectly horizontal, as from a distance they sometimes appear to be, but are somewhat downtilted in a direction a few degrees to the right of the sinking sun. And, if you are normally observant, even though untrained in geology, you would readily perceive that the very stratum you were standing on passes underground to the west beneath other similar layers of rock, which in turn, a little farther on, pass beneath still others.

A geologist would confirm that these formations do have a regional west-northwest dip and that they continue on underground for quite a long way. In fact, from the logs and samples of literally thousands of oil wells, they have been traced continuously westward beneath the High Plains and the Pecos Valley, where they lie in places more than a mile beneath the ground surface and several thousand feet below present sea

163

level. Then, some three hundred miles to the west, they finally re-emerge as outcrops in several of the Trans Pecos mountain ranges.

He would also point out that these formations are marine deposits of early Permian age, and that you were actually standing on a segment of an ancient sea floor. From the records of numerous oil tests drilled on Lambshead Ranch it is known that the Permian formations range in thickness from about 700 feet on the east side of the ranch to some 1,400 feet on the west. And, beneath the Permian formations lie older sedimentary strata almost 4,000 feet in thickness, which contain marine deposits laid down in at least three much older seas that, at widely different times, invaded the continent and spread across the Lambshead area.

People who have never learned to read earth history as it is written in the rocks or to trust the words of those who have are understandably skeptical when you talk to them about sea deposits in the dry continental interior. For certainly there is nothing in the general appearance of these rough Lambshead hilltops, hundreds of miles from the nearest sea and two thousand feet above it, to suggest that the strata ever had any closer relation to the sea than they now have. Yet we know from the overwhelming evidence provided by many scientific investigators that these strata—now hard, bone-dry layers of rocks—did start out as somewhat thicker layers of muds that settled out of the briny waters of a long-extinct Permian Sea.

I have set out here to explain something of the origin and subsequent history of interesting land features on Lambshead Ranch—a seventy-five- or eighty-square-mile tract of land in southwest Throckmorton County, Texas. My intention is to keep this account as accurate as possible and at the same time to make it understandable and believable to readers who presumably have not been much exposed to geology. Some over-simplification of important natural processes and events is unavoidable.

I mean such natural processes as the static chemical and mechanical rock decay that geologists call "weathering," a continuous process but so glacially slow-acting that it is not visually perceptible. So, not sensing that it is happening under our feet, we mostly remain blithely oblivious of it. Which is too bad, because it is, among other things, nature's primary soil-making process—and our very lives depend on the soil. Or such natural events as mountain-making, which geologists call "orogeny" or "orogenesis"—a subject of such complexity and mind-boggling immensity that no one can fully comprehend it, or, therefore, make it fully comprehensible to others.

Then there is the matter of geologic time. Cataclysmic earth events—

great floods, landslides, earthquakes, or volcanic eruptions—dramatically manifest themselves to our senses. But most geologic processes are incredibly, imperceptibly slow-acting. Hence, they can be understood and appreciated only when we have accustomed our minds to cope with the vast spans of time such events usually require to play out the role that nature designed them for. And this can mean tens of thousands, millions, hundreds of millions of years.

To gain some concept of the monumental changes in the earth surface that can be wrought by slow-acting forces operating over a geologic time interval, let us consider the following supposition: If a broad belt of earth, extending from, say, Galveston Bay northwestward through Amarillo, were rising or sinking at a uniform rate of only one inch in fifty years, none of us who live within that belt could possibly detect the movement. Yet if the entire belt continued rising or sinking at the same slow rate for, say, five million years (a quite moderate geologic time span), the end result would be, depending on whether the land had risen or sunk, either a new mountain range towering a mile and a half above its surroundings or a new inland sea more than a thousand fathoms deep severing Texas diagonally into two parts.

The pre-eminent rule of nature is change, not balance or permanence of any of its various forms. All earth features are constantly changing, some much more slowly or swiftly than others. Polar ice caps expand and contract enormously with the passing of the ages, and so do continents and oceans. Landforms of all kinds—hills and valleys, mountains and seas—come into existence and are thereafter constantly modified and eventually destroyed. No earth feature remains forever the same.

The internal and external earth forces that bring about changes in its landforms are, like geological time, of magnitudes that strain our perception. Who among us, for instance, could pretend to comprehend the awesome internal forces that folded a three-thousand-mile stretch of North America into the Rocky Mountain ranges, or who can conceive of the eons of time that the external agents of erosion—wind, ice, and running water—will require to completely wear them down? No one can, of course, but we know of the existence of those forces because we have observed their results.

A good deal is known about the history of the Rocky Mountains, and they can serve us here to dramatize important geological concepts. They began forming some seventy or eighty million years ago, which is within the most recent 2 percent of earth's history, and that makes them quite youthful as mountain ranges go. But even as they began to emerge the forces of erosion set about to destroy them; the magnificent Rockies were doomed from their inception. They will have an inconceivably long life span as human time is measured, but eventually they will be worn down to base level; they must share the fate of the scores of other and older long-extinct ranges that once reared above the earth. Old Time passes through the mountains and leaves a plain in his wake.

Comparable in magnitude to mountain-making upheavals are major down-warpings of the earth's crust that create immense basins in which inland seas are formed. And any new sea so created is, like the mountains, doomed to ultimate extinction—to share the fate of such older ones as the Permian Sea, wherein the rock strata of Lambshead Ranch were born. That will come about because of three implacable natural forces: erosion, transportation, and deposition. Working in unison, these forces will keep on grinding away at mountains and hills and other uplands and transporting the resulting pulverized rock material away to fill in the seas.

Once we come fully to appreciate, if not fully to understand, that earth features both great and small come and go, that like ourselves they have a limited tenure on earth, we have the beginning of perception that creation is a timeless, ongoing process. We need some conception of natural, slow-acting, and mostly invisible forces operating over vast lengths of geologic time in order to understand the nature and history not only of major earth features, but also of such lesser landforms as those on Lambshead Ranch. For it is time to return to the Permian Sea and the great body of sedimentary rocks it spawned.

Rivers from surrounding land masses discharged their waters into the sea. The flow from some of the rivers was laden with sand grains, which soon settled into layers on the sea floor. Waters from others, loaded with suspended particles of silt and clay, intermingled with the saline sea waters, and these fine-grained particles eventually settled to the bottom as layers of mud. In some places, the layers accumulated to a thickness of several tens of feet. Then, as time passed and the sea water warmed, evaporation increased its salinity to a point where it could no longer hold in solution all the calcium-carbonate it had brought in from the mother ocean, so part of it settled out as limey solids on top of the older layers of sediment.

This process (greatly over-simplified here) was repeated over and over. Layers of sand, and of clay muds of various thicknesses derived mainly from the surrounding land mass, alternated with layers of limey mud derived from their previously dissolved state in sea water and from uncountable billions of similarly limey sea shells of various kinds and sizes that became incorporated in these muds.

Some of the more abundant shells were of tiny, highly ornamented, wheat-grained sized, one-celled organisms called "fusulinids." Shells of various other kinds of sea life, including several species of large ammonites, which are flat-coiled like the modern South Sea nautilus, were also present. Nearly all these early Permian species became extinct before the earliest dinosaurs appeared on earth.

As eons passed, these layers of mud became buried beneath a great thickness of later deposits whose tremendous weight gradually compressed and squeezed out most of their contained sea water. The ejected waters probably carried with them droplets of oil and gas that had generated from organic matter contained in the muds. A natural self-cementing process, which geologists call "lithification," probably accompanied this dewatering stage of the muds. Eventually, we can only guess when, the muds became rocks—strata of sandstone, limestone, and shale with essentially their present hardness and texture. It was much later, on the order of 40 million years, before the Permian Basin was eventually completely filled with sediments, and its entire area was once again a part of the continental land mass.

There were subsequent geologic events, of course, most notable of which was the Cretaceous sea advance that inundated our area and buried with a new succession of marine strata all the Permian rocks. That sea inundated all of Texas and much of the remainder of the North American continent, in fact. But some 70 million years ago, it, too, finally filled and dried up. Since then the region has remained high and dry and subject to erosion, which has no doubt removed a very considerable thickness of rocks that formerly overlay the presently exposed Lambshead strata. Such eroded intervals create time gaps in the geological record, which is why it often has been said that reading earth history from the records in the rocks is like reading the history of civilization from a book that has some of its chapters missing. It was not until comparatively recent time, perhaps during the past 100,000 years, that the present outcropping formations began to emerge and the principal land features started to take shape, assuming the forms we now know.

The marine organisms that lived in the ancient Permian sea left us a highly important legacy—oil and natural gas. Petroleum is formed by the bacterial decomposition of the soft parts of certain marine organisms, both plant and animal life. The organic oils so released go through complex natural chemical changes that convert them to the various hydrocarbon compounds of which crude oil and natural gas are composed. These compounds tend to collect in underground reservoirs and in some places form commercially extractable deposits. Several such deposits have been discovered and developed on the Lambshead land during the past half-century.

One of these is the Stone Ranch Tannehill Sand Field. According to geologist Bill Burton of Abilene, Texas, who knows a great deal about the petroleum geology of this region, the Tannehill Sand Reservoir is in the basal Permian strata about 1,300 feet below the surface, but even this quite small and shallow reservoir has already produced more than 650,000 barrels of oil.

There are other small oil and gas fields on the ranch, some of which produce from reservoirs in Pennsylvanian strata underlying, and older than, the Permian beds, and others from reservoirs in the still deeper and older Mississippian formations. Some of the most prolific oil reservoirs described by Bill Burton are tall, chimney-like fossil reefs that grew in a shallow Mississippian sea. These reefs, being highly porous, contain a remarkably large reserve of oil despite their decidedly limited bulk. Standing buried and hidden in solid rock a mile or so beneath the surface, these reefs must be exceedingly elusive targets at which to aim a drill bit.

But oil and gas are not the only geologic resources that users of this land have enjoyed. Some of the Permian limestone beds exposed on the ranch are cut into blocks by two sets of strong, vertical joints that intersect each other at right angles. An excellent example of this can be seen in the clean-washed spillway at the dam of the large ranch pond, or earthen tank, a mile or so south of ranch headquarters. The spillway has a natural floor of a cross-jointed limestone stratum, which prominent intersecting fractures have cut into remarkably symmetrical squares and rectangles, though these jointed blocks still remain closely fitted together in the form of a superbly fashioned pavement. It looks for all the world like the work of a master mason, as indeed in a sense it is.

In early pioneer times, such customary building materials as sawed lumber and bricks could be obtained only at high cost and from distant sources, and barbed wire for fencing had not yet been invented. What a blessing to the early settlers it must have been to find near at hand such durable and attractive stone already providentially cut into joint blocks of suitable dimensions and smoothness for building their splendid homes and stout fences, which still grace the Clear Fork country today.

Nearly all the limestone outcroppings seen on the ranch exhibit strong vertical jointing, though it is by no means everywhere of such symmetry as seen at the spillway exposure. The joints or fractures not only facilitated quarrying of building stone, but also, and more importantly, have been a major factor in shaping the land features as we see them today, and especially in creating the favorable upland soil conditions that support the ranch's valuable range vegetation.

Prominent, near-vertical banks and bluffs seen at various places on the ranch reflect fracture-controlled erosion. A pronounced zone of strong fracturing, including both joints and faults, was also a major factor in determining the tortuous course of the Clear Fork River through and around the Lambshead area.

Just when and how these fractures formed, I do not know. But presumably they resulted from some kind of internal stress or strain caused by folding or other structural deformation of the strata. In the places I have observed them, the prominent fractures seem to appear only in relatively brittle limestone members and are either missing entirely or quite inconspicuous in the more elastic beds of shale.

By far the largest, most important, and perhaps also most interesting land feature of the Lambshead Ranch is the major valley of the Clear Fork of the Brazos River it encloses and bounds. And the first thing we should know about the geologic history of the Clear Fork is that it is flowing in its own self-made valley—a valley-making operation that has been going on for quite a long time, something on the order of a half-million years.

How the Clear Fork, or any mature stream, actually began we of course do not know. Origins of things are apt to be obscure, and the Clear Fork's is in no way an exception. Obviously it started small. We may surmise that some sections of its main trunk and tributaries could have originated as deeply worn animal trails. (There were a great many heavy, hoofed animals capable of trail making around at that time, as we shall presently see.) When the hoof-worn trails became rain-swollen into rivulets, as I presume frequently happened, the rushing waters further eroded them, deepened and widened and eventually transformed them into gullies, which in turn were eventually enlarged to the status of creeks, now integral segments of the Clear Fork's developing drainage system.

It would be a mistake to assume that the valley-making process proceeded at a uniform rate. Stream erosion depends on the action of running water; the rate of erosion depends on swiftness of current and volume of flow; and flow volume depends on run-off from rainfall. So climate is a controlling factor in stream erosion, as it is in many other natural processes, and that behooves us to consider briefly the role of climate in the development of the Clear Fork Valley.

During the parts of Pleistocene time (the Ice Ages) when the Clear Fork Valley was initiated and developed to approximately its present form, the climate was radically different from that of the present. It was a maritime, sub-humid, and equable climate, in contrast to the continental, semi-arid, and extremely variable climate we now have. This can be deduced from the fossil bones of extinct species of strange and wonderfully varied land animals that inhabited this area during much of Pleistocene time.

Vertebrate fossils have been found in stream and pond deposits at numerous places along the different forks of the Brazos, but the largest and most significant collections were made by paleontologists Claude Hibbard and Walter Dalquest, who have also identified the many fossil bones.

Along with species similar to or identical with animals recently extant in the region—such as raccoons, cottontails, coyotes, cougars, gray wolves, alligators, slider and soft-shell turtles, garfish, channel catfish, and bull-head catfish—are a number of extinct species known to us only through their preserved skeletal parts. These include three species of camels, one a giant species unbelievably enormous; two species of horse, one of which is also a giant form; the imperial elephant, perhaps the largest elephant species that ever lived; a somewhat related proboscidian, called stego-mastodon; and a huge saber-tooth cat, a variety that habitually preyed on young elephants.

But more significant as climate indicators were the numerous fossils of animals whose normal habitat is tropical and subtropical regions: tapirs; glyptodons, a giant extinct species of armadillo; three kinds of ground sloths; the Mexican scavenger eagle, *Caracara*; a variety of turkey closely related to a recent form living in the Yucatan peninsula; and numerous bones of two kinds of giant herbivorous land tortoises, one called *Geochelone*, a six-foot-long beast as large as, if not larger than, the famed monster tortoises Darwin discovered on the Galapagos Islands, and another almost equally large, called *Gopherus*.

It is Dr. Hibbard's opinion that the *Geochelone* tortoise could not have survived in a climate where the temperature ever fell below freezing. I am not qualified to judge the validity of that opinion, but it seems convincingly clear that such a large number and variety of tropical creatures could not have survived here over the long time they are known to have been present except in an equable and humid climate. Obviously it took lush vegetation, and plenty of it, to sustain so many grazing and browsing creatures, and lushness requires humidity.

Such distinctly moist conditions undoubtedly accelerated chemical rock decay, especially of the soluble limestones, and that greatly facilitated mechanical erosion in the valley-carving process. Valley erosion surely proceeded more uniformly and rapidly during such wet stages than during drier, later stages. The more regular and abundant source of moisture of that climatic regime probably maintained a perennial flow in all but the smaller streams.

Our present climatic system seems to have dominated this region, and all of the southern Great Plains, for at least the last eight thousand years or so. It is characterized chiefly by extreme variations in both precipitation and temperature and by irregularly alternating, multiyear intervals of abnormal wetness or dryness. Some conception of this can be gleaned from weather records of the general area. Annual rainfall at Abilene during this century has ranged from a low of 9.8 inches in 1956 to a high of 48.8 inches in 1941, a variation factor of about 500 percent; and the temperature at Seymour has ranged from a record low of −14°F to a record high of 120°F, a remarkable maximum range of 134 degrees. Comparable extremes are recorded at other stations of the area.

But anyone who wants to get a deeper and more lasting perception of the vagaries of climate in this country should try scratching out a living by raising dryland crops or livestock here during one of our four- or five-year droughts; or try salvaging crops, livestock, and wildlife from the bottomlands during a great flood like the one of August, 1978.

Throughout this climatic regime the Clear Fork Valley erosion could proceed only by fits and starts. In periodic severe droughts, the flow in the channel declines to a trickle and finally ceases entirely; then, of course, stream erosion also ceases. But when the rains come again, as eventually they always do, there will be rises on the river, and the processes of erosion are again set in motion.

Sometimes torrential rains in the upstream watershed cause devastating floods that increase a thousandfold the normal rate of water erosion. The record flood of August, 1978, previously mentioned, not only caused extensive channel and floodplain erosion; it also severely damaged ranch buildings and other property and caused extensive loss of wildlife.

There is geological evidence of prehistoric floods of comparable severity, which leads us to speculate on what effect they could have had on the lives of aboriginal red men. These great floods seem to occur commonly during, or at the break-up, of prolonged drought. Under such conditions both Indians and wildlife would have been concentrated along the river, as it would have been the last surviving refuge habitat of the area. It seems likely that both Indians and native animals were occasionally caught by surprise and enveloped by flood waters. But whether or not there was much loss of human life in deluges, there was undoubtedly always heavy loss of desperately needed wild plant and animal food resources.

In making its twenty-five-mile crossing of the neighboring county of Jones, southwest of Lambshead, the Clear Fork maintains an east-southeast course in the general direction of its ultimate emptying place in the Gulf of Mexico. Then, at Lake Fort Phantom Hill, it makes an abrupt right-angle shift and heads for Oklahoma. And it maintains that aberrant north-northeast course for forty miles to Reynolds Bend in Lambshead Ranch. There at last it shifts back to a general south-southeast course toward its confluence with the trunk section of Brazos River.

Now, why should the Clear Fork take such an amazing, roundabout detour away from its logical route to the Gulf? The answer seems to be that it follows, not the shortest route between source and mouth, but the path of least resistance to erosion. When it was developing its valley, it encountered, near present-day Lake Fort Phantom Hill, the outcrop belt of hard, erosion-resistant Permian limestones, a formidable barrier athwart its established course. So it selected an easier route: it simply shifted to a north-northeast course and cut a long segment of valley in the outcrop belt of easily erodable shale beds.

But eventually, in order to fulfill its destined rendezvous with the Gulf, the river had to somehow make its way across that broad limestone barrier. This it finally accomplished, in the Lambshead area, by probing out sections of the limestone that had been greatly weakened by extensive jointing and faulting. In achieving this crossing, the channel had to shift back and forth from one short zone of fracture-made weakness to another, which accounts in large part for the tortuous meanders in the present river channel across Lambshead.

Mark Twain called the Mississippi "the crookedest river in the world, since in one part of its journey it uses up one thousand three hundred miles to cover the same ground that the crow would fly over in six hundred and seventy-five." That is scarcely two miles of journey for each one mile of advance. Had Mr. Twain seen that segment of the Clear Fork that journeys through and around Lambshead Ranch, he would have learned what a really crooked river looks like. It uses up forty-eight miles between the point where it enters Throckmorton County and the point where it leaves it—a straight line, or crow flight, distance of only thirteen miles— three and a half miles of travel for each mile of advance.

Alluvial shoals form where a segment of stream channel has been made shallower by being partially refilled with alluvium, such as sand, gravel, cobbles, or boulders. They occur commonly in two different ways: on flattened gradient sections of river channel where the velocity of the current is suddenly slackened to a point where it deposits alluvium it no longer has the energy to transport, and at the junction of tributary streams with the river. The best example of an alluvial shoal I have seen on Lambshead Ranch is at the mouth of Paint Creek, a long, intermittent tributary that joins the Clear Fork on its north side about four miles upstream from Reynolds Bend.

Through its well-developed dendritic pattern of tributaries, Paint Creek drains a watershed of about one thousand square miles, including the south half of Haskell County and the north half of Young County. When heavy rains fall over most or all of the watershed, the creek rises quickly to flood stage, and the rushing torrent flows through its main channel across Lambshead's Paint Pasture and empties into the river. In this manner large volumes of coarse, angular pebbles and boulders are dumped into the Clear Fork at the confluence of the two streams, where the creek's high-energy currents are suddenly slackened. The accumulated alluvium from repeated floods has partially filled the river channel for several hundred feet downstream from the creek's mouth, thus forming a major shoal, which also functions as a natural low-water dam of the river.

When the Clear Fork is on a rise, or flooding, the tortuous twists and turns of its channel deflect the current first against one bank and then the other, and by this lateral erosive process the banks are continuously undercut and resteepened. For this reason, along most of the stream's course through Lambshead, the banks are uncommonly precipitous, in places practically vertical, and stand from thirty to fifty feet high. Obviously, at such places it is impossible for either people or the larger mammals to cross from one side of the stream to the other, or even to gain access to channel waterholes.

But here and there are short stretches where both banks slope enough to permit fairly easy access to the channel, and where this condition coincides with a shoaled section of the channel, a natural low-water crossing or fording place is formed. The crossings are valuable assets to ranch people, for, except at high-water stages, they provide easy access to livestock pastured on both sides of the river. They are also useful watering places for all kinds of domestic animals and are much used by deer and other wildlife, as numerous game trails and tracks reveal.

There is no reason to believe that the river's condition in this area during the prehistoric period of Indian occupation was appreciably different from the way it is now, except that during the earliest stage it carried a continuous and larger volume of flow. Who can doubt that these natural shoal crossings, or others much like them, served aboriginal hunters as ideal spots for waylaying deer and other game? Obviously they were also extensively used by Indians to cross back and forth to hunt and forage on whichever side of the river seemed most bountiful.

In addition to their travel-facilitating function, the shoals—especially the large alluvial kind like the one at the mouth of Paint Creek—functioned as natural dams that impounded in the upstream channel deep holes of water. These served in the past, as now, as reserve water supplies during droughty times when the flow of the river ceases. The deep pools must also have had special significance for the Indians as a source of food during stressful times, for they were a suitable habitat preserve for the stream's exceptionally abundant supply of fish and turtles that so impressed early explorers and settlers.

Carving out the Clear Fork Valley was a remarkable earth-moving operation, and it was accomplished exclusively with nature's own tools. In performing that feat, the river's most difficult and time-consuming task undoubtedly was the cutting of its swath through the hard limestone outcrops on Lambshead Ranch. As we have seen, the river had to first break down the rock strata into separate slabs and boulders, and in this it was aided by jointing and fault fractures that had previously weakened the rocks, especially where tree roots had grown into them and spread the adjoining slabs farther apart. Then, ever so gradually, it had to wear down the slabs and boulders, by the milling action of its currents, into particles of transportable fineness. Only then could it ingest and carry them away to their new resting place in the Gulf of Mexico. In this manner the Clear Fork carved out and transported away several cubic miles of rock from only that segment of its valley that crosses the Lambshead area.

How remarkable and evocative of contemplation it is that these rocks, born a quarter-billion years ago as muds in an ancient sea, are being gradually returned to another sea, there to form a new generation of mud layers, destined, eventually, to be restructured into new but distinctly different rock strata. One important respect in which they will differ is that the marine organic matter, such as sea shells, fish bones, and algae, that are being entrapped in these new mud layers are very unlike those found in the parent rocks. Sea life, like land life and everything else in nature, is forever, inexorably changing.

The dramatic destructiveness of the comparatively rare great floods previously discussed should not blind us to the overall benefits of normal, wet-season flooding. During its latter stages of valley development, the river channel seems to have deepened very little, if at all. But it has meandered extensively, impinging at many places against the bedrock of valley walls. In those segments of the valley where the wall rock was readily erodable because of inherent softness or extensive fracturing, this lateral erosion widened the valley appreciably, in some places to about two miles.

Flooding of these broad bottomlands during the valley-widening process—which is still in progress—has occurred countless times, and each flood has left an incremental deposit of alluvium spread over the area that was inundated by its slack water. As this process was repeated over and over, the alluvial mantle continued to build up, until it is now in places at least fifty feet thick. It took the Clear Fork something like ten thousand years to lay down that broad alluvial floodplain on the floor of a valley it had spent many more tens of thousands of years carving out of sterile bedrock. But the floodplain is now incomparably the richest and most productive land on the ranch. What a marvelous thing is a river—especially when it is flowing boldly and doing its destined work.

FLORA AND FAUNA OF LAMBSHEAD RANCH

By A. S. JACKSON

>&&&&&&&&&&&&&&&&&&&&&&&&&&&&&&&&&&&&&&&&&&&&&&&&&&&&&&&&&<

The Early Years

FLORA

BEFORE AND DURING the early settlement of the West Texas Rolling Plains, a range of natural influences widely different from those of today were at work, and the differences in plant and animal communities must have been great.

The journals and reports of explorers and army men (they were often the same) who traveled the plains abound with references to great areas grazed clean by buffalo, to sweeping prairie fires, and to prairie dog towns of vast dimensions. Albert Pike (*Albert Pike's Journeys in the Prairies* [1832]) described effects of the close-herd grazing of buffalo: "We were now fairly in the broad open prairie among the buffalo. . . . You may see them on each side of you as far as your sight will extend, . . . Where they have passed, the ground looks as if it had been burnt over" (p. 72).

The journal of Sam P. Newcomb, appended to *Interwoven* by Sallie Reynolds Matthews (1936), is a daily record of a trip in 1864 from the Clear Fork in Stephens County to the San Saba River and back. On March 30, the party encountered many buffalo on grazed-off range and later the same day had to search on burned-off range for grass for their horses.

Prairie fires were started by lightning, by Indians, and by careless travelers. Captain Randolph B. Marcy, on an expedition in 1854 out of Fort Belknap to the headwaters of the Trinity, Wichita, and Brazos rivers, wrote in his journal of July 18, "For several days past we have seen extensive fire on the prairie to the southwest and supposed it was made by some of Pah-hah-eu-ka's band" (*Thirty Years of Army Life on the Border*, p. 197).

Prairie fires did not end with early settlement. Jacksboro's *Frontier Echo* on December 22, 1876, noted that the entire garrison at Fort Richardson had been called out to protect the fort's hay supply from a prairie fire. "Sunday," it said, "extensive fires were to be seen south, east, and west from here. Much damage has resulted from these fires, which nine times out of ten are caused by careless campers who are too lazy or careless to

176

put out their camp fires." On February 23 of the following year, the *Frontier Echo* noted, "Night before last the northern sky was brightly illuminated by prairie fires. . . ." And the next month, March 23: "It is estimated that prairie fires which have swept the county from one side to the other have destroyed nearly if not quite 50 miles of fencing." Fencing was barely under way in 1877, and the fences were probably rail or plank. On March 12, 1879, the editor of the *Frontier Echo*, who had followed the edge of settlement west to Fort Griffin and changed the name of his paper to the *Fort Griffin Echo*, was quoted by the Galveston *Daily News*: "For several days the whole country has been burning as well as the greater part of Throckmorton County."

In an interview with me (1940), L. H. Hardy, pioneer druggist and rancher in Throckmorton County, recalled often seeing a red glow all around the horizon, "as if the whole world was burning." In his view, ranchers were divided on the question of burning off the old grass as late as 1902. He described the method of setting the grass on fire. A heavy rope, soaked with kerosene for several feet at one end, was dragged by a man on horseback. Hardy believed that prairie dogs helped prevent spread of mesquite and that they did little damage to grassland under early conditions.

The late George Newcomb, who was born at Fort Griffin, said to me in an interview (1945) that he had burned out all the river country from Hayford to the west pasture, burning sagegrass waist-high to a man on horseback. He believed that the tall grasses went out in the decade 1880–1890. His "sagegrass," as indicated by relic stools on river benches today, was probably Indiangrass.

In 1944, historian J. R. Webb interviewed Henry Herron, a Fort Griffin pioneer. About 1877 Herron went to work cutting wood from the scrubby mesquite on hillsides and washes about two miles north of Albany. "Nearly all the mesquites," he said, "were to be found then growing in the draws and rough places in this section. . . . We thought the prairie fires prevented them spreading. In those days we protected the mesquites for firewood and later, for posts" ("Henry Herron, Pioneer and Peace Officer," *West Texas Historical Association Year Book* 20 [1944], 27).

If we are to credit accounts of early cowboys and ranchers in Throckmorton County, one or more of the tall grasses were once more common on the divide country than they are today—little bluestem or a mixture with Indiangrass and big bluestem. These are all decreasers under grazing, but, paradoxically, their regrowth is stimulated by burning. Today on Lambshead relics of these grasses increase in wet years or when a pasture is rested from grazing. Once when Reynolds Bend was thus rested, little bluestem increased greatly.

The tall grasses when mature and dry are unpalatable to cattle and were likely so to buffalo. Stands of old, tall grass would have burned hotter and thus have been more of a deterrent to mesquite. The heat with which a cowchip burns may have been equally a factor in preventing or slowing the spread of mesquite. During the drought of the 1930's, cow-chips on many ranges were loaded with mesquite seeds.

Prairie dogs remained numerous in Throckmorton County well into the 1900's. B. F. Reynolds, describing Throckmorton County in the *Texas Almanac* (1904), wrote, "About one-third of the county is susceptible to cultivation and the balance is fine grazing land when protected from prairie dogs and the grass given a chance."

Range scientists today are studying the ecology of fires in grassland, and others are experimenting with depletion grazing as a part of rotation formulas. Ranchers in the flint hills of Kansas are again spring-burning tall grass range after an interlude of several decades of abstaining from what had been a long-time practice.

FAUNA

Establishment of Camp Cooper and, subsequently, Fort Griffin, un-doubtedly brought heavy pressure on the wildlife populations in their vicinity. It was a common practice for military commanders to choose special hunters from the ranks to keep the mess supplied with wild meats. Indians encamped near both forts probably depended to some extent on the larger game species.

Along the looping turns of the Clear Fork, game remained plentiful into the 1890's. On December 28, 1894, the *Albany News* described a hunt sponsored by the Texas Central Railroad Club. Equipage consisted of three trail wagons, buggies, carriages, and horses. Chasing antelope and wild horses was part of the fun, and the Clear Fork afforded fine fish-ing. Trophies included horns of bucks and antelope, boars' tusks, and many skins and pelts. The account concludes, "Mr. Hamilton will send a number of skins and tusks to the northern owners to show what a hunter's paradise the Texas Central Railroad enters at its northern terminus." At this time, Shackelford and Throckmorton counties were among the 130 counties exempt from the General Game Law of Texas.

Species that have vanished in the Clear Fork area since those early years include the buffalo, the gray wolf, the panther, the river otter, and the prairie chicken. If the twelve or fourteen deer still holding out during 1939 in the upper reaches of the Clear Fork were the result of a private restocking attempt, as some believe, then the deer were also extirpated.

During the severe drought of the 1930's, cowboys on the SMS Ranch northwest of Throckmorton roped a strange animal in a drying pool in Elm Creek. It was identified as a very old, near-toothless river otter, perhaps the last of its kind in Throckmorton County. J. N. Condron, a man of excellent memory who had been foreman of the ranch in the 1880's, told me in an interview (1936) that river otters were common on Elm Creek when he came to the county but were all trapped out by 1888. He remembered their slides and thought that they had been numerous in other streams of the county.

Both Condron and Hardy agreed that prairie chickens once migrated into Throckmorton County from the north during severe winters. Neither man recalled seeing a prairie chicken or nest during the summer. Hardy said he killed his last prairie chicken about 1894.

Antelope were also common, much hunted during the early settlement of Shackelford and Throckmorton counties. Their presence in great numbers substantiates recollections of the earliest residents that the country was largely open prairie, for antelope will not long remain in a brushy area.

The Galveston *Daily News* carried many exchange items concerning wildlife and hunting in the Clear Fork country during the 1870's. On January 30, 1879, for example: "Messrs. Sebastian and Webb of Stephenville, have returned from attending court in Shackelford, and report game abundant. From the door of the Boone House in Albany, they saw a herd of antelope on the mountain, while fish and turkeys seem abundant. A few white swans and canvasback ducks have been seen on the streams." On February 8, the *News* again reported: "Mr. George Reynolds informs that a herd of antelope of fully five hundred came to his place during the recent storm and took shelter on the lee side of his stone fence. He managed to kill two of them. They went from there to Mr. Lockey's place, and that gentleman killed three at one shot." Condron and Hardy agreed that the last antelope in Throckmorton County were killed in a general hunt on the SMS Ranch in 1910. They were shot out, so these men said, to put an end to all too frequent hunting excursions and reckless shooting, which endangered cattle.

Of all the larger game that once existed in Throckmorton County, only the wild turkey still exists, an autochthonous species with an unbroken lineage in the same habitat.

The Scene Today

FLORA

Trees, shrubs, and vines: forest association. The true forest on Lambshead is limited to the nearly thirty miles of the winding Clear Fork. The dominant tree here, in distribution, size, and importance as a source of food for humans and wildlife alike, is the pecan (*Hicoria pecan*). Its nut ranks high in the list of winter foods of wild turkeys, the larger ducks, raccoons, fox squirrels, feral hogs, and a host of smaller mammals and birds that profit from the wasteful feeding habits of the hogs. Turkeys and mallards swallow the pecan nut whole; their gizzards are capable of breaking up the shell. Signs have been found that white-tailed deer may eat pecans. The tallest pecan trees are preferred winter roosts of the wild turkeys.

Many of the pecan trees on the Clear Fork died during the drought of the 1950's. And more recently, numbers of bankside trees were undermined by the flood of August, 1978. Unfortunately, the larger pecan trees are not being replaced by younger growth.

In past years the population of turkeys and feral hogs has consumed prodigious crops of pecans. As leader of a game management project on Lambshead, I noted on January 20, 1946: "The quantity and availability of pecans on the unit [Lambshead Ranch] exceeded estimates, and a diminishing supply is still available. . . . No commercial harvest of pecans was authorized on Lambshead, the crop being left as key food for the population of wild turkeys and hogs. As a sample of production two men were allowed to gather pecans in the West Pasture's river bottom near ranch boundary where turkeys were difficult to protect. The men gathered 870 pounds of nuts in two days, taking not more than an estimated 10 percent of the pecans in a mile of river bottom."

Translated into a total river length within ranch limits, this meant the incredible sum of 261,000 pounds of pecans. Even allowing as much as a 50 percent error on the plus side, the estimate still points to the importance of the pecan as a wildlife food where the range of species supplying mast food is narrow.

Another important member of the riverine tree community is the gum elastic, better known as chittam (*Bumelia lanuginosa*). Chittam grows as a large, thorny, rough-barked tree or as a thicket-forming shrub. Both forms blossom in June, long after danger of frost-kill. The fruit, a black, bitter-tasting drupe, often persisting after leaf fall, is an important food of turkeys, bobwhite quail, raccoons, and songbirds.

Sugar hackberry (*Celtis laevigata*) and net-leaf hackberry (*Celtis reticulata*) are common in the bottom vegetation, although the former may have been introduced. Both have edible fruits once used by the Indians and now loved by many birds. The honey mesquite (*Prosopis juliflora*) rounds out the list of woody plants that provide mast food for wildlife.

Other forest plants belonging to the river-bottom association are American elm (*Ulmus americana* var. *americana*); western soapberry, also known as wild china (*Sapindus drummondii*); black willow (*Salix nigra*); buttonbush (*Cephalanthus occidentalis*); poison ivy (*Rhus toxicodendron*); and greenbrier (*Smilax bono nox*). All these species add to the mix of wildlife shade and cover and minimize erosion.

Transition zone. Bluffs, rocky hillsides, and ravines adjacent to the river have their own representative species of woody plants. Prominent among them is foresteria (*Foresteria pubescens*), a beautiful bowerlike shrub, sometimes called elbowbush because its branches droop to the ground at acute angles. It is excellent bobwhite cover. Sometimes in close association with elbowbush is white shinoak (*Quercus sinuata* var. *breviloba*). Red haw (*Crataegus* sp.) is a small tree with limited occurrence on Lambshead. Its small, apple-like fruit is soon consumed by turkeys and other wildlife. Mexican buckeye (*Ungnadia speciosa*) is another shrub with showy blossoms. Blooming in early spring before fully leafing out, it becomes a giant, rose-colored bouquet. The fruit—small, marble-sized, in three-lobed capsules—seems unattractive as food for wildlife.

Other associates are fragrant sumac (*Rhus aromatica*), netleaf hackberry, and mesquite. More local in occurrence are redberry juniper (*Juniperus pinchotii*), catclaw acacia (*Acacia greggii*), feather dalea (*Dalea formosa*), Chickasaw plum (*Prunus angustifolia*), ivy treebine (*Cissus incisa*), balsam gourd (*Ibervillea lindheimeri*), prickly-ash (*Zanthoxylum* sp.), and joint-fir (*Ephedra antisyphlitica*). Finally, there are straggling relics of the tree that gave its name to the creek that ran by Stone Ranch, the little walnut (*Juglans microcarpa*). A few specimens still spring from ancient stumps above the ruins of the old Stone Ranch.

Two plant communities of this transition zone have special interest to the curious botanist. Above MK Canyon in the West Pasture, a steep slope is covered with a dense tangle of large white shinnery oak. Too tightly laced and on an uncomfortable slope, this oak thicket remains unknown, unexplored, and the most mysterious wildlife habitat on Lambshead. Once an attempted climb into its fastness was abandoned when slick-worn trails and the stench of wild boars discouraged the adventure.

The other unique community is an established colony of redberry juniper, which gives the name Cedar Point to a gravelly promontory overlooking the river's course. These trees are exceptionally large for the species. A few, no doubt spread by birds, have secured footholds on rimrock ledges downriver from the parent colony.

Alluvial floodplain and upland prairie. Here the mesquite is the dominant woody plant, occurring in varying densities where the first settlers recalled open vistas. Lote-bush (*Condalia obtusifolia*) is found in close association with mesquite and seems to resist control measures even more than mesquite. A few solitary round groves of large live oaks grow along the eastern margin of the ranch. Here and there, little groups of netleaf hackberry grow, more commonly in the valley. Mistletoe (*Phoradendron serotinum*) is a parasite on the older mesquite. Both mistletoe and hackberry are spread by birds.

Grasses. A wide variety of grasses are native to Lambshead. Cattle can pick and choose the more nutritious species at any season. Plants differ in their ability to bring up and store specific minerals from the soil. Even forbs, the so-called weeds, serve a valuable role in this respect. Some, notably Texas filaree, provide supplementary forage. Others go deep for minerals, adding directly to the diet or, decaying, add minerals to the topsoil. Some sources term rescuegrass an introduced species, first identified in 1806, but the date of introduction is unknown. It has been included as a native here. According to Grant Foreman (*Marcy and the Gold Seekers* [Norman: University of Oklahoma Press, 1939]), in October, 1849, Marcy found the valley of the Clear Fork covered with several kinds of grass that remained green all winter, causing the Indians to come there in the autumn to fatten their horses. Rescuegrass is the major grass in the plant association that makes winter grazing in the Clear Fork bottoms analogous to winter-wheat pasturage elsewhere.

The data below are old (1940), and the list is not to be considered complete for Lambshead. The need for this article arose in a season when neither condition of the grass or the time allotted allowed an inventory. The dates of flowering are approximate, varying with rainfall and temperature. Lyndon Parker, district conservationist for the U.S. Soil Conservation Service, kindly reviewed my list and added eight species.

Big bluestem	(*Andropogon furcatus*)	July–September
Buffalograss	(*Buchloë dactyloides*)	May–September
Canada wildrye	(*Elymus canadensis*)	June–July
Curly mesquite	(*Hilaria belangeri*)	May–September
Fall witchgrass	(*Leptoloma cognatum*)	May–July
Gummy lovegrass	(*Eragrostis curtipedi-cellata*)	May–June
Hall's panicum	(*Panicum hallii*)	late May–mid-July
Hairy grama	(*Bouteloua hirsuta*)	June–September
Hooded windmill-grass	(*Chloris cucullata*)	March–September
Indiangrass	(*Sorgastrum nutans*)	August–early October
Littlebarley	(*Hordeum pusillum*)	mid-April–early June
Little bluestem	(*Andropogon scoparius*)	August–September
Meadow dropseed	(*Sporobolus asper* var. *hookeri*)	
Purple threeawn	(*Aristida purpurea*)	late March–August
Red lovegrass	(*Eragrostis oxylepis*)	June–October
Rescuegrass	(*Bromus uniloides*)	mid-April–July
Sand dropseed	(*Sporobolus cryptandrus*)	May–September
Sand paspalum	(*Paspalum stramineum*)	mid-June–October
Sideoats grama	(*Bouteloua curtipendula*)	May–September
Silver bluestem	(*Andropogon saccharoides*)	June–September
Switchgrass	(*Panicum virgatum*)	mid-June–early October
Tall dropseed	(*Sporobolus asper*)	
Texas bluegrass	(*Poa arachnifera*)	late April–early June
Texas cupgrass	(*Eriochloa sericea*)	
Texas wintergrass	(*Stipa leucotricha*)	late April–early June
Tumblegrass	(*Schedonnardus panicu-latus*)	April–mid-July
Tumble windmill-grass	(*Chloris verticillata*)	May–August
Vine mesquite	(*Panicum obtusum*)	mid-June–mid-September
Western wheat-grass	(*Agropyron smithii*)	late May–June
White tridens	(*Tridens albescens*)	May–August

Wild flowers. Space limitations here permit neither photos nor descriptions for assistance in identifying flowers of Lambshead. A number of books on Texas wild flowers are available, all of which contain useful information and any one of which will help in identification of a few of the local wild flowers. The best field guide to Lambshead flowers is *Roadside Flowers of Texas*, with paintings by Mary Motts Mills, text by Howard S. Irwin (Austin: University of Texas Press, 1961). Mrs. Wills lived in Abilene for many years, and her book includes watercolor paintings and descriptions of approximately sixty of the species common to Lambshead Ranch. The wild flowers discussed and listed below are only a part of those native to the ranch.

Flowers named here were chosen because they are showy and eye-catching, can be viewed from the roadside without a search, and, except for the daisies, are different enough from the others to simplify identification. Many are annuals that appear early in the spring, produce seeds before competition of the grasses sets in, and then fade into obscurity. Successional plants for the most part, their seeds lie dormant in the soil until certain patterns of weather and land use combine to awaken them. When this happens, they may literally blanket a landscape with a single color.

Some of the spring landscape painters are Texas filaree (*Erodium texanum*), lavender to purple; popweed (*Lesquerella gordonii*), golden yellow; Indian blanket (*Gaillardia pulchella*), scarlet with yellow markings; huisache daisy (*Amblyolepis setigera*), yellow-orange; plains coreopsis (*Coreopsis tinctoria*), yellow-red-brown; and Mexican hat (*Ratibida columnaris*), yellow with cone-shaped centers.

First to appear in the spring are Texas filaree and popweed. April is their month, with the others not far behind.

More regular in appearance from one year to the next are little garden-sized communities of a single species. Such "gardens" show sometimes at regular intervals along ranch roads. Among these are the primroses (*Oenothera* sp.), yellow and white; winecups (*Callirhoë involucrata*), varying from white to deep purple; foxgloves (*Pentstemon* sp.), white to pale blue; rockdaisy (*Melampodium leucanthum*), white; and prairie gentian (*Eustoma grandiflorum*), deep blue to purple.

Still other wild flowers are either mixers or loners. Some grow as if they had been sowed from a package of mixed seed; others as widely spaced colonies of a single species. Eryngo (*Eringium leavenworthii*), purple; and gay-feather (*Liatris punctata*), purple, are good examples of the latter. Both bloom in the fall.

Many autumns, broomweed (*Amphyachyris dracunculoides*) takes over, coloring vast ranges with yellow. Observed singly, broomweed, like the mesquite, is an attractive plant. Its tiny seeds, produced in great quantities, are rich in protein, and in severe winters it has sustained countless generations of bobwhite quail. Broomweed is the first plant to cover drought-damaged range. Its shallow root system and thin shade seem to aid rather than retard recovery of the perennial grasses. However, its flammability makes it a serious fire hazard.

The following is a list of some of the more beautiful wild flowers of Lambshead Ranch. They have been photographed and the transparencies made a part of the ranch library.

Actinella daisy (*Tetraneuris linearfolia*), yellow, April
Annual buckwheat (*Eriognum annum*), red-brown in fall, August–
   September
Arkansas daisy (*Aphanostephus skirrhobasis*), white, April–June
Black-eyed susan (*Thunbergia alata*), red-yellow, May
Bluecurls (*Phacelia crenulata*), blue, May–June
Blue salvia (*Salvia azurea*), blue, June to fall
Bluestem prickly poppy (*Argemone intermedia*), white, June–September
Broadleaf milkweed (*Asclepias latifolia*), rose, May–June and later
Button-bush (*Cephalanthus occidentalis*), white, spherical, June–August
California filaree (*Erodium cicutarium*), pink, April
Catclaw acacia (*Acacia greggii*), a small shrub with yellow catkins, May
Clammy-weed (*Polanisia dodecandra* var. *trachysperma*), pink, May–July
Dakota verbena (*Verbena bipinnatifida*), lavender, May
Dotted gayfeather (*Liatris punctata*), purple, July–October
Drummond skullcap (*Scutellaria drummondii*), blue to purple, May–June
Erect dayflower (*Commelina erecta*), blue, May–August
Feather dalea (*Dalea formosa*), perennial small bush with tiny leaves, tiny
   blue blossoms, June
Fendler's pentstemon (*Pentstemon fendleri*), blue, May–June
Fluttermill (*Oenothera missouriensis*), yellow, April–May
Golden corydalis (*Corydalis aurea*), yellow, April–May
Golden dalea (*Dalea aurea*), yellow-crowned spikes, May–June
Honeysuckle milkweed (*Guara suffulta*), white and scarlet, May–June
Horsemint (*Monardia* sp.), yellow to lavender, mostly pink, June–July
Mexican buckeye (*Ungnadia speciosa*), shrub to small tree with deep pink
   to rose blossoms, April or May
Plains daisy (*Aphansotephus ramossissimus*), white, April–June
Plains larkspur (*Delphinium vivescens*), white to pale lavender, April–May
Popcorn milkweed (*Asclepias asperula*), greenish, May–June
Prairie spiderwort (*Tradescantia occidentalis*), light blue, May–June

Purple thistle (*Cirsium ochrocentrum*), rose to lavender, May–June
Redhaw (*Crataegus* sp.), a small tree with white blossoms, May
Rhombic primrose (*Oenothera rhombipetala*), yellow, May–June
Sawleaf daisy (*Prionopsis ciliata*), yellow, June–August
Sensitive brier (*Schrankia uncinata*), vine-like, with pink balls, June–September
Showy evening primrose (*Oenothera speciosa*), white or pink, April–May
Showy milkweed (*Asclepias speciosa*), rose, May–June
Silver-leaf nightshade (*Solanum elaeagnifolium*), violet to blue, April to summer
Skeleton plant (*Lygodsemia texana*), rose, June–July
Snow-on-the-mountain (*Euphorbia marginata*), white-edged leaves, summer into frost
Star thistle (*Centaurea americana*), pink to lavender, June
Sweet gaillardia (*Gaillardia suavis*), reddish-brown, May
Texas sleepy daisy (*Xanthisma texanum*), yellow, May–June
Texas star daisy (*Lindheimera texana*), yellow, April–July
Turkey peavine (*Astragalus nuttallianus*), violet pea-shaped flowers, April–May
Two-leaf senna (*Cassia roemeriana*), yellow, May–June
Unicorn plant (*Martynia louisianica*), pink, sticky, June–September
Yucca (*Yucca angustifolia*), greenish-white, May–June

Cacti. The cactus family represents an efficient adaptation to low and infrequent rainfall. Leaves have been lost and their function in chlorophyll making taken over by fleshy, succulent stems. Pulpy stems store water in times of drought, and a waxy coating prevents evaporation. These features, plus a protective armor of vicious spines, make the cacti a most successful plant group.

Lambshead Ranch lies far north of the real cactus environment in Texas, and its cactus population consists of relatively few species. Two—Engelmann prickly-pear and tasajillo—are common on the ranch and abundant enough to be of economic importance in a negative way. Two others, the devil's head cactus and a cholla (pronounced "choya") are individually conspicuous and hazardous to contact but relatively scarce. Another two cacti, possibly more, are small species of the type sought by commercial collectors for sale as pot plants. These are seldom seen unless searched for when in bloom.

The Engelmann prickly-pear (*Opuntia engelmannii*) needs little description. The most common cactus in the Southwest, its gorgeous rose-like flowers have been photographed and published in countless books and magazines. The blossoms are large, two to four inches in diameter, opening in May on Lambshead. A rich yellow in the morning, they turn to burnt orange for a short life of one to five days, depending on sunlight and temperatures at the time. Candy and jellies have been made from the urn-shaped russet fruit, and a poultice made from the boiled stems is a folk remedy for snakebite, wounds, and infections. Seeds of prickly-pear have been found in the crops of bobwhite quail collected for study of summer food habits.

If a prickly-pear uses up its growth energy, it adjusts by dropping some of its joints. Fallen joints may die or, more likely, take root and become a new plant at the margin of the parent plant. This is a form of progressive multiplication that can result in large colonies in a short time. In periods of severe drought or on arid range, ranchers burn off the spines and make cattle food of prickly-pear. The plant thus becomes of economic value.

On ranch land managed for dependable production of grasses, prickly-pear colonization devours ground space better utilized for grass production. Eradication of prickly-pear is a part of the management policy for Lambshead Ranch, and over the years a great deal of labor and expense has been devoted to "pear" control.

Tasajillo cactus (*Opuntia leptocaulis*) is also known by the common names pencil cactus, finger cactus, and Christmas cactus, the last name derived from the fact that the scarlet fruit hangs on until Christmas, an unlikely possibility on Lambshead because of the fruits' attraction for wild turkeys. Tasajillo is an erect, bushy plant, commonly growing to a height of three to four feet. The joints are pencil-thin and three to four inches in length. Slender, sharp spines spring from the base of each joint. Blossoms are greenish-white, one-half to three-quarters of an inch in diameter, and not especially attractive. The fruit is scarlet, about one-half-inch in diameter, abundant, and an important fall and winter food of Lambshead's wild turkeys.

The devil's head cactus (*Echinocactus texensis*) is usually found on Lambshead as a solitary specimen, which suggests that its propagation depends upon ingestion by wildlife. The plant is round as a pie plate and six to eight inches, sometimes more, in diameter, shaped like a low, rounded mound. Thirteen to twenty-five vertical ribs radiate from the center, each rib bearing one or two clusters of heavy, flattened, very hard sharp spines. Each cluster consists of six spines in a flattened circle like the spokes of a wheel, with a seventh projecting from the center. The flowers are pink to yellowish-rose, followed by scarlet fruits. If abundant, the devil's head would be a dangerous nuisance to man or beast.

Cholla cactus (*Opuntia* sp.) fortunately seldom occurs on Lambshead. Cholla is a squat, many-branched cactus whose cylindrical joints are linked like loosely-joined sausages. Each joint has tubercles spirally arranged, bristling with long straw-colored spines barbed for one-way travel—into the victim who unwisely comes in contact. Cholla spreads when the joints hitch a ride on cattle or other animals, to be finally dropped and take root in a new location. The sometime common name, "jumping cholla," comes from the seeming eagerness with which the joints attach themselves to an unwilling victim. The cholla on Lambshead has not been identified. It appears to be an intermediate form between *Opuntia spinosior* and *O. versicolor*.

Two small species of cactus, seldom noticed except when revealed by showy blossoms, occur on Lambshead. At other times they blend with the rocky environment best suited to them. One, believed to be a species of *Echinocereus*, is cylindrical, solitary, and reaches a height of six inches or more. Its blossoms of rose-purple are striking. The other (*Mammillaria* sp.) is round, biscuit-shaped, and three to four inches in diameter. At its center it is only an inch or two above the ground.

FAUNA

Wild turkeys. Lambshead's wild turkeys are justly ranch showpieces. Native wild stock, they are elegant, streamlined game birds, at home with their predators and competitors alike. They run or fly with equal ease.

In December, 1953, a male turkey was collected from a Lambshead flock, prepared as a museum skin, and submitted to the Smithsonian's Museum of Natural History. There it was compared with specimens collected by early naturalists before the plains were settled. It was pronounced an excellent specimen of the Rio Grande race, *Meleagris gallopavo intermedia*. The wild turkeys of Lambshead ranch are as pure a strain of the Rio Grande race as exists in Texas. No doubt the reason lies in the isolation of the riverine habitat and the fact that the area has had the regard and protection that goes with continuity of land ownership.

July 1, 1944, a six-year research and management project for the wild turkey was initiated under a cooperative agreement between owners of a large block of the turkey habitat and the Texas Game Agency, now the Parks and Wildlife Department. The program was carried out principally on Lambshead Ranch. I was the project leader and was in residence on the ranch for two years. Management involved supplemental feeding, predator control, and better control of night-hunting poachers.

During the last four years of the project, 1946–1950, 505 turkeys were trapped for restocking vacant habitats in eight counties. Landowner agreements to protect the releases covered a total of 772,000 acres. Except for Freestone County, all releases resulted in established populations. The restoration attempt in Freestone County was unwise, as the Rio Grande race of turkeys was never native in East Texas and the climate proved too humid.

The 505 turkeys taken from Lambshead represented surplus production; the population at the end of the program period was high, close to the carrying capacity of the habitat. Ranch policy has been to carry out a moderate degree of predator control and to continue some supplementary feeding. Waste of annual increase has been accomplished by controlled hunting. Turkey hunting was legalized in 1957, and by the end of the 1979 season, 1,250 turkeys had been harvested with no charge to the hunters. An additional 100 turkeys have been provided the Texas Parks and Wildlife Department for use in experimental stockings.

How the wild turkeys survived the flood of August, 1978, remains a mystery. The high population in autumn, 1979, attests to the ability of this splendid game bird to cope with almost any hazard except those created by man.

White-tailed deer. Restoration of deer to Lambshead began in October, 1941, with release of 20 white-tails from an Edwards Plateau source. Two more releases, the last in December, 1944, brought the total to 111. This, again, was the result of a cooperative agreement between the landowners and the Texas Game Department in which the former ensured protection from hunting until such time as the increase was judged adequate. The deer were slow in taking hold in a different environment but, once adapted, increased rapidly.

Deer hunting in Throckmorton County was legalized in the mid-1950's. Up to and through the 1979 season, 1,152 bucks and 585 does have been harvested on Lambshead Ranch. Hunting is by permit control, with no charge to the hunter. Here the owners' policy has been to prevent overpopulation with consequent deterioration in the quality of the deer.

Bobwhite quail. On Lambshead, as elsewhere near the western limits of its range, the bobwhite numbers rise and fall with variations in annual rainfall and weed successions. Unlike the wild turkeys, quail are short-lived birds, and failure of one season's nesting brings about a sharp decline in fall populations. Quail management on Lambshead would be impractical and is not needed. The conservative grazing pressure on ranch pastures, based on dry-year carrying capacity, ensures against sudden declines in bobwhite populations. A secondary effect of the extensive ranch-road development on the ranch in recent years has been an increase of food-bearing plants. The soil disturbance at road margins results in stands of weeds that provide key winter food for bobwhites and mourning doves. Best of these are western ragweed, Texas croton, snow-on-the-mountain, bluestem prickle-poppy, buffalo bur, and clammy-weed.

Mourning doves. Mourning doves are prolific producers in mesquite habitats. Their favorite nesting platform is the bowl-shaped crotch of first limbs. Lambshead has a greater summer than winter population of doves, since most of the nesting population and its increase migrate south.

Furbearers. Coyote, gray fox, bobcat, raccoons, striped skunks, opossum, and badger have all been trapped at one time or another on Lambshead.

Rodents, hares, and rabbits. Only old information on Clear Fork rodents can be reported here. During the winter months of 1938–1939, several overnight trips were made to Reynolds Bend to collect rodents and an occasional bird for museum skins. Lines of snap-traps were set, and the following catches were made: gray wood rat (*Neotoma micropus*), deer mouse (*Peromyscus maniculatus*), white-footed mouse (*Peromyscus leucopus*), Merriam's pocket mouse (*Perognathus merriami*), hispid pocket mouse (*Perognathus hispidus*), and hispid cotton rat (*Sigmodon hispidus*).

These and others were principals in the singular eruption of rodent populations in the eastern counties of the Rolling Plains in 1958. The increase was minimal on Lambshead but incredible from the town of Throckmorton north, where ranges were covered with tall dense stands of the annual grass, Japanese brome (*Bromus japonicus*).

The fox squirrel (*Sciurus niger*), common jackrabbit (*Lepus californicus*), and eastern cottontail (*Sylvilagus floridanus*) round out the list of more common mammals native to Lambshead Ranch.

Birds. The birds listed below have, with a few exceptions, been recorded as common over a long period of years. The exceptions, marked with an asterisk, were unusual or rare. Any dedicated birder working for a life list could double the number in four seasons.

American coot	Baldpate duck
Arkansas kingbird	Baltimore oriole
Bald eagle	Barred owl*

Belted kingfisher

Bewick's wren

Blue-winged teal

Brewer's blackbird

Broad-winged hawk

Cardinal

Carolina chickadee

Common cowbird

Common crow

Common grackle

Downy woodpecker

Eastern bluebird*

Eastern meadowlark

Golden-fronted woodpecker

Great blue heron

Great horned owl

Green-winged teal

Killdeer

Ladder-backed woodpecker

Lark bunting

Lark sparrow

Least sandpiper

Mallard duck

Mississippi kite*

Mockingbird

Painted bunting

Pied-billed grebe

Red-shafted flicker

Red-tailed hawk

Ring-necked duck

Roadrunner

Robin

Scissor-tailed flycatcher

Screech owl

Slate-colored junco

Sparrow hawk

Swainson's hawk

Texas nighthawk

Upland plover*

Verdin*

Vermilion flycatcher*

Vesper sparrow

White-crowned sparrow

White-necked raven

Wilson's phalarope*

Yellow-billed cuckoo

Yellow-legged plover*

The bald eagle is a rare winter resident of Lambshead's more remote river country. A pair of adults wintered there in 1944–1945 and occasionally since. Not rare, but a seeming oddity in prairie country, is an active nesting colony of great blue herons.

Reptiles. Common turtles of the Clear Fork and ranch ponds are the snapping turtle (*Chelydra serpentina*), midland painted turtle (*Chrysemys picta belli*), soft-shelled turtle (*Tryonyx* sp.), and western box turtle (*Terrapene ornata*). The common lizards are the Texas horned lizard (*Phrynosoma cornutum*), mountain boomer (*Crotaphytus collaris*), six-lined race runner (*Cnemidophorus sexlineatus*), and southern prairie lizard (*Sceloporus undulatus*).

The most common snakes on Lambshead are the common garter snake (*Thamnophis sirtalus*), eastern yellow-bellied racer (*Coluber constrictor flaventris*), diamondback water snake (*Nerodia rhombifera*), hog-nose snake or spreading adder (*Heterodon nasicus*), Texas bull snake (*Pituophis sayi*), and diamond-backed rattlesnake (*Crotalus atrox*). Uncommon are the little pigmy rattlesnake (*Sistrurus miliarirus*) and broad-banded copperhead (*Agkistrodon contortrix laticinctus*).

Amphibia and Fishes. The common frogs are the bull frog (*Rana catesbiana*), southern leopard frog (*Rana sphenocephala*) and little cricket frog (*Acris crepitans*). Toads seem scarce on Lambshead and are seldom seen, but in August, 1938, the Throckmorton County range thronged with young plains toads (*Bufo cognatus*). Twenty years later it happened again, an instance of the fascinating natural dynamics of the region.

Fishes of the river are the channel catfish (*Ictalurus punctatus*), the flathead catfish (*Pylodictis olivarius*), the blue catfish (*Ictalurus furcatus*), the buffalo (*Ictiobus bubalus*), and the mosquito minnow (*Gambusia* sp.). The long-nosed gar (*Lepisosteus osseus*) is a fish of no value.

Fishes of the many ponds on Lambshead are the large-mouthed bass (*Micropterus salmoides*), bluegill sunfish (*Lepomis macrochyrus*), and the catfishes mentioned above. All have been planted in the ponds, of course, many of them by grateful fishermen. Lambshead's fishing, like the hunting, is generously shared with friends and neighbors of the surrounding area.

INITIAL RUN OF THE BUTTERFIELD OVERLAND MAIL
ACROSS LAMBSHEAD, 1858
By WATERMAN L. ORMSBY

WE ARRIVED at [Fort] Belknap on Wednesday, the 22d of September, at 5:25, in just four hours behind the time in which we should have made it, but still twenty-seven hours ahead of the time-table time—which, considering the mules, I thought was doing wonders for the first trip. . . .

Our course led us for forty miles through plains whose sterile plainness was only varied by clumps of black oaks or weeds and coarse grass, with hardly a house or field to beguile the dreary spectacle. The only objects of interest passed on the road were a train of government mules, a Comanche Indian woman riding "straddle," and herds of cattle taking care of themselves. This woman, by the way, was the only one of the blood-thirsty Comanche Nation that I had the pleasure of seeing, though terrible tales are told of their deeds of blood in this section of the country, in the way of stealing stock and taking the scalps of straggling travellers. Some of the settlers, here, say that these acts of depredation are often committed by the Comanches on the reservation, with arms furnished by our Indian agents—while the northern Comanches get the credit of it.

The Clear Fork of the Brazos was not very clear, but even its muddy waters were a grateful boon for a bath while our horses were being changed at the station on the banks. Here were in progress of erection a log hut for the station keeper and help, and a corral, or yard, in which to herd the mules and catch them for harnessing. Dr. Birch, the mail agent, had everything in readiness, so that I had to finish dressing in the wagon— so short was the delay. They changed wagons, however, and took a heavier loaded one—which I thought was bad policy.

Our next stopping place was at Smith's station, twenty-three miles from Clear Fork, on the banks of a small creek. No house had been built yet, those at the station living in tents. They had nearly finished a fine corral for the stock, making it of brush (as no timber could be had) and filling in the chinks with mud. Our supper consisted of cake cooked in the coals, clear coffee, and some dried beef cooked in Mrs. Smith's best style. We changed horses or mules and swallowed supper in double quick time and were soon on our way again.

Our road from Clear Fork lay for a time through a little valley, and wound among the hills almost on a level. . . . I noticed two bluffs. . . . But they were mere hills, as most of our road lay through rolling plains covered with good grass and mesquite timber—a sorry landscape, I assure you. Our way was, however, much enlivened by "Big Dick," our driver, . . .

Our next stopping place was at Phantom Hill, a deserted military post, seventy-four miles from Fort Belknap and fifty-six from Chadbourne, on the road between the two. It was, I believe, . . . destroyed by fire by the soldiers in 1853, on the occasion of their being ordered to some other post. Over half a million dollars' worth of property was destroyed at the time; yet after a pretended investigation no conclusion was arrived at as to the cause of the diabolical deed. It was said that the officers and men were heartily disgusted with the station and wished to make certain of never going back; that, as they were leaving the fort, one of the principal officers [the last commandant, Lieutenant Newton C. Givens, who marched the troops out of the fort on April 6, 1854] was heard to say that he wished the place would burn down; and that the soldiers, taking him at his word, stayed behind and fired the buildings. Two things are pretty certain: first, that the soldiers did not like the place; and second, that whether accidentally or not, it burned down just as they left it.

Most of the chimneys are still standing, and as they reflected the light of the full moon as we drove up might well become the title of "Phantom Hill." . . .

The station is directly in the trail of the northern Comanches as they run down into Texas on their marauding expeditions. To leave this and other stations on the route so exposed is trifling with human life, and inviting an attack on the helpless defenders of the mail. As I have already said, there will be designing white men as well as Indians whose cupidity must be overawed by adequate military protection. Let but this be afforded, and I predict for the mail route a complete success, as well as a rapid settlement of the many fertile and desirable spots along the line.

We had expected to find a team of mules in readiness for us at Phantom Hill, but as they were not there we had to proceed with our already jaded animals until we could meet them on their way towards us. Our mules had brought us already thirty-four miles at a good pace, but we had to go fifteen miles further, or half way to Abercrombie Peak [Mountain Pass], before we met another team. The road was across a smooth plain studded with the everlasting mesquite timber. . . .

We stopped at the station called Abercrombie Pass, to get breakfast, which consisted of the standard—coffee, tough beef, and butterless short cake, prepared by an old Negro woman, who, if cleanliness is next to god-liness, would stand but little chance of heaven. There is an old saying that "every man must eat his peck of dirt." I think I have had good measure with my peck on this trip, which has been roughing it with a vengeance.

Leaving Abercrombie Peak, our road led through a rugged pass in the mountains, and up rather a steep hill, which I supposed of course had an incline on the other side. But what was my surprise on reaching the top to find a broad plain stretching before us. The keeper of the next station [Valley Creek], as well as of that at Abercrombie Peak [Mountain Pass] was appropriately named Lambshead, for he had a drove of 300 sheep grazing, growing, and increasing without expense to him, while he was attending to other duties.

Notes on Sources

Chapter 1

MY PRINCIPAL SOURCES for the archaeology of the Lambshead range were Dr. Cyrus N. Ray and Glen L. Evans. On several occasions in the 1940's, Dr. Ray took my husband and me to Clear Fork culture sites and discussed with us their significance. Most recently, Glen L. Evans, geologist and archaeologist, examined with us the evidences of archaic and more recent Indian cultures and the geological features of what is now Lambshead Ranch. Also helpful on the period before the arrival of Marcy in 1849 were the discussions of Spanish explorers in Ben O. Grant, "Explorers and Early Settlers of Shackelford County," *West Texas Historical Association Year Book* 11 (1935), 17–35; Joseph Carroll McConnell, *The West Texas Frontier* (vol. I); and Walter Prescott Webb and H. Bailey Carroll (eds.), *The Handbook of Texas*.

Of course the most important sources on Clear Fork country at mid-century are Marcy's own account in *Thirty Years of Army Life on the Border* of both his 1849 and 1854 explorations (especially pp. 206–213) and that of his secretary, W. B. Parker, *Notes Taken during the Expedition Commanded by Capt. R. B. Marcy, U.S.A., through Unexplored Texas in the Summer and Fall of 1854* (especially pp. 184–211). Waterman L. Ormsby's description of the country in the October 31, 1858, issue of the *New York Herald* supplements Marcy's reports. Ormsby's piece is excerpted in the Addenda.

Another contemporary account of the Clear Fork country is that of Brevet Captain John Pope, who kept a diary of the expedition sent by the secretary of war to explore a southern route for a transcontinental railroad. Pope, who was there in April, 1854, shared Marcy's enthusiasm for the land's agricultural potential and describes the Stem farm (*Report ... upon the Portions of the Route Near the Thirty-Second Parallel, Lying between the Red River and the Rio Grande*, in *Reports of Explorations and Surveys to Ascertain the Most Practicable and Economical Route for a Railroad from the Mississippi River to the Pacific Ocean*, Sen. Exec. Doc. 78, 33rd Cong., 2nd Sess., 1855, vol. 2, app. A, pp. 85–87).

The description of Stem's trading post and rancho comes from Marcy's, Parker's, and Pope's accounts, with additional details on the farming operation from Thomas Lambshead's letter to Indian Commissioner George W. Manypenny, May 1, 1856, in Kenneth F. Neighbours, "Chapters from the History of Texas Indian Reservations," *West Texas Historical Association Year Book* 33 (1957), 14–16. Pope notes that the agency building was made of logs.

Valuable background material on the Texas Indians, specifically the Comanches, came from Marcy's *Thirty Years of Army Life*, Rupert Norval Richardson's *The Comanche Barrier to South Plains Settlement*, and Ernest Wallace and E. Adamson Hoebel's *The Comanches: Lords of the South Plains*. Marcy and Neighbors' examination of possible reservation lands and their meeting with Sanaco, Tecumseh, and the Comanche bands are in both Marcy's and Parker's 1854 accounts. Here as elsewhere biographical information on Robert S. Neighbors comes from Kenneth F. Neighbours' excellent study, *Robert Simpson Neighbors and the Texas Frontier, 1836–1859.*

Chapter 2

The transactions on which I have based my discussion of landholdings are recorded in Texas General Land Office, Titles and Deeds for Throckmorton County, 1850–1910, available on microfilm; *Abstracts of All Original Texas Land Titles Comprising Grants and Locations to August 31, 1941*; and the Texas General Land Office maps (1859, 1885, and 1898) that include Lambshead range and the Comanche Reservation. The 1898 map is also in the Southwest Collection, Texas Tech University, Lubbock, Texas, as are the microfilm and abstract. Neighbours, *Robert Simpson Neighbors*, cites the surveys and abstracts listing the location of Stem's house in the Records of the General Land Office, Austin, Texas.

General biographical information on Jesse Stem was drawn from Watt P. Marchman and Robert C. Cotner, "Indian Agent Jesse Stem: A Manuscript Revelation," *West Texas Historical Association Year Book* 39 (1963), 114–154; Grant, "Explorers and Early Settlers" (pp. 17–35); and Rupert Norval Richardson, *Frontier of Northwest Texas, 1846 to 1876* (pp. 77–85). Neighbours (p. 101) places Neighbors in Seguin, where he could have met Stem. Dr. Richardson shared additional insights in an interview (August 18, 1979). Don H. Biggers in *Shackelford County Sketches* mentions local legend concerning Stem, whom he refers to as Shell or Snell. Description of the Stem farm is drawn from the same sources used in chapter 1.

Stem's goals and plans for the future in western Texas are stated in his own words in a series of letters to his friend Rutherford B. Hayes and various members of his own family. These letters, the originals for which are held in the Rutherford B. Hayes Memorial Library in Fremont, Ohio, are reproduced in Marchman and Cotner, "Indian Agent Jesse Stem," and photostats are available at the University of Texas Archives in Austin.

For the Koweaka episode I have drawn on Parker's *Notes Taken . . .* and Richardson's *Frontier of Northwest Texas*. Parker arrived six months after the event. Richardson had access to the copies of the Stem material, which includes an 1853 letter to Koweaka. Sibley's letter to his wife is quoted by Richardson (p. 83).

Stem's reports to the U.S. Indian Office are summarized by Richardson (pp. 77–78). In *Interwoven*, Sallie Reynolds Matthews quotes Parker verbatim on Stem's death (pp. 164–165; I have relied here and elsewhere on the second and third editions). In addition to Parker, I have used the discussion and documents in Marchman and Cotner's article on Stem. McConnell, *The West Texas Frontier*, presents a slightly different version (I, 280–281). Neighbours describes Major Neighbors' reaction to Stem's death and cites McConnell on the removal of Stem's remains to Washington, D.C. (*Robert Simpson Neighbors*, pp. 113, 284).

Chapter 3

Thomas Lambshead's association with the Peters Colony is discussed by Seymour V. Connor in *The Peters Colony of Texas* (p. 307). Connor cites a letter from Willis Stewart to William G. Hale that refers to W. S. Peters' being in London (p. 28); the Navarro County census (p. 96); and a letter from Peters to Hedgcoxe (p. 307). Lambshead's certificate is recorded in File 12, Colony Contracts File, General Land Office; no titles were issued until 1854 (p. 91). These documents offer the earliest evidence of Lambshead's arrival in northwest Texas.

Lambshead's patent at Round Mountain is recorded in Throckmorton County Titles and Deeds, vol. 25, p. 808, Throckmorton County Courthouse, and Nealey Abstract Company, Throckmorton, Texas. I have pinpointed its location on the 1859 map in the Texas General Land Office, Austin, Texas, and have walked the land with Watt Matthews and Joseph

E. Blanton. Though it would appear logical for Lambshead to have established a homestead here, there is no record or recollection of the place ever having been occupied or of any structure having been built upon it prior to the 1880's, when it became headquarters for the Reynolds Cattle Company.

Lambshead's two letters are reproduced by Neighbours, "Chapters from the History of Indian Reservations" (p. 15), and *Robert Simpson Neighbors* (p. 193). McConnell, *The West Texas Frontier* (I, 201), mentions the location of the ranch and notes Lambshead's appointment as commissioner. Eliza Johnston's remarks are from Charles P. Roland and Richard C. Robbins, "The Diary of Eliza (Mrs. Albert Sidney) Johnston: The Second Cavalry Comes to Texas," *Southwestern Historical Quarterly* 60 (1957), 486.

Sources for Lambshead's association with the Butterfield Stage stands are Roscoe P. and Margaret B. Conkling, *The Butterfield Mail, 1857–1869* (I, 128; II, 333); and Waterman L. Ormsby's October 31, 1858, article in the *New York Herald*. John Irwin's comments on the stage stand are from his 1934 interview with J. R. Webb, J. R. Webb Collection, Rupert N. Richardson Library, Hardin-Simmons University, Abilene, Texas. On Lambshead Ranch, the Butterfield Trail is marked by two limestone monuments, one where the trail enters the ranch at the relay station near the mouth of Lambshead Creek and another at Butterfield Gap where it leaves the ranch.

The chaotic state of the frontier is summarized by William C. Holden, "Frontier Defense in Texas, 1846–1860," *West Texas Historical Association Year Book* 6 (1930), 35–64.

Dr. Rupert Richardson told me that Thomas Lambshead was mentioned as an "out man" in an 1850's newspaper account of Clear Fork country (interview, August 18, 1979). Richardson said that Lambshead Creek was named for Thomas Lambshead, and then the valley for the creek. The naming of Lambshead Ranch and its more recent history come from Watt R. Matthews and from numerous interviews with him and his brother and sisters (1975–1981), including a summary of such data (February 23, 1980).

Chapter 4

Background information on Robert S. Neighbors comes essentially from Neighbours' *Robert Simpson Neighbors*. I also found helpful the manuscript material, news items, photographs, and memorabilia in the Major

Robert Simpson Neighbors Collection, Archive Department, Texas Memorial Museum, Austin, Texas.

Two biographies, Marquis James's *The Raven: A Biography of Sam Houston*, and Llerena Friend's *Sam Houston: The Great Designer*, complement each other on Houston's life and political performance. The summary on Houston in *The Handbook of Texas* and from these other sources, notes the partnership between Houston and Neighbors in working out the destiny of the Texas Indians. The definitive studies of Texas Indian policy during both the Republic and statehood are Anna Muckleroy's "The Indian Policy of the Republic of Texas," *Southwestern Historical Quarterly* 25 (April, 1922), 229–260; 26 (July, October, 1922, and January, 1923), 1–29, 128–148, 184–206; and Lena Clara Koch's "The Federal Indian Policy in Texas, 1845–1860," *Southwestern Historical Quarterly* 28 (January, April, 1925), 223–234, 259–286; 29 (July, October, 1925), 19–35, 98–126.

The treaty of September 28, 1843, with the Comanches is in the treaty casket in the vault of the Texas State Archives. The "ring" is unknown, though it may have been one belonging to Houston.

Neighbors' knowledge of the Comanche language is well documented. In 1847 he was asked to furnish a chapter on the Comanches and a vocabulary of numerals for a study of U.S. Indians authorized by Congress (Kenneth F. Neighbours, "Letters and Documents about Fort Belknap," *West Texas Historical Association Year Book* 35 [1959], 157–158).

His comments on the February 14, 1843, meeting with the Comanches, his problems resulting from the intercourse laws, his proposals on Indian policy, and the Texas *Gazette*'s remarks are from Neighbours, *Robert Simpson Neighbors* (pp. 42, 40, 84, and 107, respectively).

Chapter 5

Newton C. Givens, builder and owner of the Stone Ranch, is best described by Parker, *Notes Taken . . .* (pp. 215–216). Givens and the Stone Ranch are discussed by Biggers, *Shackelford County Sketches* (pp. 57–59, 103–104), and by Carl Coke Rister, *Fort Griffin on the Texas Frontier* (pp. 33–36). In an article for the *Abilene Reporter-News*, August 18, 1959, A. C. Greene mentions Givens and the old Stone Ranch in relation to Camp Cooper.

Givens' acquisition and ownership of the land on which he built his headquarters was confirmed by examination of land grants for Throckmorton County in *Abstracts of All Original Texas Land Titles Comprising Grants and Locations to August 31, 1941*, vol. 2, Southwest Collection.

McConnell, *The West Texas Frontier* (I, 201), provided additional information.

In describing the buildings of the headquarters, I have drawn on discussions in Matthews, *Interwoven* (pp. 27–30); the diaries of Samuel P. and Susan Reynolds Newcomb, typescript copies in the Watt R. Matthews Collection, Albany, Texas, and microfilms in the Southwest Collection; Phin Reynolds, "The Old Stone Ranch," *Abilene Reporter-News*, December 25, 1938; J. R. Webb, "Chapters from the Frontier Life of Phin W. Reynolds," *West Texas Historical Association Year Book* 16 (1941), 119–120; Biggers, *Shackelford County Sketches* (56–61); and Watt Matthews' recollections from the early 1900's. We have often visited the site, and my husband, a builder of some experience, helped interpret how Givens must have put together and actually built the Stone Ranch.

Chapter 6

Principal sources for the history and status of the Texas Indians and the various governmental policies leading up to the establishment of the reservations were Muckleroy, "Indian Policy of the Republic of Texas"; Koch, "The Federal Indian Policy in Texas, 1845–1860"; Richardson, *The Comanche Barrier* and *Texas: The Lone Star State* (pp. 150–152); James, *The Raven* (pp. 98–116, 379, 384); Friend, *Sam Houston* (pp. 82, 180, 198, 205, 264, 282, 295, 303–304); Wallace and Hoebel, *The Comanches* (pp. 293–303); and McConnell, *The West Texas Frontier* (I, 210–285).

The actual exploration and establishment of the Texas Indian reservations are thoroughly treated by Marcy, *Thirty Years of Army Life* (pp. 206–223); Parker, *Notes Taken . . .* (pp. 183–211); and Neighbours, *Robert Simpson Neighbors* (pp. 104, 132–164), who also discusses the activation of the Comanche and Brazos reservations and the response of the Indians settled there.

Chief Tecumseh and his wives are described firsthand by Parker (p. 180) and Marcy (p. 210). Colonel J. K. F. Mansfield's inspection of Camp Cooper in July and August, 1856, includes a useful report on the Comanche Reservation (Report to the Adjutant General's Office, 1856, in Adjutant General's Files, 1780's–1917, National Archives, Washington, D.C.; also reproduced by M. L. Crimmins, "Colonel J. K. F. Mansfield's Report of the Inspection of the Department of Texas in 1856," *Southwestern Historical Quarterly* 42 [1939], 127, 373).

Biographical information on John R. Baylor is drawn from *The Handbook of Texas* and from J. Evetts Haley, *Men of Fiber* (pp. 6–7).

Chapter 7

Accounts of just when Camp Cooper was established and by whom, Johnston or Hardee, are conflicting. Carl Coke Rister, *Robert E. Lee in Texas* (p. 16), gives no date for Johnston's arrival but states he left Major Hardee at Camp Cooper with two squadrons. In his article on Camp Cooper in *The Handbook of Texas*, Rister gives the date as January 3, 1856, mentions three companies of cavalry left there, but says nothing of Hardee. Neighbours, *Robert Simpson Neighbors* (p. 166), notes that Johnston advanced with two cavalry squadrons toward Camp Cooper on December 31, 1855. McConnell, *The West Texas Frontier* (I, 77), gives January 2, 1856, as the date Robert E. Lee arrived there. Biggers, *Shackelford County Sketches* (pp. 62–63), gives a confusing account with no date or details and assigns the name Camp Cooper to the entire Comanche Reservation.

The best sources seem to be Johnston's wife's diary (Roland and Robin, "The Diary of Eliza Johnston," pp. 486–487), and Colonel J. K. F. Mansfield's Report to the Adjutant General's Office, 1856, Adjutant General's Files. Mrs. Johnston details the arrival of Colonel Johnston, his family, and four companies of troops on January 2, 1856, and the departure the next day. Ordered to inspect the Department of Texas in 1856, Colonel Mansfield arrived at Camp Cooper on July 31, 1856, and inspected it with Colonel Robert E. Lee on August 1–3. His report says the camp was established January 2 by Lieutenant Colonel W. J. Hardee. Colonel M. L. Crimmins, a respected military historian, has edited the report in the *Southwestern Historical Quarterly* 42 (1939) 369–373. I have examined a copy of Mansfield's handwritten report and, after comparison with other sources, it seems logical to accept it along with the corroborative data in Eliza Johnston's diary: that Camp Cooper was located by Johnston on January 2, 1856, and Hardee was left to establish and build the tent post there.

Useful descriptions of Camp Cooper during Lee's stay were Mansfield's report and Rister's *Robert E. Lee* (pp. 55–58), which includes a May 24, 1857, inspection report by Lieutenant Herman Biggs and a June 30, 1859, report by Lieutenant I. F. Minter, both of which reveal improvements made by Lee. Lieutenant William E. Burnet, who was stationed at Camp Cooper, also briefly describes the post as it was in 1859 (Raymond Estep, "Lieutenant William E. Burnet Letters: Removal of the Texas Indians and the Founding of Fort Cobb, Part II," *Chronicles of Oklahoma* 38 [1960], 379).

Lee's arrival and tour of duty at Camp Cooper are described by Rister,

Robert E. Lee (pp. 19–94); Neighbours, *Robert Simpson Neighbors* (pp. 165, 169–170); and Mansfield. The visits with Tecumseh are detailed by Rister, *Robert E. Lee* (pp. 19–21) and *Fort Griffin* (p. 22), and Neighbours, *Robert Simpson Neighbors* (p. 169), who adds more details about Tecumseh's role as leader and "host chief" of the reservation (pp. 172–176 passim, 182, 185). A granite monument erected on Lambshead Ranch in 1936 during the Texas Centennial commemorates the conjectured place Lee and Tecumseh met when Lee came to call.

The change of command and Lee's estimate of Neighbors are recounted by Rister, *Robert E. Lee* (pp. 22–23, 42).

Cause for Indian enmity, especially of the Comanches, toward the whites is made plain by Holden, "Frontier Defense, 1846–1860" (p. 53), and Rister, *Robert E. Lee* (pp. 25-26), who quotes the chiefs' complaint.

The drought of 1857 and its effects are discussed by Mansfield; Rister, *Robert E. Lee* (pp. 35–39, 53–54); and J. Evetts Haley, *Fort Concho and the Texas Frontier* (p. 64).

The timbre of Lee and the officers stationed with him at Camp Cooper is evaluated by Rister, *Robert E. Lee* (pp. 22-23); Haley, *Fort Concho* (p. 64); Neighbours, *Robert Simpson Neighbors* (pp. 165–166); and M. L. Crimmins, "Camp Cooper and Fort Griffin," *West Texas Historical Association Year Book* 17 (1941), 32–33.

The relocation of Camp Cooper is discussed by Rupert N. Richardson, "The Saga of Camp Cooper," *West Texas Historical Association Year Book* 56 (1980), 20–21; by Rister, *Robert E. Lee* (pp. 86–87, 89); and by Neighbours, *Robert Simpson Neighbors* (p. 204). Neighbours gives additional details of Leeper's correspondence in his 1955 University of Texas doctoral dissertation, "Robert S. Neighbors in Texas, 1836–1859: A Quarter Century of Frontier Problems" (II, 492–493).

John B. Hood's remarks on Lee's friendship, from his *Advance and Retreat*, are quoted by Rister, *Robert E. Lee* (pp. 87–88). Neighbours, *Robert Simpson Neighbors* (p. 186), notes that George Stoneman assumed command on Lee's departure.

Chapter 8

Conditions on the Indian reservations, including efforts at agriculture, and education at the Clear Fork reserve are fully discussed by Neighbours, *Robert Simpson Neighbors* (pp. 157–185 passim, 205–207), and his "Chapters from the History of Indian Reservations" (pp. 11–12). Barbara Ledbetter, "Zachariah Ellis Coombes: The Samuel Pepys of the Texas Frontier," *West Texas Historical Association Year Book* 44 (1968), 68–77, reproduces the diary Coombes, a teacher at the Brazos Agency, kept from October 7, 1858, to April 27, 1859. Coombes, an observant gossip, reveals much about both Indians and agency personnel.

The involvement of Baylor, Givens, and Nelson in the lives and destinies of Neighbors and the reservation Indians is examined in exhaustive detail by Neighbours, *Robert Simpson Neighbors* (pp. 155–273), and I have relied heavily upon his account for my own. Varying points of view are presented by McConnell, *The West Texas Frontier*, (I, 275, 284, 292–293, 313, 325); Richardson, *Texas: The Lone Star State* (pp. 150–152); Holden, "Frontier Defense, 1846–1860" (pp. 58–61); Haley, *Men of Fiber* (pp. 1–11) and *Charles Goodnight: Cowman and Plainsman* (p. 22); and Estep, "William E. Burnet Letters" (pp. 370, 378, 381).

Baylor's letter to his sister is quoted by Neighbours, *Robert Simpson Neighbors* (pp. 180–181). Haley's characterization of him is from *Men of Fiber* (p. 6). Carl Cannon's introduction to James Pike, *Scout and Ranger: Being the Personal Adventures of James Pike of the Texas Rangers in 1859–60* (p. xiv), notes the troubles that followed his removal.

Enmity between Indians and whites is recounted by McConnell, *The West Texas Frontier* (I, 218–234); James Buckner Barry, *A Texas Ranger and Frontiersman: The Days of Buck Barry in Texas, 1845–1906* (pp. 106–117); and Haley, *Fort Concho* (pp. 59–67). The William Holden episode, which I have taken from McConnell (I, 288), is also mentioned by Barry (p. 111).

Rip Ford's endorsements of the reserve Indians, Leeper, and Ross are from his November 22, 1858, affidavit to Hawkins, quoted by Neighbours, *Robert Simpson Neighbors* (pp. 205, 221). His convictions regarding the renegade ring, the undated *Herald* quote on the same subject, and his warning to Runnels are also from Neighbours (pp. 208, 234).

Accounts of the Mason-Cameron massacres and the effect on the settlers are given in bloody detail by Neighbours, *Robert Simpson Neighbors* (p. 200); McConnell, *The West Texas Frontier* (I, 293–296); Richardson, *Frontier of Northwest Texas* (pp. 195–196); and Haley, *Charles Goodnight* (pp. 25–26).

The letter found on Page's body is reproduced in full by Holden, "Frontier Defense, 1846–1860" (pp. 58–60), and summarized by Richardson, *The Comanche Barrier* (p. 258).

Neighbours, *Robert Simpson Neighbors* (pp. 223–225); McConnell, *The West Texas Frontier* (I, 313–316); and Haley, *Charles Goodnight* (p. 26), all relate the attack on Choctaw Tom's party by Garland and his men.

Neighbors' accusation of Baylor and Nelson is quoted by Neighbours (pp. 225–226).

The assaults on the reservations are described by Neighbours, *Robert Simpson Neighbors* (pp. 239–246); McConnell, *The West Texas Frontier* (I, 325–327); and Haley, *Charles Goodnight* (pp. 26–31). Plummer's official report is quoted by Neighbours (pp. 240–241), who admirably details the aftermath and departure from the reservations (pp. 271-279). The inventory of Comanche property is noted by Richardson, *The Comanche Barrier* (p. 257).

Leeper's daughter's lively description of the Comanche departure is from Joseph B. Thoburn, "The Coming of the Caddos," *Sturm's Oklahoma Magazine* 11 (1910), 66–67, and Jeanne V. (Leeper) Harrison, "Matthew Leeper, Confederate Agent at the Wichita Agency, Indian Territory," *Chronicles of Oklahoma* 47 (1969), 245–246. It is also quoted by Neighbours, *Robert Simpson Neighbors* (pp. 274–275), as is Major Neighbors' own description of the exodus (p. 275) and of the country into which he delivered his charges (p. 278).

Sources for the disposition of the troops accompanying the exodus are Neighbours, *Robert Simpson Neighbors* (pp. 272–275, 277), and Estep, "William E. Burnet Letters" (pp. 277, 378–380, 383–384). Additional sources for the removal and the events leading up to it are Richardson, *The Comanche Barrier* (pp. 243–259) and *Frontier of Northwest Texas* (pp. 193–205); Wallace and Hoebel, *The Comanches* (pp. 297–308); and Cannon, introduction to Pike's *Scout and Ranger* (p. xv). Corporal Pike was among the Rangers who accompanied the departing Indians. William E. Burnet went along as quartermaster to the expedition and describes the preparation at Camp Cooper in letters of July 28 and 29 and September 5 and 15, 1859 (Estep, "William E. Burnet Letters," pp. 376–379).

Chapter 9

Neighbors' letters to his wife describing his own plans and his leave-taking from the Indians are quoted by Neighbours, *Robert Simpson Neighbors* (pp. 279, 280). The return of Major Neighbors, agents Leeper and Ross, their families, and other employees, and the attack by Indians and renegades are recorded by Cannon, introduction to Pike's *Scout and Ranger* (pp. xv–xvi); Harrison, "Matthew Leeper" (pp. 247–249); and Neighbours, *Robert Simpson Neighbors* (pp. 280–282).

My account of the assassination of Neighbors is drawn primarily from Neighbours, *Robert Simpson Neighbors* (pp. 282–292), and his "The Assassination of Robert S. Neighbors," *West Texas Historical Association Year Book* 34 (1958), 38–49. Briefer accounts of the removal, return, and assassination are included in Estep, "William E. Burnet Letters" (p. 384); Holden, "Frontier Defense, 1864–1869" (pp. 58–60); and McConnell, *The West Texas Frontier* (I, 333–334). William Burkett's September 14, 1859, letter to Mrs. Neighbors is quoted by Neighbours, *Robert Simpson Neighbors* (p. 284); facts and legends concerning events that took place immediately after the murder and information on the location of the grave are from the same source (pp. 283–284, 289). The Memorial Day ceremonies performed by the Caddos are noted in the cutline below the photograph of the Texas Centennial marker (p. 270).

The various eulogies to Neighbors, including a number I did not use, can be found in Neighbours, *Robert Simpson Neighbors* (pp. 285–291). The comment on Cornett, from a letter by J. M. Smith, is from the same source (p. 289), as are Grayson's accounting and Ford's comment (p. 290).

The situation on the Texas frontier after the removal is discussed by Walter Prescott Webb, *The Texas Rangers: A Century of Frontier Defense* (p. 172); Richardson, *Frontier of Northwest Texas* (pp. 205–212) and *Texas: The Lone Star State* (pp. 152–153); and Neighbours, "The Assassination" (pp. 47–48). Examples of the ruthless depredations against the whites on the frontier fill the pages of McConnell, *The West Texas Frontier*, volume 2.

The fates of Baylor, Nelson, and Givens have been derived from the following sources: Baylor, from Haley, *Men of Fiber* (pp. 10–12) and *Fort Concho* (pp. 101, 105), and W. Hubert Curry, *Sun Rising in the West* (pp. 53, 70–102 passim, 126); Nelson, from *The Handbook of Texas* and Neighbours, *Robert Simpson Neighbors* (pp. 226–228); and Givens, from Rupert N. Richardson, interview with author, August 18, 1979, and Neighbours, *Robert Simpson Neighbors* (pp. 217–218).

Chapter 10

The arrival of the Irwin family and their experiences on the Clear Fork are taken from John C. Irwin's interview with J. R. Webb, Webb Collection, and McConnell, *The West Texas Frontier* (I, 201); that of the Reynolds and Matthews families from Matthews, *Interwoven* (pp. 6, 10, 17, 28, 87).

The surrender of Camp Cooper is discussed by Rister, *Fort Griffin* (pp. 30–31); Barry, *A Texas Ranger* (pp. 128–144); McConnell, *The West Texas Frontier* (I, 106–107); William C. Holden, "Frontier Defense in Texas during the Civil War," *West Texas Historical Association Year Book*

4 (1928), 13; Haley, *Fort Concho* (pp. 102–103); and Biggers, *Shackelford County Sketches* (p. 65), who comments on the looting and says that Barry demanded the surrender. The citizens' report on looting appears in Rister, *Fort Griffin* (p. 31), McCulloch's in Grant, "Explorers and Early Settlers" (p. 27). Barry's Rifles command is recorded in Barry, *Texas Ranger* (pp. 128–130, 144).

The formation and activities of the Frontier Regiment are treated by Richardson, *Texas: The Lone Star State* (pp. 245–247); Webb, *The Texas Rangers* (pp. 307–309); and Holden, "Frontier Defense during the Civil War" (pp. 19–21).

The Elm Creek raid is described in the Irwin interview, Webb Collection; McConnell, *The West Texas Frontier* (II, 118–126); Rister, *Fort Griffin* (pp. 43–44); and Matthews, *Interwoven* (pp. 15, 17, 47–49).

Experiences of families who "forted up" are related by Samuel P. Newcomb in his diary for January 1, 1865, Matthews Collection; Phin Reynolds in Webb, "Chapters from the Frontier Life of Phin W. Reynolds" (pp. 115–116); Irwin interview, Webb Collection; Matthews, *Interwoven* (pp. 17–26); and Rister, *Fort Griffin* (pp. 44–58).

The Hitson episode is recounted by Phin Reynolds in Webb, "Chapters from the Frontier Life of Phin W. Reynolds" (pp. 118–119); Samuel P. Newcomb's diary, Matthews Collection; Irwin interview, Webb Collection; and Rister, *Fort Griffin* (p. 42).

In addition to Sam Newcomb's diary, information on the cattle drives comes from Haley, *Charles Goodnight* (pp. 120, 121, 184), and Matthews, *Interwoven* (pp. 25–26). General background on the early drives and the Goodnight Trail is given by Haley, chapters 8 and 9.

Information on the Cross Timbers rustlers is taken from Holden, "Frontier Defense during the Civil War" (p. 35) and *A Ranching Saga: The Lives of William Electious Halsell and Ewing Halsell* (p. 39); Cliff D. Cates, *Pioneer History of Wise County* (p. 139); Haley, *Charles Goodnight* (p. 99); and Richardson, *Texas: The Lone Star State* (p. 196).

Chapter 11

My discussion of the founding of Fort Griffin and the physical appearance of the Flat is drawn from Rister, *Fort Griffin* (pp. 62–64); Sophie A. Poe, *Buckboard Days* (pp. 30–32); and my own observations of the site today. Rister gives a detailed description of the military camp in his chapter 4.

Conrad and Rath's activities are detailed by Poe, *Buckboard Days* (p. 61), and Rister, *Fort Griffin* (pp. 149–150). Rister's chapter 9 gives a full account of hunting and the hide trade, and John R. Cook's *The Border and the Buffalo* reveals much about the hunters' experiences.

In chapters 7 and 8 of *Fort Griffin*, Rister describes in full the unsavory activities and problems of law enforcement in the Flat. (His estimate of its population appears on p. 132.) Description of the positive aspects of Griffin and of its eventual decline are also derived from Rister (pp. 196–197, 200, 204–205) and Matthews, *Interwoven* (pp. 43–64). Edgar Rye, *The Quirt and the Spur*, mentions many of the people who came through (p. 69), as does Rister (p. 194), and takes special note of Hurricane Bill Martin (p. 74). Rye devotes an entire chapter to Griffin's "wild and wooly citizens."

Haley's remarks on the outlaw gangs were made in an interview with the author, July 7, 1979. Rye, *The Quirt and the Spur* (p. 99), notes the activities of the McBride-Henderson gang, and Irwin's comments are from his interview in the Webb Collection.

Aunt Hank Smith recalled her days in Griffin in letters to her contemporaries, which Curry incorporated into *Sun Rising in the West* (pp. 138, 132, 137).

The Carl Coke Rister Papers, Texas Tech University, Southwest Collection, were a valuable source supplement.

Chapter 12

Sources for landholding on the Lambshead range include Rister, *Fort Griffin* (chapter 3 passim, pp. 128, 141–143), and the Texas General Land Office maps of 1859, 1885, and 1898.

J. Evetts Haley kindly lent me a typescript of his February 27, 1932, interview with John C. Jacobs, which is held in the Nita Stewart Haley Memorial Library, Midland, Texas. John Poe's participation in the farming venture is described in Poe, *Buckboard Days* (pp. 34–39).

Information on the trail-driving days and settlement of the Reynolds and Matthews families is taken for the most part from Matthews, *Interwoven*. Haley (*Charles Goodnight*, pp. 120, 184) mentions George Reynolds' first drive and Will's being on the Goodnight-Loving drive. Sam Newcomb's diary (Matthews Collection), as noted in chapter 10, records George's New Mexico drive.

Rister, *Fort Griffin*, discusses MacKenzie's 1874 campaign (pp. 98–124) and notes his use of Camp Cooper (p. 119).

The "boom" in housebuilding is reported by Rister, *Fort Griffin* (pp. 141–143), and treated in much greater detail by Matthews, *Interwoven*, on whom I have primarily relied for this section.

John Larn's background is mentioned briefly by Rye, *The Quirt and the Spur* (p. 103), and presented in greater detail by Phin Reynolds, unpublished interview with J. R. Webb, in "Frontier History Notes," Webb Collection. Rister, *Fort Griffin* (p. 54), and Rye, *The Quirt and the Spur* (pp. 103–104), both mention family objections to Mary's marriage. Watt R. Matthews (interview with author, May 19, 1980) told about the rumors brought back by the Reynolds brothers. Ethel Matthews Casey, in an interview on July 9, 1979, described Mary Larn and noted Larn's appeal for both men and women. The couple's devotion to each other is recorded by Mrs. A. A. Clark, "Notes," in the Nail Collection, and by Rister, *Fort Griffin* (pp. 54–55), and is attested to by the family. The quote on Larn's accomplishments and popularity is from the *Galveston News*, July 13, 1878.

For the formation of the vigilantes, I have drawn on Rister, *Fort Griffin* (pp. 146, 154); Biggers, *Shackelford County Sketches* (pp. 41–44, 89); Rye, *The Quirt and the Spur* (pp. 96–97); Ben O. Grant, "The Early History of Shackelford County" (master's thesis, Hardin-Simmons University, 1936), pp. 93–94; Leon Claire Metz, *John Selman, Gunfighter* (pp. 57–58); Wayne Gard, *Frontier Justice* (pp. 202–205); and Matthews, *Interwoven* (p. 111). Ethel Matthews Casey's remark is from the interview mentioned above.

For my treatment of the groups involved in the violence along the Clear Fork, I have relied on Matthews, *Interwoven* (p. 150), and the *Galveston News*, July 13, 1878, for the first two, and on Rister, *Fort Griffin* (chapters 7 and 8) for the last two.

Chapter 13

Sources for the variant spellings of Larn's name are Poe, *Buckboard Days* (p. 88); Henry Griswold Comstock, "Some of My Experiences and Observations on the South Western Plains during the Summers of 1871 and 1872" (typescript in Matthews Collection); Rye, *The Quirt and the Spur* (p. 101); Lieutenant G. W. Campbell to Major Jones, February 26, 1878, Adjutant General's Files; J. K. Duke, "Bad Men and Peace Officers of the Southwest," *West Texas Historical Association Year Book* 7 (1932), 55; Emmett Roberts, "Frontier Experiences of Emmett Roberts," *West Texas Historical Association Year Book* 3 (1927), 44–45; Charles A. Siringo, *A Lone Star Cowboy* (p. 268); Cook, *The Border and the Buffalo* (p. 225); Curry, *Sun Rising in the West* (p. 132); sales receipt, H. C. Smith Papers, Panhandle-Plains Historical Museum, Canyon, Texas; Phin Reynolds interview, Webb Collection; John Meadows, interview, February 21, 1928, typescript in Nita Stewart Haley Memorial Library, Midland, Texas; J. Evetts Haley, interview with author, May 4, 1979; Newton Josephus Jones, interview, March 15, 1947; John C. Irwin, interview, 1935; Henry Herron, interviews, May, 1936, and April, 1938; and Joe McCombs, "Frontier Life of Uncle Joe McCombs," ms.; the last four items are all in the Webb Collection. The Rister Papers include copies of much of this material.

The variants of Selman's name are found in Rye, *The Quirt and the Spur* (p. 106); Poe, *Buckboard Days* (p. 88); Siringo, *Lone Star Cowboy* (p. 183); and the Phin Reynolds and Irwin interviews in the Webb Collection.

Leon Metz's invaluable *John Selman, Gunfighter*, is the principal source for information on John Selman's background and activities. The diaries of Sam Newcomb and Susan Reynolds Newcomb, which contain references to Selman and his family, are in the Matthews Collection. Watt Matthews spoke with me about his family's regard for Selman (interview, May 17, 1979). Mrs. Reynolds' ride from the Stone Ranch is recounted in *Interwoven* (pp. 40–41). Metz, *John Selman* (p. 40), and Joan Farmer of Albany (interview with author, November 6, 1979) told where the widow Selman is buried. The description of Selman is from Metz, *John Selman* (pp. 22, 93).

Selman's land on Tecumseh Creek, patented about 1876, was recorded on September 30, 1879, the date of sale to J. A. Matthews (Abstract, *Texas Land Titles, Throckmorton County*, Patent No. 1577). Other information on the Tecumseh property comes from Metz, *John Selman* (pp. 124–125); Meadows interview, June 13, 1935, Haley Library; Matthews, *Interwoven* (pp. 141–142); and Watt R. Matthews, interview with author, January 10, 1980. Selman's brand is recorded in *Shackelford County Marks and Brands, 1874–1876*, Matthews Collection.

Selman's Griffin associates are noted by Rye, *The Quirt and the Spur* (p. 74), and Metz, *John Selman* (pp. 54–55), from whom the quote on Hurricane Minnie is taken. Selman's involvement with the vigilantes is documented in a letter from J. R. Webb to Mary Sutherland Lipscomb, March 8, 1947, in the Robert E. Nail, Jr., Foundation Collection, Albany, Texas.

The difficulties of farming in the area are noted in Matthews, *Interwoven* (p. 150).

The U.S. Census for 1870, a copy of which is in the Nail Collection, places John Larn and Ben Reynolds in the Newcomb household; Sallie Matthews (*Interwoven*, p. 67) notes that her brother helped out on the

Newcomb ranch. John Poe's account of Larn is from *Buckboard Days* (p. 88). Phin Reynolds' recollections are from his interview in the Webb Collection, John Meadows' from his June 13, 1935, interview in the Haley Library. Additional descriptions of community opinion were provided by Ethel Matthews Casey (interview with author, July 9, 1979) and Watt R. Matthews (interview with author, July 6, 1979).

Henry Comstock's "Experiences and Observations" details the rustling and killings that the Reynolds brothers heard about, as well as the mobbing of the Hayes outfit. Phin Reynolds' and John C. Irwin's slightly different versions of the latter are from their interviews in the Webb Collection. Emmett Roberts' account of his episode with Larn is in his "Frontier Experiences" (pp. 44–46).

Larn's Camp Cooper Ranch is marked on the 1885 and 1898 maps of Throckmorton County from the Texas Land Office. The description of Larn's house is based on Robert E. Nail, Jr., "Notes on the Larn House," Nail Collection; my interviews with Mrs. J. B. Putnam, the present owner, and with Watt R. Matthews on February 24, 1980; and my own observations. The stone fences are mentioned by Meadows in his June 13, 1935, interview in the Haley Library; by A. C. Greene, *A Personal Country* (p. 186); and by C. L. Sonnichsen, *I'll Die before I'll Run* (p. 126). Watt Matthews has discussed with me the possibility that the masons built fences elsewhere on Lambshead.

Chapter 14

Larn's association with both the stable citizenry and the lawless element has been fully discussed and cited in previous chapters, as has the formation of the vigilantes. His and Selman's joining the vigilantes and his position as chief are confirmed by a letter from J. R. Webb to Mary Sutherland Lipscomb, March 8, 1947, Nail Collection. Remarks on the role of the vigilantes come from the following sources: Phin Reynolds interview, Webb Collection; Bob Green, interview with author, November 4, 1979; Poe, *Buckboard Days* (p. 88); and J. R. Webb, "Henry Herron, Pioneer and Peace Officer," *West Texas Historical Association Year Book* 20 (1944), 33.

Larn's election as sheriff and Cruger's continuation as his deputy are recorded in Minutes of Commissioners Court, Shackelford County, I, 99. Estimates of his abilities as sheriff are from Metz, *John Selman* (p. 58); Poe, *Buckboard Days* (p. 89); and Rye, *The Quirt and the Spur* (p. 106).

Phin Reynolds interview, Webb Collection; *Frontier Echo*, April 14 and June 9, 1876; *Austin Statesman*, June 22, 1876; and Metz, *John Selman* (pp. 59–60), all remark on Larn's cleaning up the Griffin horse thieves and the McBride-Henderson gang. The newspaper report on the Griffin jail is quoted by Ben O. Grant, "Citizen Law Enforcement Agencies: A Little More about the Vigilantes," *West Texas Historical Association Year Book* 39 (1963), 158.

Metz, *John Selman* (pp. 68–69); Rye, *The Quirt and the Spur* (pp. 106, 102); and Gard, *Frontier Justice* (p. 204), all note Larn's initial popularity and the developing suspicions against him and Selman. Metz (p. 69–70) characterizes the reasons Larn continued to be backed by both friends and enemies. Irwin mentions the bribe offer in a 1934 interview with J. R. Webb, J. R. Webb Papers, Nail Collection. Metz (pp. 69–70) and the *Galveston News*, July 13, 1858, note Joe B. Matthews' loyalty toward his son-in-law. The description of Larn's double-dealing and more frequent wearing of the dark hat come from my interview with Rupert N. Richardson on August 18, 1979.

The Millet outfit is described by J. Marvin Hunter, *Trail Drivers of Texas* (I, 185, 410, and II, 815–816). Biggers, *Shackelford County Sketches* (p. 60), and Newton J. Jones, interview with J. R. Webb, March 15, 1947, Webb Collection, mention their arrival at the Stone Ranch, and Jones notes that Selman and Larn joined the outfit in suspicious activities. Biggers (p. 92) quotes Jones's description of Bland. Matthews, *Interwoven* (p. 110), comments on the cattlemen's fears. John Meadows' account of the Flat Top Mountain episode comes from his June 13, 1935, interview, Haley Library.

The killing of Bland and its aftermath are described in the Jones interview, Webb Collection; *Frontier Echo*, January 17, 1877; and Phin Reynolds interview, Webb Collection. Metz, *John Selman* (pp. 71–72), also notes the bitterness over the shooting. Cruger's appointment as sheriff is recorded in Minutes of Commissioners Court, Shackelford County, I, 112.

Reports of the disappearance of the stonemasons and the carpenter appeared in the *Galveston News*, July 13, 1878, and the *Fort Worth Daily Democrat*, July 2, 1878. John Meadows' remarks on the stonemasons are from his June 13, 1935, interview, Haley Library. Present-day estimates of the episode come from Bob Green, interview with the author, November 4, 1979, and Joan Farmer, interview with the author, November 6, 1979. Phin Reynolds' remarks are from his interview in the Webb Collection.

Metz, *John Selman* (pp. 72–73), discusses Larn and Selman's reconciliation with the vigilantes and their appointment as hide inspectors, and

John Meadows comments on their beef contract and their activities as inspectors in his Haley interview. The bonds are recorded in Records of Official Bonds, Shackelford County, Book B, pp. 54, 63, Albany, Texas; the forfeiture is recorded in Minutes of 34th District Court, Shackelford County, Book A, no. 24, p. 97, Albany, Texas.

Increasing lawlessness and active Granger involvement is described by Newt Jones in his March 15, 1947, interview (Webb Collection), as is his joining the Rangers and his arrival at Camp Sibley. Biggers' summary of vigilante efforts is from *Shackelford County Sketches* (pp. 41, 44) and is supported by Gard, *Frontier Justice* (p. 202).

The discovery of the cache of hides is related in the *Galveston News*, July 13, 1878; Irwin interview, Webb Collection; Jones interview, Webb Collection; and Campbell and Van Riper's official reports, Adjutant General's Files. Other reports put the number discovered much higher (e.g., Rye, *The Quirt and the Spur*, p. 107).

Metz, *John Selman* (pp. 79–81), discusses Bill Martin's "alliance" with the Rangers and the Rangers' subsequent removal. Fleming's letter of May 1 and Stribling's telegram of June 30 to Governor Hubbard are in the Texas State Library and Archives, Adjutant General's Files, in Austin.

Newt Jones comments in his Webb interview on Larn's breaking the truce; the increased violence is recorded in Campbell's June 16 report, Van Riper's June 15 report, and Metz, *John Selman* (pp. 84–85). Ethel Matthews Casey (interview, July 9, 1979) and the *Galveston News*, July 13, 1878, both note the settlers' fears after dark.

On the continued threat of revealing the vigilantes, I have relied on my interviews with J. Evetts Haley, December 31, 1979; Bob Green, November 4, 1979; and Joan Farmer, November 6, 1979. Newt Jones mentions the original threat in his Webb interview.

Lancaster's warrant and Larn's subsequent arrest and killing are recounted by Phin Reynolds interview, Webb Collection; *Galveston News*, July 13, 1878; *Fort Worth Democrat*, July 2, 1878; Rye, *The Quirt and the Spur* (pp. 107–113); Poe, *Buckboard Days* (pp. 91–96); Metz, *John Selman* (pp. 85–89); and others. Larn's farewell to his family is drawn from Mrs. A. A. Clark, "Notes," Nail Collection, and Irwin's interview, Webb Collection. Mary's efforts in his behalf are noted by Mrs. Clark and by Rye, who also mentions his negative verdict on bond. The Poe account says Larn was not armed and offered Cruger $500 to let his wife bring him his gun so he could shoot it out, and also notes that his legs were tied.

The pursuit of Selman, including Minnie's ride, is described by Meadows in his Haley interview and by Webb to Lipscomb, March 8, 1947, Nail Collection. Newt Jones recounts the Rangers' activities and the visit to Mrs. Selman in his Webb interview.

Phin Reynolds' account, which places Dave Barber, Cruger, and Ben Reynolds in the posse that arrested Larn and Glenn Reynolds and Howsley in the one that pursued Selman, gives the clearest description of the scene at the jail and is the source most others have relied on. Joan Farmer told me that according to J. R. Webb, one man dissented (interview, November 6, 1979).

Mary's vigil and her reaction to the gunfire are recorded in Mrs. Clark's "Notes" and by Rye. Ethel Matthews Casey (interview, July 9, 1979) talked with me about the family's grief and Larn's burial. (The old Sessions clock is still on a mantel at Lambshead headquarters.) I have seen the gravestone at the Larn place.

L. B. Carruthers' telegram to Jones from Fort Davis on June 22, 1880, regarding Selman is in the Adjutant General's Files, as is Cruger's reply of July 2, 1880.

Joe McCombs' recollection is from his 1934 interview with Ben O. Grant, contained in Grant's master's thesis, "The Early History of Shackelford County" (pp. 92–93). Watt W. Reynolds has passed on John A. ("Bud") Matthews' traditional comment on Selman and Larn, and Watt R. Matthews' remarks were made in an interview with the author, July 10, 1979.

Bibliography

Archival Material

Abilene, Texas. Hardin Simmons University. Rupert N. Richardson
    Library.
    J. R. Webb Collection.
Albany, Texas. Ethel Matthews Casey Collection.
    Robert E. Nail, Jr., Foundation Collection.
    Watt R. Matthews Collection.
    Shackelford County Courthouse. Minutes of Commissioners Court,
        vol. 1. Minutes of 34th District Court, Book A. Records of Official
        Bonds, Book B.
Austin, Texas. Texas General Land Office. Titles and Deeds for Throck-
    morton County, 1850–1910.
    Maps for Throckmorton and Haskell counties, 1859, 1885, 1898.
    Texas Memorial Museum. Archive Department. Major Robert Simp-
        son Neighbors Collection.
    Texas State Library and Archives. Adjutant General's Files.
Canyon, Texas. Panhandle-Plains Historical Museum. H. C. Smith Papers.
Lubbock, Texas. Texas Tech University. Southwest Collection.
Midland, Texas. Nita Stewart Haley Memorial Library. John C. Jacobs
    interview, February 27, 1932. John Meadows interviews, February
    21, 1928; June 24, 1933; June 13, 1935.
Throckmorton, Texas. Throckmorton County Courthouse and Nealey Ab-
    stract Company. Titles and deeds for Throckmorton County.
Washington, D.C. National Archives. Adjutant General's Files, 1780's–
    1917.

Dissertations and Theses

Grant, Ben O. "The Early History of Shackelford County." Master's thesis,
    Hardin Simmons University, 1936.
Neighbours, Kenneth F. "Robert S. Neighbors in Texas, 1836–1859: A

Quarter Century of Frontier Problems." Ph. D. dissertation, University of Texas at Austin, 1955.

Government Publications

Pope, John. *Report . . . upon the Portion of the Route Near the Thirty-Second Parallel, Lying between the Red River and the Rio Grande.* In *Reports of Explorations and Surveys to Ascertain the Most Practicable and Economical Route for a Railroad from the Mississippi River to the Pacific Ocean.* Sen. Exec. Doc. 78, 33rd Cong., 2nd Sess., 1855, vol. 2, app. A, pp. 85–87.

Interviews

Ethel Matthews Casey. July 9, 10, 11, and August 16, 1979.

Joan Farmer. November 6, 1979; January 10, July 30, August 2, 1980; September 23, 1981.

Bob Green. November 4, 1979; August 1, 1980.

J. Evetts Haley. May 4, July 7, December 31, 1979; February 23, 1980.

Watt R. Matthews. May 17, July 9–12, 1979; January 10, February 23, May 19, 1980; February 4, March 4–6, May 26, 1981.

Mrs. J. B. Putnam. February 24, May 19, 1980.

Watt W. Reynolds. July 10, 1979.

Rupert N. Richardson. August 18, 1979.

Newspapers

Abilene Reporter-News
Albany News
Austin Weekly Statesman
Dallas Herald
Dallas News
Fort Griffin Echo
Fort Worth Democrat
Fort Worth Star Telegram
Frontier Echo
Galveston News
Houston Post
San Angelo Standard-Times
San Antonio Express
San Antonio Herald
Wichita Falls Times

Books

Barry, James Buckner. *A Texas Ranger and Frontiersman: The Days of Buck Barry in Texas, 1845–1906.* Ed. James K. Greer. Dallas: Southwest Press, 1932.

Biggers, Don H. *Shackelford County Sketches.* Ed. Joan Farmer. Albany and Fort Griffin, Tex.: Clear Fork Press, 1974.

Blanton, Joseph. *True Tales of the Frontier.* Albany, Tex.: Venture Press, 1965.

Blanton, Thomas L. *Pictorial Supplement to Interwoven.* Albany, Tex.: The Albany News, 1953.

Burns, John. *Summers at Lambshead.* Privately printed, 1976.

Casey, Ethel Matthews. *Reminiscences.* El Paso: Carl Hertzog, 1979.

Cates, Cliff D. *Pioneer History of Wise County.* Saint Louis: Nixon-Jones Printing Company, 1907.

Clarke, Mary Whatley. *A Century of Cow Business: The First Hundred Years of the Texas and Southwestern Cattle Raisers Association.* Fort Worth: Evans Press, 1976.

Conkling, Roscoe P., and Margaret B. Conkling. *The Butterfield Overland Mail, 1857–1869.* 3 vols. Glendale, Calif.: The Arthur H. Clark Company, 1947.

Connor, Seymour V. *The Peters Colony of Texas.* Austin: The Texas State Historical Association, 1959.

Cook, John R. *The Border and the Buffalo.* Chicago: The Lakeside Press, 1938.

Curry, W. Hubert. *Sun Rising in the West.* Crosbyton, Tex.: Quality Printers, 1979.

De Cordova, Jacob. *Texas: Her Resources and Her Public Men.* Philadelphia: J. B. Lippincott and Company, 1858.

Douglas, C. L. *Cattle Kings of Texas.* Dallas: The Book Craft, 1939.

Friend, Llerena. *Sam Houston: The Great Designer.* Austin: University of Texas Press, 1954.

Gard, Wayne. *Frontier Justice.* Norman: University of Oklahoma Press, 1949.

Graves, John. *Goodbye to a River.* New York: Alfred A. Knopf, 1961.

Greene, A. C. *A Personal Country.* College Station: Texas A&M University Press, 1979.

Haley, J. Evetts. *Charles Goodnight: Cowman and Plainsman.* Norman: University of Oklahoma Press, 1943.

———. *Fort Concho and the Texas Frontier.* San Angelo, Tex.: San Angelo Standard-Times, 1952.

————. *Men of Fiber.* El Paso: Carl Hertzog, 1963.

Holden, William C. *Alkali Trails.* Dallas: Southwest Press, 1930.

————. *A Ranching Saga: The Lives of William Electious Halsell and Ewing Halsell.* 2 vols. San Antonio: Trinity University Press, 1976.

Hunter, J. Marvin. *The Trail Drivers of Texas.* 2 vols. New York: Argosy-Antiquarian Press, 1963.

James, Marquis. *The Raven: A Biography of Sam Houston.* Indianapolis: The Bobbs-Merrill Company, 1929.

McConnell, Joseph Carroll. *The West Texas Frontier.* 2 vols. Palo Pinto, Tex.: Legal Bank and Book Company, 1939.

Marcy, Captain Randolph B. *The Prairie Traveler: A Handbook for Overland Expeditions.* New York: Harper and Brothers, 1859.

————. *Thirty Years of Army Life on the Border.* New York: Harper and Brothers, 1866.

Matthews, Sallie Reynolds. *Interwoven.* 1st edition, privately published, 1936. 2nd edition, El Paso: Carl Hertzog, 1958. 3rd edition, Austin: University of Texas Press, 1974.

Metz, Leon Claire. *John Selman, Gunfighter.* 2d edition. Norman: University of Oklahoma Press, 1980.

Neighbours, Kenneth F. *Robert Simpson Neighbors and the Texas Frontier, 1836–1859.* Waco: Texian Press, 1975.

Ormsby, Waterman L. *The Butterfield Overland Mail.* Ed. Lyle W. Wright and Josephine M. Bynum. San Marino, Calif.: The Huntington Library, 1954.

Parker, W. B. *Notes Taken during the Expedition Commanded by Capt. R. B. Marcy, U.S.A., through Unexplored Texas in the Summer and Fall of 1854.* Philadelphia, 1856.

Pike, James. *Scout and Ranger: Being the Personal Adventures of James Pike of the Texas Rangers in 1859–60.* Ed. Carl Cannon. Princeton: Princeton University Press, 1932.

Poe, Sophie A. *Buckboard Days.* Caldwell, Idaho: Caxton Printers, 1936.

Richardson, Rupert Norval. *The Comanche Barrier to South Plains Settlement.* Glendale, Calif.: The Arthur H. Clark Company, 1933.

————. *Frontier of Northwest Texas, 1846 to 1876.* Glendale, Calif.: The Arthur H. Clark Company, 1963.

————. *Texas: The Lone Star State.* Englewood Cliffs, N.J.: Prentice-Hall, Inc., 1943.

Rister, Carl Coke. *Fort Griffin on the Texas Frontier.* Norman: University of Oklahoma Press, 1956.

———. *Robert E. Lee in Texas*. Norman: University of Oklahoma Press, 1946.

Rye, Edgar. *The Quirt and the Spur*. Chicago: W. B. Conkey Company, 1909.

Siringo, Charles A. *A Lone Star Cowboy*. Santa Fe: privately printed, 1919.

Sonnichsen, C. L. *I'll Die before I'll Run*. New York: The Devin-Adair Company, 1962.

———. *Ten Texas Feuds*. Albuquerque: University of New Mexico Press, 1957.

Wallace, Ernest, and E. Adamson Hoebel. *The Comanches: Lords of the South Plains*. Norman: University of Oklahoma Press, 1952.

Webb, Walter Prescott. *The Great Plains*. New York: Ginn and Company, 1931.

———. *The Texas Rangers: A Century of Frontier Defense*. Boston: Houghton Mifflin Company, 1935.

———, and H. Bailey Carroll, eds. *Handbook of Texas*. 2 vols. Austin: The Texas State Historical Association, 1952.

Articles

Crimmins, M. L. "Camp Cooper and Fort Griffin." *West Texas Historical Association Year Book* 17 (1941), 32–43.

———. "Colonel J. K. F. Mansfield's Report of the Inspection of the Department of Texas in 1856." *Southwestern Historical Quarterly* 42 (1939), 369–373.

———. "Robert E. Lee in Texas: Letters and Diary." *West Texas Historical Association Year Book* 8 (1932), 3–24.

Drake, Florence. "Tecumseh at the Turn of the Century." *Chronicles of Oklahoma* 38 (1960), 397–408.

Duke, J. K. "Bad Men and Peace Officers of the Southwest." *West Texas Historical Association Year Book* 8 (1932), 51–61.

Estep, Raymond. "Lieutenant William E. Burnet Letters: Removal of the Texas Indians and the Founding of Fort Cobb, Part II." *Chronicles of Oklahoma* 38 (1960), 369–396.

Farmer, Joan. "Fort Davis on the Clear Fork of the Brazos." *West Texas Historical Association Year Book* 33 (1957), 117–126.

———. "Sandstone Sentinels." *West Texas Historical Association Year Book* 34 (1958), 112–127.

Grant, Ben O. "Citizen Law Enforcement Agencies: A Little More about the Vigilantes." *West Texas Historical Association Year Book* 39 (1963), 155–161.

————. "Explorers and Early Settlers of Shackelford County." *West Texas Historical Association Year Book* 11 (1935), 17–37.

————. "Life in Old Fort Griffin." *West Texas Historical Association Year Book* 10 (1934), 32–41.

————, and J. R. Webb. "On the Cattle Trail and Buffalo Range with Joe S. McCombs." *West Texas Historical Association Year Book* 11 (1935), 93–101.

Greenwood, C. L. "Opening Routes to El Paso in 1849." *Southwestern Historical Quarterly* 48 (1937).

Harrison, Jeanne V. (Leeper). "Matthew Leeper, Confederate Indian Agent at the Wichita Agency, Indian Territory." *Chronicles of Oklahoma* 47 (1969), 242–257.

Holden, William C. "Frontier Defense in Texas during the Civil War." *West Texas Historical Association Year Book* 4 (1928), 16–31.

————. "Frontier Defense in Texas, 1846–1860." *West Texas Historical Association Year Book* 6 (1930), 35–64.

Koch, Lena Clara. "The Federal Indian Policy in Texas, 1845–1860." *Southwestern Historical Quarterly* 28 (January, April, 1925), 223–234, 259–286; 29 (July, October, 1925), 19–35, 98–126.

Ledbetter, Barbara. "Zachariah Ellis Coombes: The Samuel Pepys of the Texas Frontier." *West Texas Historical Association Year Book* 44 (1968), 68–77.

Lenamon, James. "Watt Matthews and the Texas Tradition." *Persimmon Hill* 4 (1974): 16–25.

Marchman, Watt P., and Robert C. Cotner. "Indian Agent Jesse Stem: A Manuscript Revelation." *West Texas Historical Association Year Book* 39 (1963), 114–154.

Muckleroy, Anna. "The Indian Policy of the Republic of Texas." *Southwestern Historical Quarterly* 25 (April, 1922), 229–260; 26 (July, October, 1922, and January, 1923), 1–29, 128–148, 184–206.

Neighbours, Kenneth F. "The Assassination of Robert S. Neighbors." *West Texas Historical Association Year Book* 34 (1958), 38–49.

————. "Chapters from the History of Texas Indian Reservations." *West Texas Historical Association Year Book* 33 (1957), 3–16.

————. "Indian Exodus out of Texas in 1859." *West Texas Historical Association Year Book* 36 (1960), 80–97.

————. "Letters and Documents about Fort Belknap." *West Texas Historical Association Year Book* 35 (1959), 157–158.

————. "Robert S. Neighbors and the Founding of Texas Indian Reservations." *West Texas Historical Association Year Book* 31 (1955), 65–74.

Reeves, Frank. "The Reynolds Story." *The Cattleman*, December, 1968.

Roberts, Emmett. "The Frontier Experiences of Emmett Roberts." *West Texas Historical Association Year Book* 3 (1927), 43–58.

Roland, Charles P., and Richard C. Robbins. "The Diary of Eliza (Mrs. Albert Sidney) Johnston: The Second Cavalry Comes to Texas." *Southwestern Historical Quarterly* 60 (1957), 463–500.

Thoburn, Joseph B. "The Coming of the Caddos." *Sturm's Oklahoma Magazine* 11 (1910), 63–72.

Webb, J. R. "Chapters from the Frontier Life of Phin W. Reynolds." *West Texas Historical Association Year Book* 21 (1945), 110–143.

————. "Henry Herron, Pioneer and Peace Officer." *West Texas Historical Association Year Book* 20 (1944), 21–50.

Index

Thunder (Indian), 19
Tiffin, Ohio, 9
Tin Hat Brigade, 116
Tonkawa Indians, 13, 31, 32
Torrey Brothers Trading House, 30
Treadwell, David, 106
Treadwell, H. R., 106
Treadwell, J. H., 106
Tree, Brevet Major A. D., 18
Trinity River, 30, 92
Tucker, George H., 120
Turkeys. *See* Wild turkeys
Twain, Mark, 172
Twiggs, Brevet Major General W. A., 78, 90

U.S. Highway 90, 32–33

Van Dorn, Earl, 58
Van Riper, J. E., 148–49, 153
Veracruz, 29
Vigilantes, 116, 158; and Selman and Larn, 137. *See also* Fort Griffin Vigilance Committee

Waco, Texas, 30

Waco Democrat, 63
Waco Indians, 18, 31, 45
Walnut Creek, 38, 40
Washita Agency, 81
Washita River, 78
Weatherford, Texas, 63, 86, 101, 105
Webb, J. R., 88, 93, 144, 156, 177; and Selman's name, 120
The West Texas Frontier, 23, 90
West Texas Historical Association Year Book, 177
The Whiteman, 63, 64
Whites: attitudes to Indians, 13–14; and horse stealing, 66–67
Wichita Indians, 13, 14, 18, 31, 32
Wild flowers: of Lambshead Ranch, 183–86
Wild turkeys, 180, 188–89
Williams, Henry, 83–84
Wolfforth, Sheriff Edward, 82, 85
Wood, Major W. H., 101
Worth, General W. J., 32
Wray, Judge, J. W., 104, 152

Young, Captain, 142
Young County, 44, 93